DAILY BREAKTHROUGH

ROD PARSLEY

CREATION HOUSE
Orlando, FL

DAILY BREAKTHROUGH by Rod Parsley
Published by Creation House
Strang Communications Company
600 Rinehart Road
Lake Mary, Florida 32746
Web site: http://www.creationhouse.com

All Scripture quotations are from
the King James Version of the Bible.

Scripture quotations marked NLT are from
the Holy Bible, New Living Translation.
Copyright © 1996. Used by permission of Tyndale House
Publishers, Inc., Wheaton, IL 60189. All rights reserved.

Scripture quotations marked NAS are from
the New American Standard Bible.
Copyright © 1960, 1962, 1963, 1968, 1971,
1972, 1973, 1975, 1977 by the Lockman Foundation.
Used by permission.

Scripture quotations marked ASV are from the American
Standard Version of the Bible.

89012345 BVG 8765432

IN THE BEGINNING ... GOD

In the beginning God created the heaven and the earth.

—GENESIS 1:1

I n the time it takes you to read this page, you will have entered a moment you have never experienced before. God said before we can form His name in our minds and speak it forth, He will be there! (Isaiah 65:24). Before any defeat . . . any distress . . . any sorrow . . . any pain or discouragement, God has already gone before you, making all the necessary arrangements to ensure that you will make it into the next moment of your future with Him. God never starts anything before it is finished. He's the Alpha and Omega. He knows the end before the beginning.

With God in charge, every moment can be a radically new beginning. In the next moment, if you will let God be bigger than the pain of the last moment, you will have a new beginning in Him (2 Corinthians 5:17).

Before remembering all you endured last year, think about where you are right now in God. And right where you are, God is there—greater than all your problems!

As you start this year, put God at the beginning of every day and every moment in each day. Let Him lead you through a year of victory!

LORD GOD, YOU ALONE ARE AT THE BEGIN-
NING OF MY DAY AND EACH MOMENT IN MY
DAY. TAKE CONTROL OF MY LIFE. HAVE YOUR
WAY IN MY EVERY THOUGHT AND DEED, AND I
WILL GIVE YOU ALL THE PRAISE AND THE
GLORY FOR THE NEW THING YOU WILL BE
DOING IN MY LIFE TODAY. AMEN.

GO UP

And David inquired of God, saying, Shall I go up against the Philistines? And wilt thou deliver them into mine hand? And the LORD said unto him, Go up; for I will deliver them into thine hand.

—1 CHRONICLES 14:10

Soon after David had ascended the throne of Israel, the Philistines again attacked God's chosen nation. Before sending troops against the Philistines, King David asked the Lord for His will in the situation. David desired to know if he was commissioned from heaven to engage the enemy in battle, for the steps of a good man are ordered of the Lord (Psalm 37:23). David would not move until God first moved. Only when God said, "Act!" would David take action.

King David knew it was his destiny to purge the Philistines from the land, but he wanted assurance that God would go before him to give him the victory. David understood God's perfect timing.

Once you have God's Word—the Sword of the Spirit—on the matter, you can go into battle expecting to be victorious. Determine to acknowledge Him in all your ways. Be sure His hand is on whatever you set your hand to do, and you will have total victory throughout the year.

GOD, TO YOU BELONG THE BATTLES OF THIS DAY AND EVERY DAY. I WILL NOT FIGHT UNTIL YOU HAVE SOUNDED THE TRUMPET FOR BATTLE. I WILL NOT MOVE UNTIL YOU MOVE. FOR IN YOU AND YOUR PERFECT TIMING AND WILL RESIDE EVERY VICTORY AND GLORIOUS TRIUMPH. AMEN.

LORD OF THE BREAKTHROUGH

So they came up to Baal-perazim; and David smote them there. Then David said, God hath broken in upon mine enemies by mine hand like the breaking forth of waters: therefore they called the name of that place Baal-perazim.

—I CHRONICLES 14:11

Baal-perazim literally means, "Lord of the breakthrough." Because David sought God's direction first (v. 10), he knew it was God's victory. David acknowledged God as the One who brought about his victory. He said, "I couldn't have done it if God had not gone before me."

There will be many battles to fight this year, but realize that you are not standing alone. The God you serve is the Master of the breach, and the battle is not yours, but His. When you seek God first in the matter, you can be assured of the victory.

The battle belongs to the Lord (1 Samuel 17:47). So, never defend yourself. Let Him be your strong tower, your defense, and your refuge. Why are you trying to fight battles He has already won? Put on His armor and go forth in His Spirit, not your own might and power (Zechariah 4:6).

"Submit yourselves therefore to God. Resist the devil, and he will flee from you" (James 4:7). Every time you resist temptation, you will see the devil flee from you this year. So give God the glory.

> LORD, GRANT ME THE BOLDNESS TO RESIST TEMPTATION AT EVERY TURN. I KNOW YOU HAVE GIVEN ME VICTORY OVER THE DEVIL. SO I PRAISE YOUR NAME FOR DEFEATING THE DEVIL ON THE CROSS AND GIVING ME THE POWER THROUGH YOUR BLOOD TO BREAKTHROUGH SIN AND LIVE VICTORIOUSLY. AMEN.

ABSOLUTELY FAITHFUL

And I will establish my covenant between me and thee and thy seed after thee in their generations for an everlasting covenant, to be a God unto thee, and to thy seed after thee.

—GENESIS 17:7

W e live in a time when a person's word means nothing. Marriages are dissolved daily with no regard to the vows of "till death we do part," and our courts are flooded with lawsuits.

It has not always been this way. In biblical times a covenant, sealed in blood, was a promise of enduring responsibility—never entered into lightly and never disregarded.

This is the kind of relationship we have with God. The entire Bible is a legal contract signed in Jesus' blood! When God said, "I will never leave thee, nor forsake thee" (Hebrews 13:5), He did not add "maybe" or "if." In covenant with Him, we possess His armor, His weapons, His power, and His victory!

This is the unchangeable fact of His absolute faithfulness! Study the promises of God in the light of His blood covenant and learn how sure and secure the Rock is on which you stand.

ALMIGHTY GOD, YOU ARE MY HOPE, FORTRESS, AND CONFIDENCE. THANK YOU FOR YOUR BLOOD COVENANT THAT SEALS MY FUTURE FOREVER. I WILL TRUST YOU IN EVERY DECISION. I WILL LISTEN TO AND OBEY YOUR VOICE, FOR YOU ALONE ARE FAITHFUL. AMEN.

BLOOD-WASHED

For the life of the flesh is in the blood: and I have given it to you upon the altar to make an atonement for your souls: for it is the blood that maketh an atonement for the soul.

—LEVITICUS 17:11

God did not create a sin-ridden world. But when man yielded to Satan's corruption, Adam's descendants were infused with sin's curse.

When God saw Adam and Eve's attempt to cover their nakedness, He made the first blood sacrifice, using skins from the slain animals to cover them (Genesis 3:21).

The endless cycle of blood sacrifices that ensued was a grim reminder of the chasm separating a holy God from sinful man and of man's desperate need to be cleansed. The blood of animals could not cleanse man from sin; it could only cover the sin temporarily.

Only the sinless blood of Jesus could remove the stain of sin forever. "In whom [Christ] we have redemption through his blood, the forgiveness of sins, according to the riches of his grace" (Ephesians 1:7). Praise God today because you can stand before Him with the assurance that the blood of Jesus has washed your sin away!

LORD JESUS, I CONFESS MY SIN TO YOU THIS DAY. CLEANSE ME AND WASH ME WHITE AS SNOW WITH YOUR BLOOD. I APPLY YOUR BLOOD TO MY LIFE AND MY FAMILY FOR PROTECTION, SALVATION, HEALING, AND RESTORATION. AMEN.

JR PLACE

the LORD *made a covenant with Abram.*
—GENESIS 15:18

⬥

The Hebrew word for *covenant* literally means "to cut in pieces." The ceremony required an animal to be sacrificed and cut in half. The parties to the covenant then made "the walk of death" in a figure-eight pattern between the cut pieces, symbolizing total commitment to each other. The participants then no longer lived for themselves but for their covenant partner.

God knew Abraham could never keep his part of the covenant, so He caused a deep sleep to come upon him. Jesus took Abraham's place and accomplished what Abraham could not do—establish an eternal, unbreakable covenant (Genesis 15:18).

When Jesus took the "walk of death" in our place, He became the guarantee of God's promises (Hebrews 7:22). He took Abraham's place to secure the blessings of the covenant, and He took our place at Calvary to secure our salvation. This is the great exchange: In covenant with us, we exchange our death for His life; our disease for His healing; our weakness for His strength; and our brokenness for His wholeness.

JESUS, THANK YOU FOR ENTERING INTO BLOOD COVENANT WITH ME. I KNOW THAT FRIENDSHIP WITH YOU IN COVENANT TRANSCENDS ALL OTHER RELATIONSHIPS. YOU ARE EXCLUSIVELY MY FIRST LOVE AND PASSION IN LIFE. AMEN.

AN UNBREAKABLE WORD

For ever, O LORD, thy word is settled in heaven.
—PSALM 119:89

When Joshua led the children of Israel into the Promised Land, news of their conquests spread quickly.

The terrified Gibeonites devised a plan to avoid being conquered. Several men approached the camp dressed in dirty, worn-out clothes, carrying old wine and moldy bread. They told Joshua they were ambassadors from a distant land and asked Israel to enter into a covenant with them (Joshua 9).

Later, when Joshua learned the truth, the Israelites murmured that the Gibeonites should not be spared (v. 19). But the covenant was absolutely binding. It had to be honored, even though they had been tricked!

How much more will God, whose Word is settled in heaven, honor His covenant with you! Your Word, O Lord, has settled my past, present, and future. I trust Your Word for forgiveness of past sin. Your Word has prepared me to face my present with victory and to know that my future is eternally secure in You.

> LORD, YOUR WORD IS A LAMP UNTO MY FEET AND A LIGHT TO MY PATH. I WILL HIDE YOUR WORD IN MY HEART SO THAT I MIGHT NOT SIN AGAINST YOU. WRITE YOUR WORD ON MY HEART AND ESTABLISH IT IN MY MOUTH THAT I MAY GLORIFY YOU BY YOUR WORD WITH ALL MY LIFE. AMEN.

Come Out

Now the LORD had said unto Abram, Get thee out of thy country . . . unto a land that I will shew thee.

—GENESIS 12:1

W hen God calls you into His covenant, He calls you to separate yourself from everything that hinders you from fulfilling His purpose for your life. God instructed Abraham, who came from a long line of idol-worshippers, to leave his home and go into an unknown land. God's call to Abraham required both obedience and personal commitment to Him in order to receive all that He promised.

To receive all God promised, Abraham had to leave all his past security. He had to come out of relying on what he could see and begin trusting what he could not see. "For we walk by faith, not by sight" (2 Corinthians 5:7).

Because of Abraham's faithful obedience, He became the father of the entire Jewish nation, which included the Savior of all mankind. All these blessings ensued from that moment when God said, "Come out," and Abraham replied, "Yes."

When God calls you into His covenant, He calls you to separate yourself from everything that hinders you from fulfilling His purpose for your life. Lay aside your idols of power, prestige, and position; say "Yes" to God and walk under the blessing of God's covenant with mankind!

LORD, I SAY "YES" TO YOU. WHEN YOU CALL ME OUT OF THE WORLD, I SAY, "YES." WHEN YOU ASK ME TO SURRENDER ALL, I SAY, "YES." WHATEVER YOU COMMAND, I SAY, "YES!" AMEN.

Week 2—Wednesday

SEPARATE UNTO GOD

I am the LORD your God, which brought you out of the land of Egypt, to be your God: I am the LORD your God.

—NUMBERS 15:41

God divided light from darkness, water from dry land, and the heavens from the earth. He called Abraham to separate himself from his former life. In all His determined dealings with Israel, He identified Himself as the Lord who had brought them out of bondage and set them apart (1 Kings 8:53).

When we enter a covenant relationship with God, we must also separate ourselves from our past and from our ungodly associations.

Another separation will take place in heaven, when those who have entered His covenant will be eternally divided from those who have chosen to live apart from it (Matthew 25:32).

The call to separate yourself unto God is not a punishment but a privilege.

> **LORD JESUS, SHOW ME BY YOUR HOLY SPIRIT THE THINGS I NEED TO COME AWAY FROM. SINCE I HAVE ENTERED A COVENANT RELATIONSHIP WITH YOU, I LEAVE THE DARKNESS BEHIND AND COME JOYFULLY INTO YOUR MARVELOUS LIGHT!**

NO DRY SEASON

Behold, there ariseth a little cloud out of the sea, like a man's hand. And he said, Go up and say unto Ahab, prepare thy chariot, and get thee down, that the rain not stop thee.

—1 KINGS 18:44

Are you ready for a refreshing this year from God? He will end your dry season. Your morning has come. A cloud the size of a man's hand is rising on the horizon. Laden with wind, rain, and fire, it is gathering above you. Glory and honor will crown your life, while signs and wonders will follow you into the four corners of the earth.

God is calling you to raise high the standard for living in this final generation. The time has come to plant your flag, possess the land, raise the standard, and march under the banner of the King of kings.

Your time as a standard-bearer for the King has arrived. The heavens are opening. The wind of the Holy Spirit is blowing. Holy fire is consuming all that is dross and refining all that is gold. The latter and the former rains are falling. You will reap before the sower's seed hits the ground.

LORD, I GAZE AT THE HORIZON OF MY FUTURE AND LOOK FOR YOUR CLOUD OF PROMISE. I THIRST FOR THE LIVING WATERS OF YOUR RAIN AND REFRESHING. FLOOD ME, BAPTIZE ME, AND FILL ME WITH YOUR PRESENCE THIS DAY. AMEN.

PARTAKERS OF THE PROMISE

To the end the promise might be sure to all the seed; not to that only which is of the law, but to that also which is of the faith of Abraham.

—ROMANS 4:16

A braham and his descendants looked forward to the promise of becoming a great nation, receiving blessings, having a great name, being empowered to bless others, and knowing God would curse those who cursed them. They were also promised an eternal right to occupy a land of prosperity into which God Himself would bring them.

As born-again believers, we are partakers of all those same promises through Jesus Christ. "For all the promises of God in him [Christ] are yea, and in him Amen, unto the glory of God by us" (2 Corinthians 1:20). It is the nature of God to bless us and bring goodness into our lives—"O taste and see that the Lord is good!" (Psalm 34:8).

Covenant people live under an open window of God's blessing. You have a right to live in the land of blessing and prosperity that God will lead you to when you obey the laws of the land (Deuteronomy 28).

If you are not living under the blessings of the covenant, determine today to be obedient to His commands and see Him pour out a blessing you will not be able to contain (Malachi 3:10).

> **LORD GOD, I BOW DOWN BEFORE YOU TO WORSHIP YOU AND SERVE YOU. I SUBMIT MYSELF TOTALLY TO YOUR WILL. I RECEIVE THE TRUTH THAT I AM BLESSED TO BE A BLESSING. AMEN.**

WEEK 2—WEEKEND
LEAVE LO-DEBAR

*Then King David sent, and fetched him [Mephibosheth]
out of the house of Machir, the son of Ammiel, in Lo-debar.*
—2 SAMUEL 9:5

Just as Abraham had to leave Ur, so Mephibosheth had to leave Lo-debar. Lo-debar! The very name of that place means "not a pasture." Lo-debar was the dwelling place of lack, poverty, dryness, and desolation. It was the wilderness, an empty field of no sowing and no harvest.

There was only one way out of Lo-debar. The only way out required that a prior promise be remembered and a cherished covenant be fulfilled.

When in Lo-debar, it seems that existing on stale crumbs is the only option. For Mephibosheth, Lo-debar seemed like the end of the journey, the final chapter in a tragic existence. Lame and alone, the king's descendant appeared doomed to an existence devoid of hope or harvest. He may have been born royalty, but he would die an outcast. Or would he? Against all hope, overcoming every circumstance, and beyond Mephibosheth's wildest dreams, the impossible happened. He was called out of Lo-debar by the King and from that moment on, there would be *no more crumbs!* King Jesus is calling you out of your Lo-debar today and into His kingdom. Will you leave where you are and follow Him?

JESUS, I WILL FOLLOW YOU WHEREVER YOU LEAD. I NO LONGER DESIRE TO STAY IN LO-DEBAR. I WANT TO RESIDE IN THE PRESENCE OF YOU, KING JESUS, AND TO DINE AT YOUR TABLE. AMEN.

HOW DO YOU GIVE?

Every man according as he purposeth in his heart, so let him give; not grudgingly . . . for God loveth a cheerful giver.

— 2 CORINTHIANS 9:7

G od cares about how much you give, and He cares about your attitude when you give to Him. He does not bless the so-called Christian who begrudgingly tosses a tip in the offering bucket.

Time and again the Bible tells of those who gave sacrificially, honoring Him and acknowledging Him as their provider (1 Samuel 2:1–10; Acts 10:1–4; Judges 11:30–31).

It is not the amount of the gift that is important to God, but the amount of the sacrifice in giving it. It is easy to give out of your abundance when there is no sacrifice involved. But like the widow who gave everything she had, could you do the same? (Mark 12:42–44).

Whatever you give to God—your finances, your time, or your talent—give sacrificially out of love for all He gave for you. Are you having problems recalling how blessed you are? Psalm 103:2–5 will remind you of your blessings and is today's prayer of praise:

> BLESS THE LORD, O MY SOUL, AND FORGET NOT ALL HIS BENEFITS. HE FORGIVES ALL MY INIQUITIES AND HEALS ALL MY DISEASES. HE REDEEMS MY LIFE FROM DESTRUCTION, AND CROWNS ME WITH LOVINGKINDNESS AND TENDER MERCIES. HE SATISFIES MY MOUTH WITH GOOD THINGS, SO THAT MY YOUTH IS RENEWED LIKE THE EAGLES. AMEN.

CHOSEN

For thou art an holy people unto the LORD thy God: the LORD thy God hath chosen thee to be a special people unto himself, above all people that are upon the face of the earth.

—DEUTERONOMY 7:6

When two men entered into a covenant, they acquired each other's assets, possessions, and prestige, as well as each other's liabilities, debts, and enemies. A strong, wealthy person had nothing to gain by pledging himself to someone who was weak or poor.

We have nothing God needs. Our best works are as filthy rags before His holiness (Isaiah 64:6). God receives nothing from the covenant except the one thing He desires—a relationship with His children.

God chose you to be a partaker of His covenant. In Isaiah 41:9 He says, "I have chosen thee, and not cast thee away."

Give Him all you have—your desires, dreams, sorrows, and needs—and allow Him to replace them with His abundant life. When you give Him all of you, you lose nothing of value. Make the same choice to surrender that Paul made when he wrote, "But what things were gain to me, those I counted loss for Christ. Yea doubtless, and I count all things but loss for the excellency of that knowledge of Christ Jesus, my Lord" (Philippians 3:7–8).

LORD JESUS, I PASSIONATELY DESIRE AN INTIMATE RELATIONSHIP WITH YOU. I GIVE YOU MY HEART, MY LIFE, MY HOPES, DREAMS, AND DESIRES AS WELL AS MY SIN, HURT, AND PAIN. I RECEIVE YOUR HOLY SPIRIT AND YOUR ABUNDANCE SO I MAY LIVE MY LIFE IN PRAISE OF YOU. AMEN.

WHAT'S IN A NAME?

Neither is there salvation in any other: for there is none other name under heaven given among men, whereby we must be saved.

—ACTS 4:12

Biblical names carry great significance and reveal their bearer's very nature. Before completing His covenant with Abram, God (whose name is spelled YHWH in Hebrew) took the "H" from His own name and placed it in the names Abram (Abraham) and Sarai (Sarah). In Hebrew, the "H" represents God's breath, and in so doing He breathed new life into this childless couple.

God says we are His people which are called by His name (2 Chronicles 7:14). In Christ, we have a new name. Jesus has promised, "Him that overcometh . . . I will write upon him my new name" (Revelation 3:12).

"And it shall come to pass, that whosoever shall call on the name of the Lord shall be saved" (Acts 2:21). Jesus means "God saves." Because God gave His Son a name which is above every name (Philippians 2:9), we can rejoice today that we are partakers of that glorious covenant and that even the devils are subject unto us through His name! (Luke 10:17).

I CONFESS YOUR NAME, JESUS. I REST IN THE SECURITY OF YOUR NAME. I REJOICE IN PRAISING YOUR NAME. I ACT IN THE POWER OF YOUR NAME. AMEN.

NEW WEAPONS

Do not I hate them, O LORD, that hate thee? and am not I grieved with those that rise up against thee? I hate them with perfect hatred: I count them mine enemies.

—PSALM 139:21–22

C ovenant partners exchanged weapons and pledged to fight each other's battles—the enemies of one to be the enemies of both.

We have entered into covenant with Almighty God and have taken on His enemies, wrestling not against flesh and blood, but against principalities, powers, the rulers of the darkness of this world, and spiritual wickedness in high places (Ephesians 6:12). His enemies—our flesh and the devil—become our enemies.

Jesus has given us a new set of armor and powerful weapons to stand against the forces of darkness and has given us a mandate to take His weapons and go into battle (Ephesians 6:13–17). Put on His armor today:

- His belt of truth
- His breastplate of righteousness
- His shield of faith
- His helmet of salvation
- His sword of the Spirit

Put on Christ today (Galatians 3:27). He is our truth and righteousness. He is the author and finisher of our faith. He is our salvation, and Jesus is the Word of God. So go to battle today against the enemies of the Father.

JESUS, I PUT YOU ON TODAY. YOUR ARMOR PROTECTS ME. YOUR WORD IS A MIGHTY WEAPON FOR DESTROYING THE ENEMY'S POWER. I REFUSE TO ENTER TODAY'S BATTLE UNTIL I PUT ON YOU. AMEN.

WEEK 3—FRIDAY
THE INDELIBLE SIGN

For we are the circumcision, which worship God in the spirit, and rejoice in Christ Jesus, and have no confidence in the flesh.

—PHILIPPIANS 3:3

ovenant partners symbolized their pledge by cutting into their flesh, thus creating a scar. When God entered into covenant with Abraham, he instituted a different kind of symbol.

Abraham was told to circumcise every male in his household. Throughout the history of Israel, circumcision was the indelible sign of a covenant relationship with God.

The sign of the new covenant that Jesus instituted is the indwelling of the Holy Spirit. We are recognized by the sign and seal of His Spirit within us (Acts 2:38). We are sealed with the Holy Spirit (Ephesians 1:13).

Determine to display all the fruit of the Spirit: love, joy, peace, longsuffering, gentleness, goodness, faith, meekness, and temperance (Galatians 5:22–23). The fruit of the Spirit is the very nature of Christ in you—the hope of glory (Colossians 1:27).

Boldly prepare to share the gospel with those whom the Holy Spirit gives you the opportunity to share. As a Spirit-filled believer, allow your life to point to the Greater One. He must increase while you decrease (John 3:30).

INCREASE IN MY LIFE, O LORD. BE THOU MY ALL IN ALL. SHINE THROUGH ME WITH THY FIRE. CLEANSE ME WITH THY BLOOD. MAKE OF MY LIFE A MIRROR REFLECTING THY GLORY. AMEN.

AN ETERNAL COVENANT

And David said unto him [Mephibosheth], Fear not; for I will surely show thee kindness for Jonathan thy father's sake, and will restore thee all the land of Saul, thy father; and thou shalt eat at my table continually.

—2 SAMUEL 9:7

King David's magnanimous response toward the helpless cripple Mephibosheth closely parallels how God loves us.

A covenant blessing awaited Mephibosheth that he could never even hope for in his wildest imagination. While Mephibosheth had resigned himself to a life of scraps and crumbs, his true inheritance was rooted in a covenant blessing that promised an abundant life.

Mephibosheth had to move from the desolation of Lo-debar to the palace in order to claim his blessing—and so do we! The covenant promise David made was more than a human promise to his beloved friend, Jonathan. David is honoring a timeless, eternal covenant sealed in blood and in the name of Almighty God, El Shaddai.

Jesus has sealed a covenant in His blood with You. You can feast at the table of the King of kings and Lord of lords. Will you come to His table?

LORD JESUS, WHEN I EAT THE BREAD OF YOUR BROKEN BODY AND DRINK THE CUP OF YOUR SHED BLOOD, I REMEMBER THE SACRIFICE YOU MADE ON THE CROSS TO BRING ME TO YOUR TABLE. THANK YOU FOR THE NEW COVENANT SEALED BY YOUR BLOOD FOR MY SALVATION. AMEN.

GUILTY BUT BLAMELESS

Having therefore, brethren, boldness to enter into the holiest by the blood of Jesus . . . let us draw near with a true heart in full assurance of faith, having our hearts sprinkled from an evil conscience, and our bodies washed with pure water.
—HEBREWS 10:19–22

I n the Old Testament, covenant partners would plant a tree and sprinkle it with blood as a memorial to their covenant union. The blood-stained tree that symbolizes our union with Jesus Christ was planted two thousand years ago on Calvary. This blood, was applied to the mercy seat of God. Sin was no longer covered, but cleansed.

Now when we go before the Father in our guilt, He looks upon the perfect blood on the mercy seat and says, "Guilty but blameless."

You may be carrying a burden of guilt for things you have done, attitudes you have held, or words you have spoken. Give your guilt to the Lamb who takes away the sin of the world. You can then stand before God in absolute confidence that the blood of Jesus has made you blameless.

Christ has made us partakers in His nature through His shed blood. With confidence and boldness you can come into the Holy of Holies because you are blameless in Christ Jesus.

WITH CONFIDENCE AND BOLDNESS, I ENTER INTO YOUR PRESENCE, O GOD, THROUGH THE SHED BLOOD OF JESUS. HE ALONE IS MY ATONEMENT. I PRAISE HIS NAME. AMEN.

THE PRICE OF ACCESS

And, behold, the veil of the temple was rent in twain from the top to the bottom; and the earth did quake, and the rocks rent.

—MATTHEW 27:51

To symbolize the equality of privilege and responsibility in the covenant, sacrificial animals were split from top to bottom. Each half stood for one partner in the covenant. No one was represented by the head, and no one was represented by the tail.

Our covenant with God is a contract between equals only because Jesus Christ took our place and accomplished what we could not do for ourselves. In mercy, God did not give us what we had earned. Jesus paid the price for our sin on the cross. In grace, God gave us what we could never earn. The gift of God's Son gave us eternal life.

At the moment Jesus died, the curtain in the Holy of Holies was torn from top to bottom. This symbolized that Jesus had now paid the price for man to have access to the throne room of God (Hebrews 10:19–20).

Jesus died to give you access to God. Come boldly before your Father today and receive His grace (Hebrews 4:16).

LORD JESUS, I RECEIVE YOUR MERCY AND YOUR GRACE. I CAN NEVER EARN SALVATION, BUT I TRUST YOU BY FAITH TO RECEIVE ALL YOU HAVE FOR ME. I LOVE YOU, LORD. AMEN.

COME PAST THE VEIL

*And thou shalt hang up the veil under the taches . . . and
the veil shall divide unto you between the holy place and the
most holy.*

—EXODUS 26:33

T he Ark of the Covenant was also called the Ark of
the Presence, for the presence of God was with it.
God instructed Moses to keep the Ark of the Covenant
in a room separated from the people.

Those who do not partake of the new covenant do
not understand the character of God. They may even
believe He is cruel and unyielding, indifferent and
unconcerned. But a veil of sin separates them from God.

Under the new covenant, the veil has been torn, and
God's presence is fully available to us (Matthew 27:51).
The veil of sin has been removed by Christ so that we are
liberated from sin and changed from glory to glory.
"Since this new covenant give us such confidence, we can
be very bold. . . . But whenever anyone turns to the Lord,
then the veil is taken away" (2 Corinthians 3:12, 16 NLT).

No one who receives the blood of Jesus is shut out. As
a born-again child of God, He will never turn you away.
Come boldly before Him today, through the precious
blood of Jesus, and make your needs known to Him!

JESUS, THANK YOU FOR REMOVING THE VEIL
FROM MY EYES AND EMPOWERING ME TO LIVE
IN YOUR GRACE AND PRESENCE. THROUGH
YOUR BLOOD, I BOLDLY APPROACH THE
FATHER AND DESIRE TO BE CHANGED IN HIS
PRESENCE. AMEN.

COVENANT BLOOD

I am crucified with Christ: nevertheless I live; yet not I, but Christ liveth in me.

—GALATIANS 2:20

Both parties of the covenant cut their right hands and mingled their blood, symbolizing they were now one person with a new nature.

Jesus Christ is at God's right hand (Ephesians 1:20), and His precious blood is the only blood shed for this new covenant. His pure blood replaced our polluted stream. God's own arm brought salvation (Isaiah 63:5).

To be crucified with Christ is to die to the old self. The old life is drained from me, and His pure blood fills me with new life. "And Jesus Christ was revealed as God's Son by his baptism in water and by shedding his blood on the cross—not by water only, but by water and blood (1 John 5:6 NLT).

When we enter God's covenant, we become a new creation (2 Corinthians 5:17). We receive His laws written on our hearts (Hebrews 8:10). We die to all self-centeredness and self-seeking. Everything we do— our attitudes, our motives, our every action—we surrender to the God of the covenant.

Declare with confidence today, "Yet not I, but Christ liveth in me" (Galatians 2:20). Receive a new heart from the Lord (Ezekiel 36:26).

LORD GOD, CHANGE MY HEART OF STONE INTO A NEW HEART OF FLESH. REPLACE MY HARD-NESS WITH A TENDERNESS TOWARD YOU. FILL MY HEART WITH YOUR LIVING WATERS SO THAT LIFE FLOWS THROUGH ME. AMEN.

THE OLD COVENANT

If ye will obey my voice indeed, and keep my covenant, then ye shall be a peculiar treasure unto me above all people.

—EXODUS 19:5

After four hundred years of bondage in a pagan nation, the Israelites did not understand God. Soon they returned to idol worship. From Mount Sinai, God gave them a set of laws (engraved on tablets of stone) to help them learn how to live holy lives. Yet, the first thing that Israel did was build a golden calf, breaking the first commandment. The Law reveals our sin but cannot empower us to be obedient or righteous.

Living under the old covenant clearly revealed the need for a new and improved covenant (Hebrews 8:7). The old covenant foreshadowed the greater one to come.

Jesus instituted a better and more perfect contract signed in His blood. God's commandments no longer lie rigid and cold in stone, but now live and breathe inside us (2 Corinthians 3:3).

The new covenant fulfills the prophetic promise given in Jeremiah: "But this shall be the covenant that I will make with the house of Israel: After those days, saith the LORD, I will put my law in their inward parts, and write it in their hearts, and will be their God, and they shall be my people" (31:33). Is His new covenant written on your heart?

LORD JESUS, MAKE MY LIFE A LIVING LETTER WRITTEN BY YOUR SPIRIT SO THAT OTHERS MAY SEE YOU IN ME. I DESIRE TO LIVE A LIFE EMPOWERED BY YOUR SPIRIT. MAY OTHERS ALWAYS SEE YOU IN ALL THAT I SAY AND DO. AMEN.

DON'T SELL OUT

*Then King David sent, and fetched him [Mephibosheth] out
of the house of Machir, the son of Ammiel, from Lo-debar.*

—2 SAMUEL 9:4

Mephibosheth dwelt in the house of Machir,
which means "sold out." He had sold out to his
circumstances. Have you ever said, "Well, under the circumstances, I'm doing okay." Who says you are under
your circumstances? You are more than a conqueror. But
if your circumstances dictate your lifestyle instead of
your position, then you will sell out your birthright for
your current situation instead of waiting for your future
promise. You may have settled for less, but God won't.

Like the man with the withered hand, God will
demand that you stretch forth your disability (Mark
3:1–5). Perhaps, instead, you are like the prodigal son eating with pigs, but the Father is waiting for you to come
to His feast (Luke 15:11–32). You may be eating crumbs,
but God has prepared His table for you (Luke 16:19-31).
Yes, you can run from covenant but you cannot hide.
The light of His Light will expose you. You will say with
the psalmist, "If I say, Surely the darkness shall cover me;
even the night shall be light about me (Psalm 139:11).

Don't run from the covenant. Embrace the new
covenant with Jesus as Your Lord and Savior.

JESUS, I DESIRE TO BE IN COVENANT WITH
YOU. NO LONGER WILL I SELL OUT TO THE
WORLD WITH ALL OF ITS PLEASURES AND
TEMPTATIONS. I DESIRE YOU AND YOU ALONE.
AMEN.

DELIVERANCE

And God heard their groaning, and God remembered his covenant with Abraham, with Isaac, and with Jacob.

—EXODUS 2:24

God knew the descendants of Abraham would suffer the bonds of the Egyptians for more than four-hundred years, and He even told Abraham about it when they established their blood covenant (Genesis 15:13–16).

God had a plan for Abraham's descendants before Abraham had any children. He looked forward through time and chose the land He would give to them. He foresaw the results of idolatry, and in His perfect time brought forth a covenant people to establish a holy nation.

When the cry of Abraham's descendants reached God's ears, He was ready, and He "remembered His covenant." Because of the everlasting promises He had made to Abraham, deliverance was on the way!

The promises of the covenant will never be broken. When you are in need, cry out to God. Declare your covenant relationship with Him through Christ. Fix your eyes on Jesus, not on your need. Refuse to be entombed by your circumstances because you are in covenant with the Resurrection and the Life. Rejoice in everything (Philippians 4:4). Your deliverance is on the way!

JESUS, YOU ARE MY BONDAGE-BREAKER. YOU HAVE REPAIRED EVERY BREACH. YOU ARE MY BRIDGE OVER MY CIRCUMSTANCE TO YOUR DELIVERANCE. HELP ME TO REJOICE ALWAYS, FIXING MY EYES ON YOU. AMEN.

COVENANT EXCHANGE

Know therefore that the LORD thy God . . . keepeth covenant and mercy with them that love him and keep his commandments to a thousand generations.

—DEUTERONOMY 7:9

G od promised that any of His enemies who came against Abraham must inevitably face the Lord, not just Abraham. God will fight your battles for you when you walk in covenant with Him.

When you walk in covenant, you can be confident in possessing the promises of God in your life—salvation, deliverance, healing, and prosperity all belong to you.

He has given you His Word that when you are weak, He will give you His strength. When you have no ability, He will give you His ability (2 Corinthians 12:9–10). Philippians 4:13 promises that you can do all things through Christ, who strengthens you.

What a glorious exchange:
- His strength for your weakness
- His healing for your sickness
- His salvation for your sin
- His deliverance for your bondage!

LORD JESUS, I LAY DOWN ALL THAT I AM NOT IN EXCHANGE FOR ALL THAT YOU ARE. I AM NOT ABLE, BUT YOU ARE. I AM NOT SINLESS, BUT YOU ARE. I AM NOT STRONG, BUT YOU ARE. I RECEIVE ALL THAT YOU ARE. AMEN.

THE HIGH PRIEST

Neither by the blood of goats and calves, but by his own blood he entered in once into the holy place, having obtained eternal redemption for us.

—HEBREWS 9:12

Once a year the High Priest sprinkled the blood of the sacrificial lamb on the mercy seat to atone for the sins of the Israelites. The High Priest set aside his robe and jeweled ephod when he went before God. He wore only a simple linen garment.

Jesus, the High Priest of the new covenant, laid aside His glory and was utterly forsaken by God (Matthew 27:46). Humbled and alone, He entered the Holy of Holies and applied His blood to the mercy seat.

The death of Jesus on the Cross was the final sacrifice for sin. He has broken forever the powerful hold of Satan over man! (Revelation 1:18). You do not have to submit to the works of your adversary. Your High Priest willingly shed His blood so you could be free (John 10:18).

Jesus came to destroy the works of the devil (1 John 3:8). Christ in you is greater than the adversary in the world (1 John 4:4). So you can live today in victory, overcoming every attack of the enemy.

JESUS, I AM AN OVERCOMER IN YOU. I DECLARE THAT IN YOUR STRENGTH, I WILL OVERCOME EVERY TEMPTATION, WEAKNESS, AND BONDAGE. I WILL WALK IN YOUR VICTORY. AMEN.

BEHOLD HIM

He was in the world, and the world was made by him, and the world knew him not. He came unto his own, and his own received him not.

—JOHN 1:10–11

Many Christians do not understand the privileges of the covenant and, therefore, live lives of hardship and defeat. To the spiritually blind, Jesus cannot be seen. To the spiritually deaf, He cannot be heard. To the spiritually dead, He cannot be perceived. But in Christ, your eyes and ears have been opened. You have been quickened or made spiritually alive in Christ. You know Him!

Those who live apart from Him can look right past Him and not see Him. They think the promise of abundant life is meant for when this life is over.

Like Martha at the tomb of Lazarus, they sigh, "I know he shall rise again in the resurrection at the last day" . . . while Jesus stands before them saying, "Look at me! I am the resurrection!" (cf. John 11:24–25).

Abundant life with Jesus is not in the distant future. Your covenant blessings are yours today! Jesus came that you might have life and have it abundantly (John 10:10). Stop believing the lie of the world that you are destined to lack. Christ's resources are infinite. Touch infinity today.

JESUS, YOU ARE MY ABUNDANCE. THERE IS NO LACK IN YOU. YOU ARE MY SHEPHERD, I SHALL NOT WANT. SO TODAY, LORD JESUS, REMOVE MY LACK AND FILL ME WITH YOUR ABUNDANCE. AMEN.

COMFORTER

But when the Comforter is come, whom I will send unto you from the Father, even the Spirit of truth, which proceedeth from the Father, he shall testify of me.

—JOHN 15:26

J esus Christ is the same yesterday, and to day, and forever" (Hebrews 13:8). Jesus does not change. He was not a different Jesus for John than He is for you today. When you see Him with the eyes enlightened by the Holy Spirit, you will see the same Jesus whom John knew.

The Holy Spirit makes this possible, for He was sent to show us Jesus. "Howbeit when he, the Spirit of truth, is come, he will guide you into all truth . . . He shall glorify me: for he shall receive of mine, and shall shew it unto you" (John 16:13,15).

The Holy Spirit was called alongside us to help. The Spirit is the Paraclete—the One who stands beside us. He is our Comforter, Helper, and Teacher, given to us to carry out God's part of the covenant! Welcome the Holy Spirit into your life and allow Him to lead you into all truth and wisdom (1 Corinthians 2:7).

HOLY SPIRIT, LEAD, GUIDE, AND DIRECT MY LIFE. SHOW ME JESUS CONTINUALLY. TEACH ME HIS TRUTH. COMFORT ME IN EVERY SORROW AND PAIN. DWELL IN MY LIFE WHICH IS CONSECRATED TO BE YOUR TABERNACLE. AMEN.

MIDNIGHT DELIVERANCE

And it came to pass, that at midnight the LORD smote all the firstborn in the land of Egypt.

—EXODUS 12:29

At midnight, Ruth was introduced to Boaz. At midnight, Paul and Silas sang, and heaven couldn't help but hear their song.

Too often in the middle of the night, in the midst of our darkest crisis, at the depths of our darkest valley, we allow ourselves to become upset, distraught, concerned, and anxious. God sits on His throne saying, "When you have worn yourself out through your own ability, I will be here to help you and lift you up. When you have exhausted all your natural resources, when it seems the darkest and loneliest, and fear runs rampant, you have reached your midnight hour."

When you reach midnight, how do you respond? Do you stand firm or flee? Do you complain or confess Christ? Do you seek man or God? Do you try your own solutions or trust God?

We serve a God who is so much greater than we allow Him to be. Rely on Him alone. Turn to Him. In the midnight hours of your life, God will bring your deliverance. "At midnight I will arise to give thanks unto thee because of thy righteous judgments" (Psalm 119:62).

LORD, WHEN I CRY OUT TO YOU AT MIDNIGHT, HEAR MY CRY AND ANSWER MY NEED. TEACH ME TO SEEK YOU AND NOT TO DISPAIR WHEN I FACE MY MIDNIGHT CRISES. AMEN.

ON YOUR KNEES

He that cometh to God must believe that he is, and that he is a rewarder of them that diligently seek him.

—HEBREWS 11:6

This verse does not say that God rewards casual acquaintances or with those who know something about Him. It says God rewards those who diligently seek Him. "Knowing God" means to have an intimate relationship with Him. Jesus rejects lukewarm relationships (Revelation 3:15–16). He desires all your love, all your passion, and all your commitment.

If you are in a trial where the devil has stopped you in your tracks, don't become bitter or talk about it. That will only compound the problem. Find yourself a closet. Climb up the mountain of God. Like Jacob, declare, "Lord, I will not let thee go unless thou bless me" (Genesis 32:26).

There is help to be found in the closet of prayer (Matthew 6:6). God said, "Call unto me, and I will answer thee and shew thee great and mighty things which thou knowest not" (Jeremiah 33:3).

The promises of God are "yea" and "amen" (2 Corinthians 1:20). God's promises will not fall to the ground powerless if you will fall to your knees in prayer, proclaiming God's Word with authority and speaking forth His promises.

FATHER, ON MY KNEES, I CRY OUT TO YOU KNOWING THAT YOU HEAR AND ANSWER MY PRAYERS. THANK YOU FOR THE PRIVILEGE OF PRAYER. AMEN.

YOU ARE NEVER ALONE

But he [Shammah] stood in the midst of the ground, and defended it, and slew the Philistines: and the Lord wrought a great victory.

—2 SAMUEL 23:12

E very year, Shammah tilled his field and planned his harvest. Every year the Philistines took it from him. Shammah was again preparing to harvest his crop when he saw the Philistines coming.

This time something rose within him. He strode to the edge of his property and shouted, "Stop!" The chariots screeched to a halt as the jeering Philistines asked who this defiant man was.

When he declared, "I am Shammah!" they turned and headed back over the hills. They knew all about the God of the Israelites who was not only Jehovah Nissi, their banner of victory, and Jehovah Jireh, the God who supplied all their needs . . . but they were terrified of Jehovah Shammah, the God who is present in the midst of thee.

God is with you. He never leaves or forsakes you (Hebrews 13:5). Never proceed alone. The enemy will seek to isolate you from other Christians and from the Word. Pray in agreement, for there is power when two agree in prayer (Matthew 18:19).

You are not alone. He is with you every step of the way (Matthew 28:20).

IN YOU, JESUS, I AM NEVER ALONE. LEAD ME TO OTHER BELIEVERS WHO WILL AGREE WITH ME IN PRAYER. STAND WITH ME AS I FACE THE ENEMY. BE EVER PRESENT TO MY EVERY CIRCUMSTANCE. AMEN.

UNCONDITIONAL LOVE

The LORD hath appeared of old unto me, saying, Yea, I have loved thee with an everlasting love therefore, with lovingkindness have I drawn thee.

—JEREMIAH 31:3

R eligion is man seeking God. Christianity isn't about religion, but about relationship. Desiring a covenant relationship with us, God seeks us out. He loves us unselfishly and unconditionally. Being in covenant relationship with Him doesn't do anything for God. He does not need us, nor can we do anything for Him. Rather, God pursues us out of *agape*—unconditional love. In fact, He is driven to give to us.

I love my wife, Joni, with unconditional love. That means I love her whether or not she acts loving toward me. It also means that I love her whether or not I feel like it. I am in covenant relationship with her through marriage. I have promised to love her "for better or worse." And I am a driven husband. I am driven to give: to give her love, material necessities, and every luxury I can lavish upon her. The covenant I have with Joni imparts my every blessing to her.

In a much greater way, God is driven to give to us. His very nature of love compels Him to be a giver.

"God is love. In this was manifested the love of God toward us, that God sent his only begotten Son into the world, that we might live through him" (1 John 4:8b–10).

FATHER, I LOVE YOU WITH MY WHOLE HEART, SOUL, MIND, AND STRENGTH. I PRAISE YOU FOR MANIFESTING YOUR LOVE IN CHRIST JESUS. FILL ME WITH LOVE FOR OTHERS. AMEN.

IT IS GOD'S BATTLE

If, when evil cometh upon us . . . we stand before this house, and in thy presence . . . and cry unto thee in our affliction, then thou wilt hear and help.

—2 CHRONICLES 20:9

O utnumbered and surrounded, the nation of Israel faced disaster at the hands of the Moabites and the Ammonites. But King Jehoshaphat called them to get serious with God—to repent, fast, and cry out to God. He reminded God of His covenant of friendship with His people.

When we feel we are in a situation we cannot possibly overcome by our own power, that is the time we, like Jehoshaphat, are to bow our knee and acknowledge the source of our strength. When things get tough, we resist the temptation to get tougher and try to win in our own strength. Rather, we humble ourselves and seek God.

Because you are a joint heir in the covenant, you will receive the same response Jehoshaphat received: "Be not afraid nor dismayed by reason of this great multitude; for the battle is not yours, but God's" (2 Chronicles 20:15).

Do you feel overwhelmed today by a problem beyond your strength and abilities? If so, then turn to the problem-solver. As a joint heir with Christ, be not afraid. The battle belongs to Him!

JESUS, HELP ME TO STOP TRYING TO FIGHT EVERY BATTLE IN MY OWN STRENGTH. TEACH ME HOW TO TURN TO YOU IN EVERY BATTLE OF LIFE. AMEN.

WEEK 6—FRIDAY

HE CHOSE YOU

He hath chosen us in him before the foundation of the world, that we should be holy and without blame in him in love.

—EPHESIANS 1:4

The devil likes to condemn us and keep us down by whispering in our ears, "Look at you trying to act as if you're somebody when you know you're nobody! You've come from nowhere, and you're going nowhere." The devil uses the same old tactics in every battle. He deceives, lies, accuses, and seeks to destroy us.

When he does, remember David faced similar attacks from the enemy. When Samuel came to visit David's family, his father, Jesse, didn't even call him from tending the sheep (1 Samuel 16:11). Samuel came to anoint a king, but no one in David's family believed that he had the right stuff to be king. His brothers were older, wiser, taller, more handsome, and more experienced. Saul and his men laughed when David wanted to take on Goliath.

What David accomplished in his life for God had nothing to do with where he started and everything to do with the fact that God picked him out. Be not dismayed—regardless of your circumstances, God will take you out of wherever you are and bring you to wherever He wants you to be.

LORD, YOUR CALLING ON MY LIFE IS GREATER THAN ANY MAN CAN BELIEVE. I CANNOT LOOK TO OTHERS FOR MY SELF-ESTEEM OR SELF-WORTH. SO, LORD, I TURN TO YOU. IN YOU, I AM ROYALTY! AMEN.

STRAIGHT AHEAD

And he said unto me, My grace is sufficient for thee: for my strength is made perfect in weakness.

—2 CORINTHIANS 12:9

W hen the Israelites wanted to go back to Egypt, Moses said, "There isn't anything there for you any more. God's purpose and plan for you is straight ahead." Refuse to allow your past to dictate your future. Remember, there's nothing in your past to go back for— your past must be buried along with your sin. Give your present and your future to God.

The future is unlimited in God. You don't have to feel bound by the things that once bound you. You have Someone inside you who is greater than anything you will ever face.

One of the best things that can happen to you is to face an obstacle that is impossible to overcome by yourself. Then, when you are victorious, everyone must say, "It was God."

God is never in retreat. He is continually advancing His kingdom, moving forward in His divine plan and purpose. God wants to bring you all the way through, sustaining you in the midst of every trial. Rejoice, because blessing, strength, and enabling power are straight ahead (Jeremiah 29:11).

JESUS, I DECLARE THAT MY FUTURE IN YOU IS FILLED WITH GOODNESS. I KNOW THAT MY TOMORROW IN YOU IS GREATER THAN ANY- THING I CAN IMAGINE. AMEN.

STRENGTH IN WEAKNESS

Therefore I take pleasure in infirmities . . . for Christ's sake: for when I am weak, then am I strong.

—2 CORINTHIANS 12:10

A pastor who was accomplishing great things for God was asked the key to his success. Everyone thought he would respond with, "You need charisma," or "the ability to relate to people." They were astounded when, instead, he replied, "I have found the most important characteristic for anyone who wants to accomplish great things in the kingdom of God is weakness." No accomplishment of eternal value in God's kingdom is a result of men's efforts. It is a result of God using individuals who cannot do things by themselves.

Remember, if you can do it, then you don't need God. Become radically dependent upon Him. Your independence from God gives Satan a foothold into your life. Your weakness recognized and admitted is the Spirit's opportunity to use you as His vessel for ministry and service.

As you start your day, put God in charge. Ask Him to do what you cannot do through your own ability.

ALMIGHTY GOD, I ACKNOWLEDGE THAT IN YOU ALONE IS ALL STRENGTH, POWER, AND ANOINTING. I NEED YOU AND CAN DO NOTHING WITHOUT YOUR PRESENCE. SHOW ME MY WEAKNESSES AND FILL ME WITH YOUR STRENGTH TO ACCOMPLISH YOUR WILL. AMEN.

PREPARE FOR THE HARVEST

Behold, the days come, saith the LORD, that the plowman shall overtake the reaper, and the treader of grapes him that soweth seed.

—AMOS 9:13

Do you see it? The sower will overtake the reaper. God's promised harvest is that sowing and reaping will happen at the same time. Souls and abundance to the saints is coming quicker than we can preach, or sow. Time is caught up in an accelerated process. "Then shalt thou call, and the LORD shall answer; thou shalt cry, and he shall say, Here I am" (Isaiah 58:9a). Notice the immediacy of God's response.

The closer we get to the end of the age and the imminent return of Jesus, the shorter time becomes. The time is coming when seed time and harvest will be the same time.

Not only will we reap what we sow suddenly, but God will also multiply the sowers' seed. "Now he that ministereth seed to the sower both minister bread for your food, and multiply your seed sown, and increase the fruit of your righteousness" (2 Corinthians 9:10). That means that whenever we sow seed, God comes behind us and sows more. He brings such multiplication and increase to our sowing that before our seed can hit the ground, we are reaping a harvest.

LORD, THANK YOU FOR THE HARVEST. EQUIP ME BOTH TO SOW AND TO REAP AND TO EXPECT ALWAYS YOUR ABUNDANT HARVEST. AMEN.

BROKEN FOR YOU

The cup of blessing which we bless, is it not the communion of the blood of Christ? The bread which we break, is it not the communion of the body of Christ?

—1 CORINTHIANS 10:16

After two parties entered into a covenant, they celebrated by sharing a memorial meal. Using wine to represent the blood of the slain animal and bread to symbolize its flesh, they fed each other to symbolize becoming one.

At the Last Supper, Jesus identified Himself as the sacrificial animal whose blood would seal the new covenant, and He invited His disciples to partake of Him fully (Matthew 26:26–28). His eternal, unchanging covenant is still inviting the lost to receive Him fully and be saved.

When you celebrate the Lord's Supper, remember the covenant sealed with the blood of your Savior. His body was given and broken for you. His blood was shed for the remission of your sins. His sacrifice at Calvary assured your eternal place in God's kingdom.

In celebrating His Supper, remember His sacrifice. Welcome His presence. And celebrate His coming. His covenant meal points to His past atonement on the cross . . . His presence in You through the Holy Spirit . . . and His coming again to take you home.

JESUS, WHENEVER I PARTAKE OF COMMUNION, I WILL REMEMBER THE CROSS. I WILL COME INTO YOUR PRESENCE WELCOMING THE HOLY SPIRIT. AND I WILL CELEBRATE THE JOY OF YOUR RETURN TO TAKE ME HOME. AMEN.

THE FULLNESS OF TIMES

That in the dispensation of the fulness of times he might gather together in one all things in Christ.

—EPHESIANS 1:10

O ur eternal God created time to provide a measuring stick by which mortal men could recognize seasons in Him (Genesis 1:14), and a means by which they could gauge their own mortality.

Right now you have time—your most valuable commodity—but the time is quickly approaching when Jesus Christ will come to announce that time is no more.

You are a steward of every second in every minute God has given you. We are to redeem the time we have been given because the days in which we live are evil (Ephesians 5:16). Seize every opportunity to allow God to work His work in you. See each trial as an opportunity to become more Christ-like. See each day as one in which you can become stronger spiritually. Don't waste one second of your God-given time.

We serve a God of design, intention, and purpose. Be sensitive to His prompting and leading, and allow Him to guide you into fulfillment of your divine purpose.

FATHER, THANK YOU FOR EACH MOMENT YOU HAVE GIVEN ME. HOW I DESIRE TO LIVE EACH AND EVERY MINUTE FOR YOU. AMEN.

OUR VICTORY FLAG

. . . that ye may stand perfect and complete in all the will of God.

—COLOSSIANS 4:12

God is a faithful Father. He has a plan for you. Within that plan is the promise of provision. "Where there is no vision, the people cast off all restraint" (Proverbs 29:18 ASV). The vision—the plan of the Father—sets the parameters for our provision, protection, and peace. God will take care of you, as long as you stay in the vision.

When you step into your plan, you step out of His and the protection and provision it supplies. In Colossians 2:10 Paul writes, "We are complete in Him." In Colossians 4:12, Paul prays that we might stand perfect and complete in all the will of God.

If we become complete in the will of God, we march in His plan and provision—because He has, in eternity, laid out our tomorrow, secured its borders, and planted a victory flag in the middle of it. Defeat is not part of God's plan for you.

Live in God's plan for you: "For I know the plans I have for you," says the Lord. "They are plans for good and not for disaster, to give you a future and a hope" (Jeremiah 29:11 NLT).

LORD, I SURRENDER ALL MY PLANS TO YOUR PLANS. I KNOW YOUR PLANS FOR ME ARE PERFECT, GOOD, AND COMPLETE. AMEN.

DON'T GET LOST

And he wist not that the Lord was departed from him.
—JUDGES 16:20

When God gives you a particular strength, gift, or talent, guard against it becoming a weakness to you. You can reach the point where you say, "I can do this by myself. I don't need God."

Nebuchadnezzar made that statement and lost his kingdom (Daniel 4:28–37). Sometimes we lose our direction. We think we can do what God has called us to do without His anointing and His presence. Until we get out of the way, He can do nothing in us or through us. The power to accomplish great things for God only comes through His presence and anointing.

When Samson heard Delilah say, "Get up Samson, the Philistines are upon you," he thought, *I'll just get up and shake myself as other times* (cf. Judges 16). I believe what follows is one of the saddest verses in the Bible. It reveals that the Spirit of God had departed from him . . . and he didn't even know it.

Only when we recognize our weakness can we recognize God's strength. Acknowledge the One who has made His overcoming power and wisdom available to you.

LORD, WHEN I LOSE MY WAY, BRING ME QUICKLY BACK TO MY SENSES. HELP ME TO KNOW IMMEDIATELY WHEN I HAVE STRAYED FROM YOUR STRAIGHT AND NARROW PATH. HELP ME NOT TO LOOK TO THE RIGHT OR THE LEFT BUT TO FIX MY EYES ALWAYS ON YOU. AMEN.

A GETHSEMANE LIFESTYLE

. . . nevertheless not as I will, but as thou wilt.
—MATTHEW 26:39

God will orchestrate circumstances to cause us to surrender our will to His. Surrender never comes without a struggle. Your soul—your mind, will, and emotions—will struggle with your spirit for control of your thoughts and actions.

We struggle because we don't know tomorrow. We can only see today, but God knows and understands tomorrow the same way as we know and understand yesterday. We do not know what tomorrow holds, but we do know Who holds tomorrow!

Why do we often resist our heavenly Father's plan? Because in order to operate in that plan, we must live a Gethsemane lifestyle. Just as Jesus struggled in the Garden of Gethsemane, we too must come to the point where we are willing to say, "Not my will, but Thine be done." We must come to the point of surrendering our will and acknowledging and accepting His will at work in our lives.

Have you bowed your knee in surrender, or are you still struggling for control of your tomorrow? Living a Gethsemane lifestyle is a continual dying to soul, to self, and to the flesh, and surrendering completely to God's will.

FATHER, I OFFER YOU THE SACRIFICE OF MY SOUL—MY MIND, WILL, AND EMOTIONS. I DESIRE THE MIND OF CHRIST. I WANT TO DO YOUR WILL. I SEEK TO FEEL ACCORDING TO YOUR DESIRES. I EMPTY MYSELF OF ME AND ASK YOU TO FILL ME TO OVERFLOWING WITH YOUR HOLY SPIRIT. AMEN.

BURN BRIGHTLY

As long as I am in the world, I am the light of the world.
—JOHN 9:5

J esus said, "While I have been here, the kingdom has been here, and light has been shining in darkness. I'm leaving soon, but don't worry. I'm going to light candlesticks that will shine into the darkness, decadence and degradation. Even though darkness presses in around them, it cannot extinguish their light."

You say, "I don't have a dollar to change." What an opportunity for your light to shine! The doctors say you will not live much longer. What an opportunity to burn brightly! "I lost my job." What an opportunity! When things are darkest in your life, you have the opportunity to shine the most brightly for Jesus. Refuse to give your attention to the dark areas in your life. Look to the Light—Jesus Christ—who dispels all darkness and lights your life as a powerful witness for Him.

LORD JESUS, YOU HAVE MADE ME A CANDLE TO LIGHT THE DARKNESS OF THIS WORLD. HELP ME TO EMBRACE THE NIGHTFALL SO I CAN SHINE THROUGH THE DARKNESS, SHEDDING YOUR LIGHT IN THE HEARTS OF THE LOST AND DRAWING THEM INTO THE BRIGHTNESS OF YOUR PRESENCE. AMEN.

It's Your Decision

Greater is he that is in you, than he that is in the world.

—1 JOHN 4:4

Before you were born again you were a stranger to the covenants of promise, without God and without hope—just who the devil said you were!

But when you bowed your knee to Christ and called Him Lord of your life, you became the righteousness of God in Christ. In Christ you are forgiven, washed, reconciled, and redeemed.

It doesn't matter what the world says about you. The world cannot tell you the truth. The only reliable source of truth is the Truth—Jesus Christ. So, it doesn't matter what others say about you, and it doesn't even matter what you may have said about yourself in the past.

What matters is what God says about you in His Word. You must decide whether to believe God or to believe the lies of the devil concerning who you are in Christ.

Choose to believe the Word of God. Say out loud right now, "I am a child of the King. I am royalty." Trust Him to bring His Word to pass in your life, for greater is He that is in you than he that is in the world!

> **FATHER, THANK YOU FOR MAKING ME YOUR CHILD. I WILL CONTINUALLY CONFESS WHO I AM IN YOU. MY IDENTITY FOR ETERNITY IS ANCHORED IN YOU. AMEN.**

WORK OF FAITH

Every time we think of you, we thank God for you. Day and night you're in our prayers as we call to mind your work of faith, your labor of love, and your patience of hope.

—I THESSALONIANS 1:2–3 TMB

The faith of the Thessalonians was well known. Paul tells us their success was because they followed the example of the apostles.

They laid down their idols and abandoned the false worship they were taught from childhood. They gave themselves wholly to serving with deep devotion the one, true God. Although they came under great persecution for their faith, Paul exhorted them not to waver because God had given them the ability to overcome.

Our work of faith is not what we do but what God does in us. We must yield ourselves to the work of His Spirit in us. "Whereunto I also labour, striving according to his [Christ's] working, which worketh in me mightily" (Colossians 1:29). Christ is working in your mightily today.

Because you have a new identity, you can laugh in the face of the devil, and like the Thessalonians, be a sign and wonder to a hurting world. Christ's mighty works will be manifest in your life all around you to see and to give praise to the glory of God.

WORK MIGHTILY IN ME, O LORD. TAKE MY FAITH, HOPE, AND LOVE IN YOU AND USE ALL THAT I SAY AND DO FOR YOUR GLORY. AMEN.

LABOR OF LOVE

Beloved, let us love one another: for love is of God; and every one that loveth is born of God, and knoweth God. He that loveth not knoweth not God; for God is love.

—I JOHN 4:7–8

G od's response to our work of faith is His release of His life into us—overcoming, world-creating, death-defying love. The Greeks call it *agape* love, distinguishing it from *philos* (brotherly) love, *storge* (family) love, and *eros* (carnal) love.

Agape, God's love, is unconditional love with no strings attached. The Thessalonians labored in service to the true and living God, and His love was their inspiration (1 Thessalonians 1:3,9). *Agape* loves even when the one loved does not return love. *Agape* loves even when the circumstances or situations around us tell us to hate or respond with revenge.

His love is the life within us that drives us to do what we do. We do not witness because of some legalistic jargon written hundreds of years ago. We witness because we are in love with a Savior who died for us and made us alive. We labor because His life is being expressed through us. That love constrains us and becomes the inspiration of our labor also.

JESUS, YOU ALONE ARE THE SOURCE OF MY LOVE. I LOVE NOT BECAUSE I MUST BUT BECAUSE YOU FIRST LOVED ME. THANK YOU FOR LOVING ME EVEN BEFORE I EVER KNEW YOU. AMEN.

BUILD AN ALTAR

And Moses [put your name in his stead] built an altar, and called the name of it Jehovah-Nissi [God is my Banner].

—EXODUS 17:15

I challenge you right now to build an altar where you live, work, or worship. Stop what you are doing. Build an altar. Put on that altar the sin of leaving the banner of God unattended and failing to raise high the standard. Cover yourself and your altar with the banner of His love, crying out for His mercy and forgiveness.

After the altar there's a time of equipping and preparing, of training and conditioning for the battle. Get ready. Over the hill a battle rages. Around the corner the enemy sets an ambush and lies in wait. Get ready. Don't climb the hill or turn the corner without building an altar and raising high your standard. Don't go blindly into the battle.

Get under Jehovah Nissi. You are not the moon or the sun. You have no power on your own. But you can leave the night behind. You can become as fair as the moon and as clear as the sun. You can march in that terrible, awesome army of God, raising high His banner of victory. But a standard-bearer's initiation begins at the altar where he is washed in Jesus' blood, cleansed by living water, and exposed to His light.

JESUS, I LONG TO MARCH IN YOUR ARMY, TO LIFT YOUR STANDARD HIGH, AND TO BE UNDER YOUR BANNER. I BUILD AN ALTAR TODAY AND MAKE OF MYSELF A LIVING SACRIFICE TO YOU. AMEN.

CHARACTER-BUILDING LOVE

I say unto you, Love your enemies, bless them that curse you, do good to them that hate you, and pray for them which despitefully use you, and persecute you.

—MATTHEW 5:44

Never forget that while you were yet a sinner, Christ died for you (Romans 5:8). It is easy to get caught up in the cares of the world, forgetting how much our heavenly Father loves us.

Rejoice today in a love so deep and sure that death could not extinguish it. His love stretches from time eternal and reaches out to you with grace and mercy. That same love has been shed abroad in our hearts by the Holy Spirit.

God wants us to not only recognize our responsibility to operate in all the gifts of the Spirit, but He also expects us to validate those gifts by living a lifestyle that glorifies His name. That means loving our brother when our brother is unlovable.

Is there someone unlovable in your life? Think about that person today. Ask God to bless and touch that person. Ask the Spirit to reveal to you a way to show His love to that unlovely person today. Determine to reach out to today with the love of Jesus.

> **JESUS, GIVE ME LOVE FOR THE UNLOVELY PEOPLE IN MY LIFE. TEACH ME HOW TO LOVE THEM WITH YOUR UNCONDITIONAL LOVE. AMEN.**

ENDURING LOVE

*If I speak with human eloquence and angelic ecstasy but
don't have love, I'm nothing but the creaking of a rusty gate.*

—I CORINTHIANS 13:I TMB

Gifts are temporary, but love endures. God takes
an entire chapter to tell us, "If you don't love
each other, you can forget all the rest of it." If you are
not caring for your brother, God couldn't care less about
your prophesying.

There is a dying world that doesn't care how well you
sing or how eloquent your word of wisdom is. They are
dying, seeking New Age gurus, sticking needles in their
arms and drowning in a cesspool of pornography, because
they need someone to love them!

God desires that you reach out to them with His
love. They don't need your judgments, accusations, or
criticisms. They need Christ. Only He can set them free
from their bondages, diseases, or sin. Love them the way
God loves you.

The love of God at work in and through you is more
powerful than all the gifts of the Spirit rolled up
together.

JESUS, FILL ME WITH YOUR LOVE. HOW I
DESIRE TO LOVE OTHERS THE WAY YOU LOVE
ME! USE ME AS AN INSTRUMENT OF YOUR
LOVE. AMEN.

GET READY

They marvel at how expectantly you await the arrival of his Son . . . Jesus, who rescued us from certain doom.

—1 THESSALONIANS 1:10 TMB

———

The Greek word *amaneno* translated "await" here is still used in the Greek language today to stress the eagerness of the waiting as well as the readiness of those who are waiting. Paul commended the Thessalonians for their faithful service as they waited for the Lord's return.

Like the Thessalonians, we too are to be ready when Christ returns for the church. How? Through service—our labor of love.

We are admonished in Romans 10:12 to "prefer one another and again" in Hebrews 10:24 to "consider one another." The writers were telling us not to be so wrapped up in ourselves and what we are doing, that we have no time to lend a hand to those in need.

Give yourself wholeheartedly in service to God and His people, and you will be ready for the Lord's return. Don't wait to be served before you serve others. Give without expectation of return. God will reward you and take care of your needs.

JESUS, TEACH ME TO SERVE OTHERS THE WAY YOU SERVED. I DESIRE TO BE YOUR SERVANT AND TO PREFER OTHERS OVER MYSELF. AMEN.

INCREASING POWER

For as the body is one, and hath many members, and all the members of that one body, being many, are one body, so also is Christ.

—1 CORINTHIANS 12:12

Your brain provides every electrical impulse required by your internal and external organs to function rhythmically and powerfully with one another.

Your hand can move independent of the body. But adding your wrist, arm, shoulder, torso weight, and movement increases the hand's impetus, power, and capabilities.

Although you are complete in Christ, you must be joined to the body of Christ to be functionally complete and to accomplish His will.

When you occupy your place in the body of Christ, your significance multiplies by the entirety of the body of the living, resurrected Christ. By joining yourself to the body, you increase in Him as you decrease in self. "A spiritual gift is given to each of us as a means of helping the entire church" (1 Corinthians 12:7 NLT). You are gifted to serve others. You are blessed so that you may be a blessing to others.

When the devil sees you, a fitly joined member of the body, he knows the body is in full operation under the Lord Jesus Christ, head over all things to the church.

LORD, USE THE GIFTS YOU HAVE PLACED IN ME TO SERVE OTHERS. I AM WILLING TO BE YOUR VESSEL OF MINISTRY IN ORDER TO BLESS OTHERS. AMEN.

KINGDOM VISION

He saith unto them, But whom say ye that I am? And Simon Peter answered and said, Thou art the Christ, the Son of the living God.

—MATTHEW 16:15–16

W hen Peter called Jesus "the Son of the living God," he was saying, "You are the king; this is Your kingdom. You are in control. Everything You say will come to pass. No person can deny You. No devil can withstand You! No circumstance can stop You!

"You are the healer, deliverer, redeemer, the one who ransoms, the lily of the valley, and the bright and morning star. You are hope to the hopeless and help to the helpless. You are a father to the orphan and a husband to the widow! To those who walk the dark night, You are the bright, morning star, the light of the world! You are the Anointed One whom Israel has sung songs about for four thousand years! You are the King of kings and the Prince of Peace! You are who we have hoped for, sung for, prophesied for, believed for, and waited for!"

Who do you say He is? Speak out His name and give Him praise for all that He has done for you.

> I PRAISE YOU, LORD JESUS. YOU HAVE REDEEMED MY LIFE FROM THE PIT AND HAVE SET ME ON SOLID GROUND. YOU ARE MY HOPE AND MY REDEEMER. HOW I PRAISE YOUR NAME. AMEN.

A WAY OF LIFE

Repent ye therefore, and be converted, that your sins may be blotted out, when the times of refreshing shall come.

—ACTS 3:19

Repentance is not a negative message, but one of covenant blessing. When you allow your heart to indulge in lust, pride, rebellion, or selfishness you cut yourself off from His covenant.

Sin does not destroy God's love for us. He loves us with a love that is incorruptible (Romans 5:8), but you can go to hell with God still loving you. Just as confession is more than lip service to God, salvation is more than forgiveness of your sins. It is a lifestyle in which you choose to become God's own possession. The only way you can ever enter into His covenant and stay in that covenant is to love Him with all your heart and to have no idols before Him.

If God is not first in everything, you need to change your mind about God and toward God. Then and only then will your heart be free to abandon itself to loving Him. He is a jealous God and will allow no other gods in your life. Destroy all of your idols and live totally for God.

LORD, I REPENT OF MY PAST SINS AND IDOLS. I TURN AWAY FROM THE WAYS OF THE WORLD AND SEEK TO LIVE SOLELY FOR YOU. FORGIVE ME, CLEANSE ME, AND MAKE ME NEW THROUGH THE BLOOD OF CHRIST. AMEN.

AN ARMY OF REPENTANCE

Who is she that looketh forth as the morning, fair as the moon, clear as the sun, and terrible as an army with banners?

—SONG OF SOLOMON 6:10

Without repentance, your refreshing, revival, and restoration cannot come. The gift of the Holy Spirit cannot come. "*Repent,* and be baptized every one of you in the name of Jesus Christ for the remission of sins, and ye shall receive the gift of the Holy Ghost" (Acts 2:38, italics added).

People vainly seek the presence of God without first repenting. But God hates sin. He demands, "Be holy: for I the Lord your God am holy" (Leviticus 19:2). Be certain of this: You cannot know His presence without first turning from your sin and guilt. Repentance was the first adamant message of the early church: "*Repent* ye therefore, and be converted, that your sins may be blotted out, when the times of refreshing shall come from the presence of the Lord" (Acts 3:19, italics added).

We must forsake, rebuke, and reject the shadows of sin threatening to pull us back into the obscure darkness. We must abandon old wells—wells from the world, from past sin, from religious tradition. We will never be "the terrible army of banners" until we first repent.

> JESUS, I REPENT OF ALL MY PAST AND I
> REJECT THE NIGHT OF RELIGIOUS TRADITIONS
> AND THE WAYS OF THE WORLD. I SEEK TO
> WALK IN YOUR LIGHT AND MARCH IN YOUR
> ARMY. DRAFT ME TO DO YOUR WILL IN YOUR
> WAY. AMEN.

WE HAVE THE KING

They all continued with one accord in prayer and supplication.

—ACTS 1:14

⬤riginally, five hundred people witnessed the resurrection, but only one hundred and twenty stayed in Jerusalem as Jesus commanded to wait on Him—doing what He said, where, when and how He said to do it. Of these, three hundred and eighty missed Pentecost because they did not obey the King. Don't miss the visitation of the Holy Spirit in your life because of disobedience.

The church was born as the other one hundred and twenty people poured themselves out in humble obedience. They said, "Anyone who has the keys of death and hell must have the keys of the kingdom. If He has the keys of the kingdom, He must be the King of the kingdom!"

They didn't have a great building. They didn't have a head preacher . . . no choir, no radio, no television, and no Bible. They didn't have anything but a King! And if you have the King, He brings the kingdom with Him!

That's all we need! We don't need another building, another program, another lecture, another sermon, another tape series, nor another book! All we need is the King.

KING JESUS, I SUBMIT TO YOUR AUTHORITY AND WILL IN MY LIFE. I DESIRE FOR YOU TO RULE MY WHOLE BEING. ESTABLISH YOUR KINGDOM IN MY LIFE. AMEN.

DON'T LET GO

And Jacob was left alone; and there wrestled a man with him until the breaking of the day.

—GENESIS 32:24

The name Jacob means "deceiver, supplanter, liar, or thief." All his life Jacob had lived up to his name. When conflict arose from his deceitful actions against his brother, he didn't see any way out. In fear and desperation, he returned to Bethel. He climbed the mountain where he first made an altar to the Lord, and it was there that the angel of the Lord wrestled with him.

Jacob said to the angel, "It took too long to find you, I'm not letting you go!" In that struggle, Jacob was forever changed. God gave Jacob a new nature. He carried God's mark, and He carried a new name—Israel.

When God takes hold of us, old things pass away, and all things become new in Christ (2 Corinthians 5:17). He made all things new for Jacob, and He will do the same for you. Seek God with all your heart. Refuse to let go until you have been forever changed.

JESUS, CHANGE ME. MAKE ME A NEW CREATION BY THE POWER OF YOUR SPIRIT. DESTROY THE OLD AND MAKE ME NEW. AMEN.

ABUNDANT LIFE

Lord, thou hast heard the desire of the humble: thou wilt prepare their heart, thou wilt cause thine ear to hear.

—PSALM 10:17

Great revelation doesn't come without preparation. You cannot plant an acorn in concrete and expect to grow a majestic oak tree. In the same way, you cannot expect great revelation until you have prepared your heart to receive it. The soil of your heart must be prepared to receive the seed of God's Word. Your heart's soil is prepared by repentance, prayer, study of the Word, worship, and seeking God's face.

Revelations are released for specific needs at certain times. The Reformation was based on one simple truth: "The just shall live by faith." This was the message the world of Martin Luther's day so desperately needed to hear.

God chose the '40s, '50s, and '60s of this century to say, "I am still your healer." God's revelation for our generation is a truth that has been abused, ridiculed and misunderstood: Our God is a God of abundance.

His abundance was not placed on earth to satisfy our fleshly desires, but rather, to establish His kingdom. Pray for the Holy Spirit to lead you into a lifestyle of abundant, kingdom living.

JESUS, I PRAISE YOU FOR THE ABUNDANT LIFE YOU ARE GIVING ME. I DESIRE TO HEAR YOUR VOICE AND SEEK YOUR FACE. AMEN.

HE'S IN YOU

God would make known what is the riches of the glory of this mystery . . . which is Christ in you, the hope of glory.

—COLOSSIANS 1:27

The Tabernacle is a perfect picture of the coming of Christ and that He wants to live in you. The glory of God dwelt in the Holy of Holies. The very presence and tangibility of God resided within that holy chamber. Once a year the High Priest entered to sprinkle the blood of animals as an atonement for the sins of the people (Hebrews 9:7).

The Holy of Holies and the Ark of the Covenant itself have been transferred from a shittim-wood box, overlaid with gold. God has engraved those tablets not on tablets of stone, but on the fleshly tablets of your heart.

He has laid deity over your humanity and sent you out into the world as a living, breathing, moving Ark of His covenant! Jesus Christ, the Anointed One, and His anointing reside in you. You are being transformed from glory to glory. "But we all, with open face beholding as in a glass the glory of the Lord, are changed into the same image from glory to glory, even as by the Spirit of the Lord" (2 Corinthians 3:18).

JESUS, CLOTHE AND TRANSFORM ME WITH YOUR GLORY SO THAT ALL I DO MAY GIVE GLORY AND HONOR TO YOUR NAME. AMEN.

TRANSFORMING LIFE

What? know ye not that your body is the temple of the Holy Ghost which is in you, . . . and ye are not your own?

—1 Corinthians 6:19

When you were born again, the Spirit of God took up residence in you, and He imparted His very nature and being into your spirit. God left the man-made Holy of Holies and made you, the born-again believer, the temple of His presence.

You are in vital union with the Father. You have life in you today to transform your marriage, your relationship with your children, and your finances. There is life in you right now to heal your body. "In him was life; and the life was the light of men" (John 1:4). Take hold of this powerful truth today and begin to express His life.

We have been built up a holy habitation of the Lord, and He is building His dwelling place out of living stones. As His tabernacle, the presence of God goes wherever you go. You can bring those around you into His presence at any time and in any place. You bring life, healing, power, and deliverance into the lives of others through His indwelling presence. Is Jesus touching others through you?

JESUS, INDWELL ME AND OVERFLOW ME TOUCHING ALL THOSE AROUND ME. TEACH ME HOW TO KEEP MY TEMPLE HOLY FOR YOU. AMEN.

READY FOR BATTLE

But be ye doers of the word, and not hearers only, deceiving your own selves.

—JAMES 1:22

⚝

Y ou are in a spiritual battle every day you awaken on this earth; in the midst of battle there is no time to waver. The devil's plan is to take you out and put you under. He will succeed, if you walk into the battle saying, "Well, I don't know if I should go this way, or maybe I should go that way."

Indecision in itself is a choice. Sooner or later your time for decisions will run out. Make a decision today that will serve you the rest of your life. Make a decision not to be a hearer only but a doer of the Word.

Decide not to let the Word of God depart from your eyes. Keep His Word in the midst of your heart and meditate on it. Hide His Word in your heart and you will be empowered to resist sin. "Thy word have I hid in my heart, that I might not sin against thee" (Psalm 119:11). Then, when the devil launches his vilest attack, the Word will be a lamp unto your feet (Psalm 119:105). You will stand ready for battle, fortified by the Word of God.

O LORD, I HIDE THY WORD IN MY HEART, KNOWING THAT YOU WILL GUIDE AND DIRECT MY PATH IN THE WAY OF RIGHTEOUSNESS AND TRUTH. INSTRUCT ME IN THY WORD, O LORD. AMEN.

GOD'S FRIEND

Abraham believed God, and it was imputed unto him for righteousness: and he was called the Friend of God.

—JAMES 2:23

A braham was called the "Friend of God," because he believed God and willingly obeyed His direction. As born-again believers, we are already made righteous, and if we are obedient from hearts that seek to love Him, we too will be called "friends" by our Father in heaven. But if we obey God out of religious traditions, we cannot be His friend. Friendship is what religion is not. Religion is a ritual, but friendship is relationship. God's desires a relationship with us, not empty religious ritual.

Friendships are not built on fear, duty, or legalism. Instead, they are built on mutual love, respect, and trust which says, "I trust you not to do anything to hurt me. I trust you have my best interest at heart." When we trust God, it's easy to obey Him.

Jesus no longer calls us servants but friends, and He will make all things known to us. Jesus tells His disciples: "Greater love hath no man that a man lay down his life for his friends. You are my friends, if you do whatsoever I command you" (John 15:13–15).

JESUS, YOU ARE MY BEST FRIEND. I OBEY YOU NOT FOR WHAT YOU WILL DO FOR ME BUT BECAUSE I LOVE YOU SO VERY MUCH. THANK YOU FOR CALLING ME YOUR FRIEND. AMEN.

EXAMINE YOURSELF

Examine yourselves, whether ye be in the faith; prove your own selves.

—2 CORINTHIANS 13:5

I s Christ truly the Lord of your life? Are you ready to accept and act upon His Word? Are you willing to invest the time and effort necessary to receive what God has for you? Will you acknowledge the source of your supply? Can you be trusted with what He places in your hands?

God's truth about abundance only comes alive in your life when you are ready to receive it. If you said "no" to any of these questions, you need to get serious with God. Seek Him in prayer for His life-changing power to come into your heart. Tell yourself the truth. Self-examination reveals areas of your life that are still unconsecrated.

But if you have said "yes" to God and "no" to the world; if your heart is ready to receive and act on His Word; if you are ready to invest your time and energy to receive all He has for you; if you acknowledge Him as your true source and will be a worthy steward of all He gives—prepare to embark on a course of abundant life and blessing!

> LORD JESUS, I CONSECRATE EVERY AREA OF MY LIFE TO YOU. I AM WILLING TO OBEY YOU IN ALL THINGS. I SAY "YES" TO YOUR EVERY DEMAND ON MY LIFE. AMEN.

INSTRUMENT RATED

Then shalt thou understand the fear of the LORD, and find the knowledge of God. For the LORD giveth wisdom: out of his mouth cometh knowledge and understanding.

—PROVERBS 2:5–6

Pilots of small aircraft are required to be "instrument rated." This means they can fly without depending on their vision.

In a storm, pilots can lose all sense of direction. Their only hope is to lock onto their instruments and depend on the aircraft's guidance system to show them the way.

The Word of God is our spiritual guidance system. We must not depend on what we can see with our eyes or feel with our emotions. The devil attacks us in the realm of our senses, but the Holy Spirit guides us in our spirit (John 16:13). Are you trusting your sight or His?

The writer of Hebrews calls faith "the substance of things hoped for, the evidence of things not seen" (Hebrews 11:1). No matter what is happening around you, put your faith in the true, undeniable Word of the living God, and He will see you through. You will weather the storm not through "flying by the seat of your pants," but through flying with His Word as Your true compass, pointing you in the direction of righteousness.

LORD, YOU ARE NOT MY CO-PILOT; YOU ARE MY PILOT, MY AIRCRAFT, MY INSTRUMENTS, MY POWER, AND THE WIND BENEATH MY WINGS. I WILL FLY ONLY WHERE YOU SEND ME. AMEN.

OUR TRUE FATHER

For though ye have ten thousand instructors in Christ, yet have ye not many fathers; for in Christ Jesus I have begotten you through the gospel.

—1 CORINTHIANS 4:15

Any man can be a father, but it takes someone special to be a dad. A father is not a father just because he can produce a child. To be a true father he must also love, protect and provide for his child.

God says, "I am your Father and I am responsible for you. I have a plan for you." Like a loving dad, He will make whatever sacrifice is necessary to see His child birthed into and advanced in His kingdom.

God sacrificed His Son to protect and provide for you. He caused the heavens to go black and smote His Son because He knew the day would come when you bowed your knee to say, "Lord, I need you."

God not only wants to meet your material needs, but He desires to bring you fully into the abundant life of His kingdom. Abundance begins not with material blessings but the blessings of His presence and favor. In His presence is life. Apart from His presence is death. In His presence is blessing. Outside of His presence is curse. Abundance springs from resting in His grace and presence.

LORD, I DESIRE YOU MORE THAN ANYTHING, EVEN LIFE ITSELF. YOU ARE MY LIFE AND MY STRONG TOWER. I AM FILLED WITH THANKS-GIVING FOR EVERY GOOD GIFT FROM YOUR HAND. AMEN.

BEFORE YOU NEED

But when ye pray, use not vain repetitions, as the heathen do . . . Be not ye therefore like unto them: for your Father knoweth what things ye have need of, before ye ask him.

—MATTHEW 6:7–8

You serve a God who supplies your needs before you even know you have a need. He created the seed that would grow into the tree that would be crafted into the chair you are sitting on. The Almighty had you in mind long ago when that seed first fell to the ground.

If you have a need, that's proof He has already provided everything for that need to be met. Regardless of the situation you may be in at this very moment, God has already provided. Whether your children need new shoes or you do not know how you are going to pay the rent, rest in the assurance that not only will He provide, but He will stop Satan in his tracks. God knows your need. He had a plan to take care of everything before you were even born.

Take time to set aside all of your physical and emotional needs for your greatest need—your need of Him. Hunger and thirst for God. Seek Him with your whole heart. Know that when He meets with You then every need is met.

THANK YOU, LORD, FOR KNOWING AND MEET-ING ALL MY NEEDS. HOW I NEED YOU, O GOD. VISIT ME WITH YOURSELF FOR IN YOU ALL MY NEEDS ARE MET. HALLELUJAH! AMEN.

ESTABLISH YOUR HEART

And he shall be like a tree planted by the rivers of water, that bringeth forth his fruit in his season; his leaf also shall not wither; and whatsoever he doeth shall prosper.

—PSALM 1:2–3

God established His covenant in the earth, but if you are not established in His covenant, it will never do you any good. Our hearts must be established in His Word, which bonds us to the mind of Christ.

The psalmist gives us a perfect description of those whose hearts are established: Men who fear the Lord and delight in His commandments are blessed with abundance that cannot be taken away. You will reap the fruit in whatever your heart is established and rooted—fear or faith; sickness or health; poverty or prosperity; sin or righteousness. As Joshua prepared for battle, God said if he would meditate in His Word, he would prosper and be successful (Joshua 1:8).

Spend time in the Word. Hide it in your heart. Through the Word, God will chart the course for His abundance to be released into your life. Deposit these two verses in your heart:

"It is the spirit that quickeneth; the flesh profiteth nothing: the words that I speak unto you, they are spirit, and they are life" (John 6:63).

"Thy word have I hid in mine heart, that I might not sin against thee" (Psalm 119:11).

THY WORD, O LORD, I HIDE IN MY HEART. ROOT AND ESTABLISH ME IN THY WORD THAT I MIGHT PROSPER AND BEAR GOOD FRUIT FOR THY KINGDOM. AMEN.

HOMESTEAD YOUR LAND

And it shall be, when thou art come in unto the land which the LORD thy God giveth thee . . . and dwellest therein.

—DEUTERONOMY 26:1

ashab, the Hebrew word translated "dwell" in the Old Testament, means "to settle down" and "to marry." Some of us are still in courtship in the kingdom of God. God doesn't call us to a dating relationship. As the bridegroom, Jesus calls us to be His bride. He wants more than our mere infatuation. Jesus desires our passionate, fiery love.

When we marry, we set up a homestead. America's settlers knew about homesteading. It was a requirement for them to obtain title to the land they claimed, along with digging wells and planting a crop.

In the spiritual realm there is land sectioned out by God—more than enough for everyone. There are hills of healing and quadrants of joy. There are acres of ability to annihilate the forces of darkness. The soils of salvation abound.

Are you still "courting" God, or are you ready to settle down and get serious with God and homestead your promised land? In His promised land there is abundance, blessing, life, and a future. Outside of His land, there is only desolate wilderness, endless wandering, and ongoing seasons of dryness and lack. Come to the promised land.

LORD, YOU ARE MY PLACE OF DWELLING. YOU ARE MY LAND OF PROMISE AND MY FUTURE AND HOPE. AMEN.

THE SECRET

For the froward [the perverse] is abomination to the LORD, but his secret is with the righteous.

—PROVERBS 3:32

The first time I read Proverbs 3:32 I said, "Does that mean I know something I don't know?" And God answered, "Absolutely." Amos declared, "Surely the LORD God will do nothing, but he revealeth his secret unto his servants the prophets" (Amos 3:7).

Where can you find God's answer for your financial needs? Where can you go to uncover His plan for your life? You need not look far. God has hidden His secret with you!

The world will not understand the secret you possess. It is not for the unrighteous, but for those who are pure before the Lord. Although the world is sinking in debt, I am convinced the problem is not a shortage of money but morality. There is no lack of resources—only righteousness. God has established specific principles He expects us to follow. Follow His blueprint, and you will receive His blessing. His secret is Christ dwelling in you imparting to you His Spirit and instructing you in His Word.

"Even the mystery which hath been hid from ages and from generations, but now is made manifest to his saints: To whom God would make known what is the riches of the glory of this mystery among the Gentiles; which is Christ in you, the hope of glory" (Colossians 1:26–27).

LORD, I AM ETERNALLY GRATEFUL THAT YOU HAVE REVEALED EVERY MYSTERY AND SECRET IN CHRIST AND THAT YOU NOW INDWELL ME BY THE POWER OF HIS SPIRIT. AMEN.

KINGDOM FINANCES

Jesus went about all Galilee, teaching in their synagogues, and preaching the gospel of the kingdom.

—MATTHEW 4:23

God's kingdom is not a democracy. Christ is our King, and we are His loyal subjects. When we accept His Lordship, we accept His provision and His protection. When we refuse His reigning presence, we are assured of destruction. You are only the trustee of what you possess. Everything you have belongs to your King.

Again and again Jesus taught us that if we will be good stewards of what God gives us, when He returns we will be greatly rewarded.

The power to create wealth is one of God's gifts under the covenant. Jesus only intensified the terms of the covenant. If we will live faithfully under the new covenant, we will be even more effective than those who operated under the old covenant. If you will submit your finances to the headship of Christ, you will experience the prosperity, blessing, freedom, and security His authority brings.

What material possessions do you now need to surrender to the Lordship of Christ? What do you need to surrender? Surrendering everything to Him opens you to receiving whatever He desires to give to you.

LORD, I RELEASE MY GRASP ON ALL MY MATERIAL POSSESSIONS. I KNOW THAT I OWN NOTHING. I AM YOUR STEWARD, AND EVERYTHING BELONGS TO YOU. HELP ME TO GIVE THAT I MIGHT RECEIVE AND THEN GIVE AGAIN. AMEN.

MAKE AN EXCHANGE

Now the sojourning of the children of Israel, who dwelt in Egypt was four hundred and thirty years.

—EXODUS 12:40

L ife is a process of exchange. We enter to leave, go up to come down, give to receive, and die to live. God wants to make some exchanges in your life. He wants to lead you out of bondage and into your Promised Land.

The status quo is your greatest enemy of the cause of Christ. The Israelites were comfortable in Egypt and soon begged to go back. But your abundance is tied to the process of exchange. God wants you to exchange the bondage of your Egypt for the abundance of His Promised Land. He wants to bring you out of the kingdom of the world and into His glorious kingdom.

Don't stay in bondage another day. Determine to break through the boundaries the devil has raised up around you. Exchange your way of doing things for God's, and go forward with Him into your Promised Land.

LORD JESUS, I EXCHANGE EVERYTHING I AM AND HAVE FOR ALL OF YOU. I EXCHANGE MY BONDAGE FOR YOUR FREEDOM. THANK YOU, LORD, FOR THE GRACE OF EXCHANGING MY SIN FOR YOUR RIGHTEOUSNESS. AMEN.

POSSESS YOUR LAND

Therefore all they that devour thee shall be devoured; and all thine adversaries, every one of them, shall go into captivity; and they that spoil thee shall be a spoil.

—JEREMIAH 30:16

God did not drive out the inhabitants of the Promised Land. He promised the territory to the Israelites, but they had to possess it.

Any army strategist understands the meaning of possession: Enemy territory has been occupied, and the spoils of war have been taken. You are engaged in a battle against the enemy of your soul. The devil has stolen what belongs to you, and God is telling you to take it back.

Let God transform your thinking. Stop relying on your feelings and start trusting His Word and His will for your life. You may feel defeated, but Christ has already won your victory at the Cross. You may feel sick, but Christ has already healed you by His stripes. You may feel impoverished, but Christ has already laid up an eternal inheritance for you in heaven. Don't trust your feelings—trust Jesus.

Make this your season to spoil the enemy and possess your spiritual Promised Land of blessing and abundance.

GOD, I TRUST YOU, NOT MY FEELINGS, THOUGHTS, OR CIRCUMSTANCES. I REFUSE TO BELIEVE THE LIES OF THE ENEMY. AMEN.

PREPARE FOR THE RAIN

For the land, whither thou goest in to possess it . . . is a land of hills and valleys, and drinketh water of the rain of heaven.

—DEUTERONOMY 11:10–11

God was preparing His people for the land of hills and valleys, ups and downs. He was in charge. God had delivered them from Egyptian slavery, pagan religion, and bondage. The past was finished. Newness was coming.

Now God is preparing you. You can walk in the rain. You can drink from an ever-flowing well. You can leave the desert and the dry season. The past is forgiven, and the chains of bondage are broken.

At times the drought seems like it will never end. It appears that the night will last forever. Look forth, the morning is coming. You will be fair as the moon and as clear as the sun. I know you don't feel like it now, but feelings are not reality. The truth you stand on is not your feelings, not what the preacher preaches, not what any creed claims. Your truth is God's Word. He says that you will look forth as the morning and march terrible as an army with banners (Song of Solomon 6:10).

Exchange your dry season for the season of His rain, refreshing, and renewing. Exchange your defeat for victory as a mighty army marching to vanquish every foe.

LORD JESUS, PREPARE ME FOR YOUR RAIN.
POUR OUT LIVING WATER ON ME. REFRESH ME
AND FILL ME FROM YOUR FOUNTAINS THAT
WILL NEVER RUN DRY. AMEN.

A NEW CREATURE

Therefore if any man be in Christ, he is a new creature: Old Things are passed away; behold, all things are become new.

—2 CORINTHIANS 5:17

The process of exchange begins with repentance—the only passport recognized at the gates of His kingdom. To repent means "to turn from." You turn from your sin to His forgiveness; your pain to His healing; your lack to His abundance.

God's Word gives you a new realization of your resources: You are a child of more, not of less. You are a child of provision, not of poverty.

God's Word requires you to submit your will to His. The greatest barriers to His blessing are stubbornness and conceit. Believing we have all the answers doesn't give God room to work.

God's Word requires you to control your emotions. Self-discipline, combined with God's abundance, brings good stewardship.

Abundance begins with obedience. Accept God's authority over your life, and allow Him to do His transforming work in your mind.

LORD JESUS, TRANSFORM ME. RENEW MY MIND SO THAT MY EVERY THOUGHT WILL BE OF AND FROM YOU. KEEP ME IN YOUR PERFECT WILL. AMEN.

TAKE THE LIMITS OFF

Put on the new man, which after God is created in right-eousness and true holiness.

—EPHESIANS 4:23-24

E**verything in God's kingdom is in opposition to the ways of the world. To live, we must first die to ourselves, our desires, and our flesh. To receive, we must first give. To bring us out, God brings us in—out of the shadows and into His marvelous light.**

We think we can only make this much, save this much, and invest this much at this percentage rate. But our efforts only limit God. Life is not prescribed by our limits but by His limitlessness. But God promises a better rate of return. When our seed is sown in good ground we can expect a yield of some thirtyfold, some sixty, and some an hundred (Mark 4:20).

Once you begin operating in God's kingdom, the rules change; there are no limits to His abundance. Which kingdom are you living in? Are you submitted to the laws of the world? Commit to the guidance and care of your heavenly Father, and take the limits off!

FATHER, I DESIRE TO LIVE IN YOUR LIMITLESS LOVE, POWER, AND GRACE. FORGIVE ME FOR ESTABLISHING LIMITS WHERE YOU HAVE NONE. AMEN.

BE BOLD

The wicked flee when no man pursueth: but the righteous are bold as a lion.

—PROVERBS 28:1

This is the heritage of the righteous. We are warriors with enemies to overcome. One of our strongest enemies is fear. Fear stifles the church from fulfilling its destiny.

What would you attempt for God if you knew it was impossible to fail? God gave a direct order when he said, "Fear thou not" (Isaiah 41:10). It isn't an option. He also told you why you need no longer be afraid: "For I am with thee: be not dismayed; for I am thy God: I will strengthen thee; yea, I will help thee: yea, I will uphold thee with the right hand of my righteousness" (v. 10). Fear is counteracted by faith.

Perfect faith cannot exist where there is doubt concerning God's will to prosper you. When the will of God is known, faith comes alive and fear dies. Faith and fear cannot exist in the same space. Fill your heart with faith in Christ, and fear will flee.

JESUS, I RENOUNCE FEAR FOR FAITH IN YOU. I REBUKE THE SPIRIT OF FEAR AND STAND FIRM TRUSTING YOU. AMEN.

EL SHADDAI

But he saveth the poor from the sword, from their mouth, and from the hand of the mighty.

—JOB 5:15

L ike Job, who lost everything, you may feel as though you are far from God's blessing. As he sat in the ashes of ruin, Job's wife urged him to curse God and die. But Job proclaimed, "I know that my redeemer liveth!" (Job 19:25).

Job kept his eyes on God and was completely restored. The same God who brought Job back from the jaws of death and destruction can touch your life. Everything you need is already available because our God is El Shaddai, "the One who is All Sufficient."

God did not send the children of Israel into Canaan to be defeated, but to conquer. He wants your Promised Land to be conquered, and He wants to use you to conquer it. El Shaddai, the All Sufficient One, has given you all you need to possess your land. It is time for you to tell the dethroned and defeated devil, "Stand back! You have no authority. I am taking what is rightfully mine."

Prepare yourself to take back what the enemy has stolen. He has no authority over you, your family, or anything that the Lord has given you. The enemy can only take what you choose to lose. Everything you need to defeat the enemy is provided to you by El Shaddai.

EL SHADDAI, I REFUSE TO ACCEPT DEFEAT. I STAND FIRM IN THE AUTHORITY OF JESUS CHRIST AND TAKE BACK IN HIS NAME ALL THE ENEMY HAS STOLEN. AMEN.

SERVED BY GOD

For the Son of Man came not to be ministered unto, but to minister, and to give his life a ransom for many.

—MARK 10:45

J esus came not to be served but to serve. Like the father waiting for his prodigal son to come home, the Father waited for an eternity for us to come home, back into His arms. After waiting and waiting, God could wait no more. Love seeks out that which is loved. Before we could ever turn back toward home, He came to us through His Son, Jesus. He gave us everything we asked for and more. Before we asked, He died for us, offering us His eternal gift of love—everlasting life. He wants us to live forever so that He can love us forever!

Like the prodigal son, we may run to the Father, fall at His feet, and beg to serve Him. He always refuses. Instead, He picks us up, bathes us with His tears, clothes us with a white robe of righteousness washed in the blood of Jesus, puts the ring of power and authority on our finger, and ushers us into a feast fit for the King.

Do not expect to sit under the table and grab for any crumb that may fall. No, in Christ you sit at the Father's right hand—the seat of honor. And to your surprise, when you reach out to fill His cup and serve His plate, His hand stops yours. In wonderment, you look into His eyes. Then you know the truth. He seats you at the King's table for one purpose—to serve *you.*

JESUS, THANK YOU THAT I DO NOT HAVE TO SETTLE FOR THE CRUMBS OF LIFE. I REJOICE IN THE PRIVILEGE OF COMING TO YOUR TABLE WITH A FEAST FIT FOR A KING. AMEN.

THE DEVIL'S MAP

Cry aloud, spare not, lift up thy voice like a trumpet, and shew my people their transgression.

—ISAIAH 58:1

Napoleon was one of the few men who came close to conquering the world. It is said that he would gather his warlords together to study a map of the world. He would point to a little red spot in the center of the map, an island called England, and roar, "Were it not for that red spot, I could conquer the world!"

There is a red spot on the earth today, and the demons swirl in the atmosphere, shaking with rage. They point to the Cross of Jesus Christ. The devil's plans to conquer the world were thwarted at Calvary. Now those who are washed in the precious blood of the Savior stand against the forces of evil and proclaim, "Jesus is Lord!"

God's blood-bought remnant on this planet has the responsibility to point others to the Cross. We must stand up in a world filled with the devil's lies and boldly declare, "Jesus is the only way to heaven!"

JESUS, YOU ARE MY WAY, TRUTH, AND LIFE.
YOUR CROSS IS THE ONLY WAY TO HEAVEN. I
DECLARE THAT EVERY DEVIL AND DEMON
THAT CROSSES MY PATH TODAY IS DEFEATED
IN THE NAME OF JESUS. AMEN.

LIMITLESS LIVING

I beseech you therefore, brethren, by the mercies of God, that ye present your bodies a living sacrifice.

—ROMANS 12:1

W hen you are born again, you are not the person you used to be. You do not think the way you used to think or go where you used to go. No longer are you in the kingdom of this world. You have been promoted to a higher place. People like to talk about a new world order, but the best of all worlds is the one God established in His Word! When you move into His divine realm, you are no longer bound by the world's restrictions.

However, living in His kingdom is not a one-way street. Proverbs 3:5 says we are to trust in the Lord with *all* our hearts. Paul said, "I am crucified with Christ: nevertheless I live; yet not I, but Christ liveth in me" (Galatians 2:20).

Is your life partially given, or, like Paul's, fully surrendered to God? Do you say "yes" or "no" to your King? Limitless living requires limitless giving!

JESUS, HELP ME TO LIVE IN YOUR REALM
WITHOUT LIMITS SO THAT I MAY EXPERIENCE
YOUR LIMITLESS GRACE AND GIVING TO AND
THROUGH ME. AMEN.

IN SPIRIT AND IN TRUTH

God is a Spirit: and they that worship him must worship him in spirit and in truth.

—JOHN 4:24

A t the well, the Samaritan woman recognized that Jesus was a prophet, and she launched into the ongoing dispute between the Jews and Samaritans regarding the proper place to worship God. Jesus offered her a fresh way to see God, the "who" of worship instead of the "how" or "where."

As God is a Spirit, so are you. You may think you have a spirit, but you are a spirit. Jesus said we must worship God in spirit. If you try to worship God in your flesh, you will be distracted by where you are, how you feel, and what is happening around you.

While still chained in darkness, a prisoner in the dungeons of Rome, Paul rejoiced in being seated with Christ in heavenly places (Ephesians 2:6). Paul was not hallucinating! He took hold of the revelation that he was a spirit, and in the spirit he dwelt in the presence of God. If you live in the flesh you will miss it, because revelation is not received in your flesh. Take hold of this reality and learn to live, see, and hear in the spirit.

HOLY SPIRIT, PUT YOUR NEW AND FRESH REV-
ELATION IN MY HEART. I TAKE HOLD OF YOU
AND KNOW THAT I HAVE TAKEN HOLD OF
TRUTH AND REALITY. AMEN.

GOD'S MOUSE TRAPS

And it came to pass the selfsame day, that the LORD did bring the children of Israel out of the land of Egypt by their armies.

—EXODUS 12:51

God delivered the children of Israel with a strong right hand. They were on their way to the Promised Land when Moses came to them with a Word from the Lord: "We're camping by Pihahiroth, between Migdol and the sea; over against Baal-zephon, with mountains on either side; the sea in front of us and the pursuing armies of the Egyptians behind us" (cf. Exodus 14:2). The Israelites must have felt like cheese in a mouse trap when they arrived at the Red Sea.

Just because you obey the Lord does not mean you will not experience trouble in your life. God will never create a lifestyle for you that makes Him unnecessary. He may take you through some things to bring you to the place He ordained for you to be, but just when it seems you are trapped with no way out, God will exercise His mighty right hand of deliverance. His power is sufficient to carry you through to the other side.

LORD GOD, YOU ARE NECESSARY FOR MY LIFE. YOU ARE NECESSARY FOR MY FAMILY. YOU ARE NECESSARY FOR MY WORK. YOU ARE NECESSARY FOR MY CHURCH. YOU ARE NECESSARY FOR EVERYONE IN MY TOWN. HELP ME SHARE WITH THEM HOW YOU ARE NECESSARY FOR EVERY GOOD THING IN LIFE AND ETERNITY. AMEN.

HERE AM I

And when the LORD saw that he turned aside to see, God called unto him out of the midst of the bush, and said, Moses, Moses. And he said, Here am I.

—EXODUS 3:4

W hen Moses came alone to the mountain of God and encountered a bush that burned but was not consumed, he did not leave to research burning bushes nor did he try to locate someone to question who had experienced the same phenomenon. He did not ask other people what they thought God wanted to tell him. Moses turned his focus toward the bush.

Because Moses had his eyes fixed on God and his ears open to God's voice, God called out to him. God is continually calling us to turn aside and listen to His voice. He is never silent, but we cannot hear Him over the television, the tape player, or our own voices.

We must shut ourselves off from the world and give Him our full attention. James 4:8 says, "Draw nigh to God, and he will draw nigh to you." Take time for God. Seek Him in His Word. Like Moses, fix your eyes on God, open your ears to His voice and say, "Here am I."

JESUS, I LONG TO SAY TO YOU, "HERE AM I." VISIT ME WITH YOUR PRESENCE. RAPTURE MY SOUL WITH JOY. BE MY MOST INTIMATE FRIEND. AMEN.

CHANGED

In everything ye are enriched by him [Jesus].

—I CORINTHIANS I:5

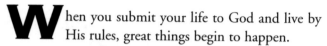

When you submit your life to God and live by His rules, great things begin to happen.

- Your income is changed: "The wealth of the sinner is laid up for the just" (Proverbs 13:22).
- Your investments are changed: "Lend, hoping for nothing again; and your reward shall be great" (Luke 6:35).
- Your giving is changed: "Give, and it shall be given unto you; good measure, pressed down, and shaken together, and running over" (Luke 6:38).
- Your life is changed: "Therefore if any man be in Christ, he is a new creature: old things are passed away; behold, all things are become new" (2 Corinthians 5:17).

The kingdom of God is filled with abundance for those who allow God to transform their lives.

Are you ready to be changed?

GOD, CHANGE ME. CHANGE MY INCOME, MY INVESTMENTS, MY GIVING, IN FACT, MY WHOLE LIFE. THANK YOU FOR THE CHANGES ONLY YOU CAN WORK IN MY LIFE. AMEN.

OUR SEED PROTECTOR

For the LORD your God is bringing you into a good land.
—DEUTERONOMY 8:7

God promised the children of Israel He would bring them into a new land, but the land was not all lush valleys. The settlers also had hills to contend with and rocky fields to till. They had to plow across inclines and deal with soil erosion when the rains came. They had to remove many rocks from their land before they could sow seed. Life in the Promised Land had many ups and downs.

Circumstances are part of God's process that brings us into His Promised Land. We are all going to experience both good times and bad.

Expect opposition, for it will surely come. Any farmer knows that after he plants his crop, the birds will be after his seed, the rabbits will be after the tender young leaves, and both will be after the fruit of the vine.

Keep your mind renewed in what God has to say about your seed, and nothing will be able to threaten your harvest—not people, not opinions, not fear, not greed, nor doubt. God says when we sow in faith, He will stand on the edge of our land and rebuke the devourer for our sakes. Sow abundantly, and trust God for your harvest.

LORD, I WILL SOW YOUR WORD REGARDLESS OF THE DIFFICULTIES OR TRIALS. TEACH ME TO SOW FAITHFULLY AND TRUST YOU FOR THE HARVEST. AMEN.

TRIUMPH FROM THE TOMB

Destroy this temple, and in three days I will raise it up . . .
but he spake of the temple of his body.

—JOHN 2:19,21

Although death gripped mankind for thousands of years, the author of life trampled death and hell. When Jesus hung on the Cross, suspended between heaven and earth, the sun was absent and the earth silent.

But on the third day, the angels watched as the resurrected Son arose with the keys of hell and death in His hands (Revelation 1:18).

Though hell comes and tempests rage, you have the assurance that regardless of whatever happens to you in this life, when your earthly body is finished you are going to wing your way to the pavilions of God's glory and station yourself in a place called heaven, where the streets are not just paved with gold but are made of it.

You have assurance of victory over death and the grave. You have the assurance of salvation from the wrath of judgment and eternal life with Christ. Go ahead and declare, "O death, where is thy sting?" (1 Corinthians 15:55).

Because you know your Redeemer lives (Job 19:25), you have the assurance that you are bound for the Father's house.

> **I PRAISE YOU, O RISEN CHRIST, FOR WINNING THE VICTORY OF DEATH AND SIN AND FOR GIVING ME ASSURANCE THAT THROUGH TRUST IN YOU, I WILL BE VICTORIOUS AS WELL. AMEN.**

YOUR SHIELD AND BUCKLER

He shall cover thee with his feathers, and under his wing shalt thou trust: his truth shall be thy shield and buckler.

—PSALM 91:4

When you are living your life on God's terms, God provides such protection that the devil won't even know your address! As long as you remain in God's kingdom, He is faithful to protect you. He is your sentry, watching over what He has entrusted to you.

"Verily, verily, I say unto you, If a man keep my saying, he shall never see death" (John 8:51). The word "keep," in the original Greek, means we are placed in a position of absolute protection.

Psalm 42:1 says, "As the hart panteth after the water brooks, so panteth my soul after thee, O God." Animals seek the water for two reasons: to quench their thirst and to hide their scent when being hunted.

When we wade out into the deep waters of covenant living, we are surrounded by His presence, protection, and provision.

Abide in Him. He is faithfully watching over the health of your children, protecting your marriage, and guarding your property. No person or thing can protect you from the enemy's attack. Only Your loving Father can shelter you and give you refuge. Run to Him. Hide under His wing and find true security in His feathers.

FATHER, HIDE ME UNDER YOUR WING AND PROTECT ME FROM ALL ATTACKS AND HARM. SPREAD YOUR WING OVER MY FAMILY, MY CHURCH, MY FRIENDS, AND ALL MY BELONGINGS. AMEN.

ONLY THE FACTS

Having the same spirit of faith . . . I believed, and therefore have I spoken; we also believe, and therefore speak.

—2 CORINTHIANS 4:13

I have met people who believe the Bible teaches that whatever we ask we can have . . . with no strings attached. They obviously have not read 1 John 5:14: "And this is the confidence that we have in him, that, if we ask any thing *according to his will,* he heareth us" (italics mine).

We can't ask outside the will of God and expect an answer. But when our request lines up with His will, we have the guarantee that He will not only hear us, but that our answer is on the way. Asking and praying in His Name means to ask and pray in His will, with His authority so that all He desires will be done in our lives.

Your hope and expectation will never rise above your level of confession. You will reap tomorrow the harvest of the words you sow today. Release your confession from a heart full of faith and belief in the God of the Word, and rest in confidence that He will hear and respond.

Begin today to pray for your life to be bound to the will of God.

CONFORM ME, O LORD, TO YOUR WILL FOR MY LIFE. BY YOUR SPIRIT, TEACH ME TO PRAY FOR YOUR WILL EVEN WHEN I DO NOT UNDERSTAND IT. AMEN.

Week 15—Friday
SELECTING YOUR SOIL

But he that received seed into the good ground is he that heareth the word, and understandeth it.

—MATTHEW 13:23

Y ou cannot expect a harvest unless you sow in good soil. Fertile soil for a spiritual harvest is a location God Himself has endorsed (Deuteronomy 26:2). God places His name where His Word is preached, where people are being saved, where there is a strong conviction of right and wrong, and where the leadership is not afraid to tell the truth about sin. Good soil is found where deliverance is preached and practiced, and where the Holy Spirit has complete liberty to move in His baptism, anointing, power, gifts, and grace.

The best seed in the world will fail if it is not watered by the Word and nourished by the Holy Spirit. Sow where there is a continual, tangible presence of the Lord. Sow into the good soil of ministry where Jesus Christ, not man or program, is lifted up.

SPIRIT OF GOD, SHOW ME WHERE TO SOW MY SEED INTO THE GOOD SOIL OF MINISTRY. HELP ME NOT ONLY TO SOW BUT ALSO TO PRAY AND WORK IN MINISTRY SO THAT YOUR NAME WILL BE EXALTED. AMEN.

STRANGE FIRE

And Nadab and Abihu, the sons of Aaron, took either of them his censer, and put fire therein, and put incense thereon, and offered strange fire before the LORD, which he commanded them not. And there went out fire from the LORD, and devoured them, and they died before the LORD.

—LEVITICUS 10:1–2

Nadab and Abihu were not chosen to be priests because of their personal integrity or worth but because God had established the priesthood in Aaron's family. Their authority was dependent upon Aaron—a right of birth.

Acting independently they attempted to offer sacrifices without their father's presence or authority, assuming their sacrifices would be acceptable to God. God recognized their offering as "strange fire," offered from the mind and imagination of man, not ordained or recognized by Him. Nadab and Abihu had overstepped their role and rebelled against the authority God had established. The result was death.

Any work undertaken in rebellion will not flourish. If your service seems to be fruitless, ask God if you are truly following His will for your life or if you are offering Him strange fire.

FATHER, I DO NOT WISH TO DO ANYTHING OF MY OWN. REMOVE ALL STRANGE FIRE FROM MY LIFE. PURIFY ME WITH YOUR FIRE. AMEN.

TO THE PRIEST

Thou shalt take of the first of all the fruit of the earth, which thou shalt bring of the land that the LORD thy God giveth thee, and shalt put it in a basket. . . . And the priest shall take the basket out of thine hand, and set it down before the altar of the LORD thy God.

— DEUTERONOMY 26:2,4

People who believe they are putting "their" money in the offering want to maintain control over it. We cannot control something we do not possess in the first place. All we have belongs to Christ. We have received everything from Him, and we are simply stewards of what belongs to Him. Be generous with what the Master has given you.

When Abraham returned from battle, he met Melchizedek, king and priest of Salem. Abraham had never seen this man before, but when they met, Abraham said to him without hesitation, "Here is my tithe" (Hebrews 7:2). Abraham had no idea how this priest was going to use the funds. His only responsibility was to obey the command of God to bring the firstfruits to the priest.

The Word says to "set your offering down" before the Lord. It doesn't say to set it down and still try to hold on to it. Let it go into the kingdom of God.

When we obey the windows of heaven are opened wide to release God's abundant blessing!

JESUS, TEACH ME HOW TO BE A CHEERFUL GIVER. HELP ME RELEASE WHAT DOES NOT BELONG TO ME SO THAT THE KINGDOM OF GOD CAN BE ADVANCED ACCORDING TO YOUR WILL. AMEN.

HE HEARS US

*And if we know that he hears us, whatsoever we ask, we
know that we have the petitions that we desired of him.*

—1 JOHN 5:15

J esus came to know God intimately by drawing
apart to pray in solitude. He had His own revelation; He recognized the Father's voice.

When Jesus walked up to the tomb of Lazarus, He
"lifted up his eyes" (John 11:41). Looking at no one but
God, He spoke to the Father and said, "I thank thee
that thou hast heard me. And I knew that thou hearest
me always."

How did Jesus know the Father always heard Him?
How did He know He could call a dead man forth from
the grave? God told Him. The Bible does not say an
audible voice gave Him directions, nor did an angel
descend with a message, nor did a prophet appear on the
scene to deliver a timely word. Jesus knew what to do
because He could hear God for Himself.

How can you hear God? Spend time alone with
Him. Talk with Him and listen for His voice. You can-
not know Him when you are separated from Him.
Come into His presence.

**HOLY SPIRIT, TAKE ME INTO THY PRESENCE.
MAKE MY DWELLING PLACE YOUR HOLY
GROUND. AMEN.**

SANCTIFIED SEED

Then thou shalt say before the LORD thy God, I have brought away the hallowed things out of mine house.

—DEUTERONOMY 26:13

T he hallowed things are those items that have been set aside and anointed by God Himself.

Belshazar took the goblets from the House of God for his party, and his guests held them high as they toasted their pagan gods (Daniel 5:4). God didn't wait to punish him. That same night his enemies invaded the land and he was slain. Tithing is a non-negotiable issue in God's kingdom. Ten percent of your earnings are ear-marked by God, and what is His belongs to Him alone.

Don't bring cursing to what God has meant to bless and prosper you. He asks us to bring Him the "hallowed things" because He separates and releases those things with miracle-working power. When God touches that money you give back to Him, He can multiply it until a mountain of obligations disappear.

Tithing is not a duty, but a joy. You are not losing what is yours. You are simply giving to God what already belongs to Him. When you tithe, you release a blessing not a curse into your house and into the House of God.

THANK YOU, LORD, FOR THE PRIVILEGE AND JOY OF TITHING. MAKE MY LIFE A BLESSING TO OTHERS. AMEN.

GOD'S VESSELS

I have been young, and now am old; yet have I not seen the
righteous forsaken, nor his seed begging bread.

—PSALM 37:25

The Lord takes pleasure in the success of His servants. Yet God's abundance is not granted so you can simply lavish it on yourself. It is given to establish the kingdom of God throughout the earth (Deuteronomy 8:18).

We are created to be vessels through which He can pour out His abundance and blessing. God looses abundance in our lives so that we, in turn, can deliver it into the earth to help bring about His kingdom.

Vessels God uses are vessels not contaminated by the ways of the world. The abundance of God overflows from vessels of gold that have been purified in the Refiner's fire.

Set your heart and your mind on becoming "a vessel unto honour, sanctified, and meet for the master's use, and prepared unto every good work" (2 Timothy 2:21).

LORD, USE ME. AS YOUR VESSEL, POUR YOUR
SPIRIT THROUGH ME. SANCTIFY AND PURIFY
ME SO THAT I MIGHT BECOME AS VESSEL OF
HONOR. AMEN.

SOWING IN FAMINE

Isaac sowed in that land, and received in the same year an hundredfold: and the LORD blessed him.

—GENESIS 26:12

Genesis tells us of a drought that came on the land, leaving nothing but parched and dusty ground. The famine it caused was so severe, Isaac and his family were ready to flee to Egypt. But the Lord had another plan and appeared to Isaac, saying, "Dwell in the land which I shall tell thee of" (Genesis 26:2).

Isaac obeyed, tilling the soil and planting his meager seed. God blessed his obedience and faithfulness with a harvest that continued until he became extremely wealthy.

"He that observes the wind shall not sow; and he that regards the clouds shall not reap" (Ecclesiastes 11:4). Those who dwell on the wind instead of the Word clutch their seed, afraid to sow. Your situation may seem hopeless, but you serve a God who created man from the dust of the ground! Trust in Him with all your might. Sow in your famine and reap a king's reward.

When we face lack, we are tempted to eat our seed instead of sowing it. But without sowing, there will be no harvest. Continue to sow in times of lack so that the future will have a harvest instead of continuing famine and dry season.

LORD, GIVE ME THE COURAGE TO SOW EVEN IN DIFFICULT TIMES. HELP ME TO TRUST YOU FOR THE FUTURE HARVEST. AMEN.

FAITH TALK

Let them say continually, let the Lord be magnified, which hath pleasure in the prosperity of his servant. And my tongue shall speak of thy righteousness and of thy praise all the day long.

—PSALM 35:27–28

Three important factors are at work in the process of possession:

Have faith. Jesus tells us to "have faith in God" (Mark 11:22).

Believe. "Whosoever shall say unto this mountain, Be thou removed, and be thou cast into the sea; and shall not doubt in his heart, but shall believe that those things which he saith shall come to pass; he shall have whatsoever he saith" (v. 23).

Pray. "What things soever ye desire, when ye pray, believe that ye receive them, and ye shall have them" (v. 24). When these elements are combined, they are more powerful than any weapon of war. You are no longer looking at what you have, but what you shall have.

Speak faith into your spirit. Remind yourself of the promises of God. Remember, God "calleth those things which be not as though they were" (Romans 4:17).

Your tongue will either announce your next victory or your next defeat. Speak victory. Refuse to open a door for the enemy's attack with your tongue.

HELP ME, LORD, TO CONFESS YOUR VICTORY WITH MY TONGUE. MAKE MY CONFESSIONS POSITIVE NOT NEGATIVE, ROOTED IN FAITH, NOT UNBELIEF OR DOUBT. AMEN.

DON'T EAT THE SEED YOU SOW

And she said, As the Lord thy God liveth, I have not a cake, but an handful of meal in a barrel, and a little oil in a cruse: and behold, I am gathering two sticks, that I may go in and dress it for me and my son, that we may eat it, and die.

—I KINGS 17:12

Now if the widow had eaten the last of her seed, she and her son certainly would have died. But she had another option. She could sow her seed instead of eating it. She could make a loaf of bread for the man of God, Elijah, and then see the promised harvest from God. Her obedience to God's command through Elijah brought her perpetual and promised harvest.

When Elijah asked her for a cake, at first the poor widow claimed that she didn't have it. But God never asks you for what you don't have; He only asks you for what you want to keep for yourself. Remember, if what is in your hand is not big enough to be your harvest, then count on it being your seed. Elijah rebuked the fear in the woman and told her to give what she had. In return, God supplied what she needed—a promised harvest of ever-increasing grain and oil.

You may have nothing left but the seed you need to sow. But until you sow, you will never experience a harvest. Sow as God commands you to sow and you will experience His future instead of your famine.

LORD, TEACH ME WHEN, WHAT, AND HOW TO SOW SO THAT MY FUTURE WILL BE FILLED WITH YOUR HARVEST AND NOT WITH MY FAMINE. AMEN.

THE SPIRIT OF REVELATION

Blessed art thou, Simon Barjona: for flesh and blood hath not revealed it unto thee, but my Father which is in heaven.

—MATTHEW 16:16–17

Peter heard the speculations of men and pondered them. Some thought Jesus was John the Baptist, or Elijah, or one of the other prophets. But when confronted with, "Who do you say I am?" Peter listened to the voice that spoke above the voices of men. Flesh and blood could not give him the right answer. Only the Spirit of God could reveal the right answer to him.

In the Book of Revelation, John repeated the words Jesus often spoke, "He who has ears to hear, let him hear." He was not speaking of physical ears, but spiritual ears tuned in to God's spirit of revelation. The Spirit was not silent, but no one was listening in the Spirit.

Learn to be led by your spirit, or you will follow the dictates of your mind and your flesh. Get in tune with your spirit, strengthening it daily with the Word. Are you listening with spiritual ears?

JESUS, I CONFESS THAT YOU ARE MY MASTER, SAVIOR, LORD, FRIEND, TEACHER, AND MY ALL IN ALL. AMEN.

BLESSED OR CURSED

For such as be blessed of him shall inherit the earth; and they that be cursed of him shall be cut off.

—PSALM 37:22

G od gave us clear directives for how He expects us to live. His laws are for our safety, security, and direction. Like any good father, God blesses us when we obey and corrects us when we stray.

Are you ready for the blessing and provision of God's abundance? There is only one door in which to place your key. Jesus said, "I am the door: by me if any man enter in, he shall be saved, and shall go in and out, and find pasture" (John 10:9). What are we promised when we walk through the door? Jesus tells us in the next verse: "The thief cometh not, but for to steal, and to kill, and to destroy: I am come that they might have life, and that they might have it more abundantly" (v.10).

The blessing of God is promised for those who obey His Word. As you submit your life to His authority, He will bring you into the fullness of His abundant life.

JESUS, I AM READY AND WILLING TO OBEY YOU. OPEN YOUR DOOR FOR MY LIFE THAT I MAY WALK INTO YOUR BLESSINGS AND ABUNDANCE. AMEN.

ON EAGLE'S WINGS

As an eagle stirreth up her nest, fluttereth over her young, spreadeth abroad her wings, taketh them, beareth them on her wings: So the LORD alone did lead him, and there was no strange god with him.

—DEUTERONOMY 32:11-12

God compares His relationship with Israel with the eagle who observes the feathers of its young to determine when they are ready to fly—and then deliberately pushes them out of the nest.

Often we do not know when we are ready to step out in faith, but God does. When we need to step out in faith, He will thrust us out of the nests of comfort and ease we have constructed for ourselves. As in the manner of a young eagle soaring for the first time, we can also soar because we know it is His timing and He is right there with us as we go forth.

As the eagle leads her young from the nest, she flies under them, guiding their journey. And if they become weary, she carries them home on her wings. When we cannot go on any longer, He carries us to our destination. You can always count on His strength that will never let you fall.

LORD, TEACH ME TO FLY. PUSH ME OUT OF EVERY NEST THAT I CONSTRUCT TO KEEP MYSELF FROM RISKING FAITH AND TRUSTING YOU. AMEN.

JOURNEY TO THE JORDAN

And it came to pass after three days, that the officers went through the host; and they commanded the people, saying, When ye see the ark of the covenant of the LORD your God, then ye shall remove from your place, and go after it.

—JOSHUA 3:2–3

Joshua stood on the banks of the Jordan and told the Israelites to get ready—in three days, they would cross the Jordan and invade Jericho.

This was a giant step of faith, but Joshua prepared them for what God had in store. When it came time to move, the Ark of the Covenant went before them. As the feet of the priests touched the waters, the waters were cut off, and they crossed safely.

Notice that after the preparation came the stepping forth. Israel had to move through the waters and into the land. Though God had given them the land, they still had to possess it. When God moved, they moved. When He stopped, they stopped. Each step of the way, they had to listen to God.

We miss the moving of God when we do not prepare ourselves and watch for what God is doing. When God gets ready to move, He takes those who are willing and have prepared themselves as holy, pure vessels. Will you be ready when God moves?

LORD, I DO NOT WANT TO MOVE UNTIL YOU MOVE. I DO NOT WANT TO GO FORTH INTO BATTLE UNPREPARED. EQUIP ME TO POSSESS THE LAND AND TO HEAR YOUR VOICE CLEARLY. AMEN.

WATER YOUR SEED

And thou shalt go unto the priest that shall be in those days, and say unto him, I profess this day unto the LORD thy God, that I am come unto the country which the LORD sware unto our fathers for to give us.

—DEUTERONOMY 26:3

The children of Israel presented their tithes and offerings to the Lord along with their profession of faith. The priest took each man's offering before the altar as the giver recounted the story of Israel's deliverance from bondage.

The Israelites recounted their years of bondage before God liberated them. They remembered their persecution by their Egyptian masters. They remembered their deliverance and their possession of the land.

Only when you recognize the depth of your sin can you realize the breadth of His righteousness. Bring your gifts before God, acknowledging who you were before God took hold of you. Recall your deliverance through the blood of Jesus Christ. Take a moment to praise God for all of your past blessings. Keep His praise continually on your lips. Praise Him for His grace to deliver you into His kingdom.

> FATHER, I GIVE YOU PRAISE FOR ALL THE FAVOR AND GRACE YOU HAVE SHOWN ME IN THE PAST. I DECLARE YOUR BLESSINGS AS A TESTIMONY OF YOUR FAITHFULNESS. AMEN.

STUCK IN THE MUD

Then took they Jeremiah and cast him into the dungeon of Malchiah the son of Hammelech, that was in the court of the prison. . . . And in the dungeon there was no water, but mire: so Jeremiah sunk in the mire.

—JEREMIAH 38:6

J eremiah was persecuted and imprisoned on several occasions, and finally left to die in a dank, wet cistern. After years of faithfully preaching the Word of God, he was tossed into a pit of mud from which there was no escape. But God used an unlikely method to rescue him-an Ethiopian eunuch and some rotten rags (Jeremiah 38:11).

God may not rescue you the way you plan. He may not act when you expect Him to act. But He is never early and never late. God always acts at the appointed time to deliver you. Stand firm and wait on Him. When you are at the end of your rope, hold on to His Word and cling to His promises.

When you feel like the enemy has overpowered you and the world is against you, always remember that God has not forgotten you. He has given us His Word that He will never leave us nor forsake us (Deuteronomy 31:6).

You may be up to your neck in problems and so deep in debt you cannot see the light of day, but get ready . . . your redemption draweth nigh.

LORD, I AM HOLDING ON FOR YOU. THOUGH I AM STUCK IN THE MUD AND SURROUNDED BY DIFFICULTY, I KNOW THAT YOU WILL NEVER LEAVE NOR FORSAKE ME. YOU ALONE ARE MY SALVATION AND THE LIFTER OF MY HEAD. AMEN.

HOW DOES YOUR GARDEN GROW?

Jesus stood and cried, saying, If any man thirst, let him come unto me, and drink. He that believeth on me . . . out of his belly shall flow rivers of living water.

—JOHN 7:37–38

So many Christians are looking for the power of God, but you have a reservoir of power that has been poured into you, "For by one Spirit are we all baptized into one body . . . and have been all made to drink into one Spirit" (1 Corinthians 12:13).

To start that power flowing, you must first prime the pump of your soul. You have the Holy Spirit within you, but His power must be primed through prayer, worship, and praise.

Once you release the power of God, it gushes like a river. "And thou shalt be like a watered garden, and like a spring of water, whose waters fail not" (Isaiah 58:11).

Begin each day by priming your pump of Holy Ghost power, and the fruit of your spirit will flourish like that of a well-watered garden. Be a tree planted by living waters. Meditate on His Word day and night. Fill today with acts of kindness prompted by the Holy Spirit.

JESUS, I DESIRE TO LIVE THIS DAY IN YOUR POWER AND GRACE. I LONG TO HEAR YOUR VOICE, SEE YOUR FACE, AND BE AN INSTRUMENT OF YOUR GRACE. AMEN.

BEGINNING WITH THE END

I am Alpha and Omega, the beginning and the ending, saith the Lord, which is, and which was, and which is to come, the Almighty.

—REVELATION 1:8

G od has a future for you, and He will see you safely to it, if you will let Him. God shows us where we are, and He shows us where we are going to end up. He shows us A and Z, but He doesn't always show us L, M, N, O, P.

If you are going to make it through to God's palace, you are going to have to pass through the "P's": problems, perils, persecutions, and people. Rest while you can in the "R's" because the "T's" are right around the corner: trials, tribulations, and trouble.

God did not just casually declare that you are going to end up somewhere. He has a master plan, and He made a blueprint! He knows exactly what it is going to take to get you from where you are to where He said you would be! He knows your omega before alpha ever begins. God is always at your side as you traverse your course. He is the one who is, and was, and is to come. The God who was faithful yesterday will meet your needs today and already knows your tomorrow. Call on Him today.

> JESUS, I KNOW THAT YOU ARE THE SAME YES-
> TERDAY, TODAY, AND TOMORROW. YOU ARE MY
> ALPHA AND OMEGA. YOU KNOW MY BEGINNING
> FROM MY END. I TRUST YOU WITH ALL MY
> BEGINNINGS, KNOWING YOU HAVE EVERY-
> THING IN CONTROL. AMEN.

BLESS THE LORD

Bless the LORD, ye his angels, that excel in strength, that do his commandments, hearkening unto the voice of his word.

—PSALM 103:20

When the Word of the Lord goes forth you must decide immediately whether you will speak and walk in His Word or ignore it. At the moment of His Word, the Spirit discerns the intentions of your heart. God knows if you are going through the rigors of religiosity or if you are committed by faith and prayer to move out into the harvest.

This should be the declaration of your mouth:

I send forth the holy angels of God right now.

They are commissioned to minister on behalf of the heirs of salvation.

I am an heir of salvation.

I am washed in the blood of Christ.

I am blood-bought, Holy Ghost-filled, and fire-baptized.

I am not waiting to get into the kingdom of God.

I am in the kingdom now, and the kingdom is in me.

Every day you can declare under the anointing of the Holy Spirit:

IN THE POWER OF THE SPIRIT AND UNDER THE AUTHORITY OF THE WORD, I DECLARE THAT THE HOLY ANGELS GO FORTH AND BECOME REAPERS IN THE FIELDS WHICH ARE WHITE UNTO HARVEST. I BIND EVERY HINDERING SPIRIT ON MY LIFE. I RELEASE THE ANOINTING OF GOD WITH HIS ANGELIC HOSTS TO BRING IN MY HARVEST. AMEN.

YOU'RE NOT LOST

And Jesus said, Who touched me? When all denied, Peter and they that were with him said, Master, the multitude throng thee and press thee, and sayest thou, Who touched me?

—LUKE 8:45

lthough the ministry of Christ was always in a crowd, His perception was individual. He did not see the crowd; He saw the person. As desperation screamed in the ear of the woman with the issue of blood, she reached out and touched the hem of Jesus' garment. He stopped abruptly in the midst of the crowd and asked, "Who touched me . . . somebody hath touched me: for I perceive that virtue is gone out of me" (Luke 8:46).

Regardless of the crowd, you are not lost. You may feel no one knows your name, but Jesus knows your name. You see, there's something finished that you have to begin. And though the work of God may have begun in your life, God is not through with you yet.

He can see you. He knows you. He is acquainted with your uprising and with your sitting down. He has numbered the very hairs of your head. You are not lost in the crowd.

JESUS, I KNOW THAT I AM SPECIAL AND SIG-NIFICANT IN YOUR SIGHT. I DESIRE TO WALK WITH YOU EVERY MOMENT AND TO FOLLOW YOUR VOICE IN EVERY DECISION. AMEN.

DON'T PLAY AROUND

The thief cometh not, but for to steal, and to kill, and to destroy: I am come that they might have life, and that they might have it more abundantly.

—JOHN 10:10

With these words Jesus drew a line in the sand between the works of God and the works of the devil. God's work is life-giving, healing and uplifting. "Every good gift and every perfect gift is from above, and cometh down from the Father of lights" (James 1:17). Everything that steals, kills, and destroys is the work of the devil. Sickness, disease, and injury do not come from God.

Christianity is not a game that you play on Sunday and then reenter the world's game on Monday. The devil will see to you that you lose such a game. Being a Christian, a little anointed one, means that you live out Christ's life seven days and week and twenty-four hours a day. You cannot play at faith . . . you must live it!

Don't play around with salvation. You are either a child of the devil or a child of God. The devil hates his own kids. He will use you, abuse you, and destroy you, as long as you play around in his kingdom.

Draw close to God through prayer (Psalm 91:15), giving (Luke 6:38), fasting (Luke 2:37), and living right (Romans 6:13). Praise Him for your salvation that allows you to walk in victory.

> **LORD JESUS, I HAVE STOPPED PLAYING THE GAME, AND I AM IN THE RACE FOR REAL. HELP ME TO LIVE FOR YOU EVERY MOMENT OF TODAY. AMEN.**

OUR CONTENDER

But thus saith the LORD, Even the captives of the mighty shall be taken away, and the prey of the terrible shall be delivered.

—ISAIAH 49:25

When I was nine, my daddy and I used to go to a great pizza shop called Johnny's Pizza in the rough part of town where we lived. While waiting on our pizza one night, I walked over to the corner where a big leather and chain-clad Goliath was playing a bowling game. When he slid the game disc to knock down the pins, I grabbed it and slid it the rest of the way down. Growling at me, he slid it again. I grabbed the disc and helped it down the table once more.

This guy came toward me, snorting and fuming like a mad bull. As I was backing up, my daddy stepped between us and said, "Did you have something to say to the boy?"

When the devil's forces come at you, with the smoke of hell billowing from their nostrils, your heavenly Father slides in front of you and says, "If you have anything to say, you have to say it to me." Tell your Father how much you appreciate Him, and thank Him for His divine intervention.

FATHER, I AM ETERNALLY GRATEFUL TO YOU FOR EVERYTHING. FROM THE GIFT OF LIFE ITSELF TO THE GIFT OF ETERNAL LIFE THROUGH YOUR SON, JESUS. I GIVE YOU CONTINUAL PRAISE. AMEN.

ARISE

[Jesus] entered into Simon's house. And Simon's wife's mother was taken with a great fever; and they besought him for her. And He stood over her, and rebuked the fever; and it left her; and immediately she arose and ministered unto them.

—LUKE 4:38–39

The word *rebuke* in the Greek is a very strong word. It means essentially, "Stop it; that's enough." When Jesus hung on the Cross and declared, "It is finished," He announced to the underworld, "Stop it; that's enough!"

Whatever the devil has designed to sideline you—whether it's cancer, a divorce, or an affair—know that every enemy attack against you is met with the presence of God standing over you declaring, "Stop it; that's enough." Not only is Jesus standing over you, He's standing behind you, in front of you, beside you, and beneath you.

In verse 39, the fever left Simon Peter's mother-in-law and she arose. Allow Jesus to overshadow you with His presence and rebuke worry, disease, and depression. Do as Peter's mother-in-law: Arise and serve Him.

Is there a disease, worry, anxiety, or fear in your life that you need to rebuke in Jesus' name? Do it now. Don't delay. Don't lose one more minute being intimidated by the enemy. Rise and serve Jesus.

IN JESUS' NAME, I REBUKE ALL DISEASE, WORRY, FEAR, DEPRESSION, AND ATTACK AGAINST MY LIFE. I STAND FIRM IN JESUS' NAME, PUTTING ON THE FULL ARMOR OF GOD AND TRUSTING TOTAL IN HIS WORD. AMEN.

OUR PERFECT TREASURE

For God, who commanded the light to shine out of darkness, hath shined in our hearts, to give the light of the knowledge of the glory of God in the face of Jesus Christ. But we have this treasure in earthen vessels, that the excellency of the power may be of God, and not of us.

—2 CORINTHIANS 4:6–7

What is the treasure Paul is talking about? Grace—the supernatural enabling of God placed in our human vessels. Why? So that "the excellency of the power may be of God, and not of us."

God wants to display His power. The only way for Him to show that He can do what you cannot do, is to bring you to the place where you cannot accomplish what you need to accomplish on your own. When you finally say, "I am so discouraged I can't go on; I have prayed until I can't pray anymore," the supernatural enabling of God's grace will take over.

Unless you are in rebellion, everything that comes into your life is either allowed by God or sent by God. In either case, it is sent to bring you into maturity and make you more like Him. If you will receive your circumstances in that light, you will defeat every devil. You will come out of the fiery furnace not even smelling of smoke (Daniel 3:27).

GOD, I KNOW THAT YOU ARE WORKING FOR GOOD IN EVERY SITUATION OF MY LIFE. SO I ACCEPT WHERE I AM IN YOU AND SEEK YOUR GUIDANCE IN TAKING EVERY STEP. ORDER MY STEPS IN RIGHTEOUSNESS. AMEN.

YOUR AUTHORITY

Let every soul be subject unto the higher powers. For there is no power but of God: the powers that be are ordained of God.

—ROMANS 13:1

Authority is the right to use the anointing of God. You can have anointing; but without the authority to use it, it will do you no good.

You must obtain the right and the privilege to use the anointing, because it does not belong to you. It is God's anointing—and that makes a difference. It is His anointing that dissipates the fevered brow and breaks the back of cancer.

We obtain spiritual authority when we fully understand that all authority comes from God. Spiritual authority comes when we know the will of God and continually seek to know Him more.

Keep in daily fellowship with God, living in His presence, and continually learning of Him. In so doing, you will gain the authority of trusted and faithful servants walking in the demonstration and power of His anointing.

JESUS, YOU ALONE ARE FAITHFUL AND TRUE. I TRUST YOUR WORD SPOKEN INTO MY LIFE. I RECEIVE THE AUTHORITY YOU HAVE GIVEN ME OVER THE ENEMY. I WALK IN YOUR VICTORY OVER SIN, DISEASE, AND BONDAGE. I PRAISE YOU IN EVERY CIRCUMSTANCE OF MY LIFE. I RECEIVE THE ANOINTING OF YOUR HOLY SPIRIT FOR MINISTRY. AMEN.

LITTLE FAITH OR GREAT FAITH?

And he [Jesus] saith unto them, why are ye fearful, O ye of little faith?

—MATTHEW 8:26

H alfway across the Galilee, the disciples became frightened and woke Jesus, saying, "Don't you care that we perish?" Jesus stilled the storm and rebuked the disciples for not moving on in their faith. How do we grow from the "little faith" of whiny Christians to the "great faith" of Christians who are strong in their faith?

Every day that your mind is renewed in the Word of God, your soul is brought up to a higher level of faith-filled living. Your mind is more renewed in the Word of God today than it was yesterday. I don't spoon-feed my children as I did when they were babies. Don't stop with the milk of His Word; eat the meat. Devour the bread of life. The more meat of His Word that you digest, the stronger your faith will become.

God expects us to mature and become strong in our faith. The stronger we become, the more glory we give Him. Strengthen yourself in the Word, exercise your faith, and go from whining in the boat to unwavering faith.

WORD OF GOD, I HUNGER AND THIRST FOR YOU. FEED MY SPIRIT THAT I MIGHT GROW STRONG IN YOU. EXERCISE MY FAITH THROUGH YOUR TRIALS AND TEST THAT IT MAY BE REFINED IN YOUR FIRE AND BECOME LIKE PURE GOLD. AMEN.

DO YOU KNOW?

The spirit itself beareth witness with our spirit, that we are the children of God.

—ROMANS 8:16

H ere is the gospel: Man is hopelessly, eternally lost. Left to his own devices, he will not only destroy himself, but everything and everyone around him. But on a cross hung a bleeding, dying Savior who said, "I am doing this for you." We are saved through the shed blood of Jesus.

If you are saved, you will not have to ask the deacon or the preacher if you are saved, nor will you have to get a confirmation letter from your denomination to validate your salvation. You will know that you know, that you know, you are saved.

When you are saved, everything looks different. The birds sing louder and the sun shines brighter because you have been touched by God and you have been changed. The path of the righteous grows brighter and brighter!

Salvation is not a change in your social agenda. I didn't make a decision when I was eight years old; I was saved! And I may have to go to hell and back before I leave this planet, but I have what it takes to make it all the way through! I'm saved and I know that I am. Do you?

JESUS, THANK YOU FOR SAVING ME. YOU ARE MY REFUGE AND MY RIGHTEOUSNESS. I KNOW YOU AS MY REDEEMER THROUGH YOUR SHED BLOOD. THANK YOU WITH ALL MY HEART FOR SAVING ME. CHANGE, SANCTIFY, AND RENEW ME EVERY MOMENT IN YOUR PRESENCE. AMEN.

HE LOVES YOU

Jesus prayed that we would know just how much our heavenly Father loves us. He loves us just as He loves Jesus!

—ROMANS 5:8 TMB

Order your thinking, your feelings, and your ideas according to God's Word, for you are a child of God and precious in His eyes. If you see yourself as the expression of the love of God, there are things you will not do and places you will not go. Say to yourself right now, I am a child of the King. I am royalty. I have a place at His table.

We do not serve God to gain His acceptance. We serve not out of duty but out of devotion. We are accepted, so we serve God. We do not follow Him in order to be loved. We are loved, so we follow Him.

LORD JESUS, THANK YOU FOR LOVING ME AND GIVING ME A PLACE OF HONOR AT YOUR TABLE. I WILL SERVE YOU OUT OF GRATITUDE BECAUSE YOU HAVE ACCEPTED ME INTO YOUR ETERNAL KINGDOM. AMEN.

ARE YOU READY?

God also bearing them witness, both with signs and winders, and with divers miracles, and gifts of the Holy Ghost, according to his own will.

—HEBREWS 2:4

G od wants to be identified as your God. And He wants to do it with the thundering "amen" of signs and wonders that prove you serve the God you say you serve. Jesus promises that you will do greater works than He did: "Verily, verily, I say unto you, He that believeth on me, the works that I do shall he do also; and greater works than these shall he do; because I go unto my Father" (John 14:12).

Once we were lost, without hope, far away from God, but now that we belong to Christ Jesus we have been brought very near to Him because of what He did for us with His blood (Ephesians 2:12–13). The cross was the price of access into the presence, power, anointing, and glory of God!

When you meet God and He meets you, the anointing that destroys every yoke is manifested, and your miracle is on its way as sure as the sun will come up tomorrow.

Welcome Him now and give Him free reign in every aspect of your life . . . and get ready for your miracle.

LORD, YOU HAVE COMPLETE FREEDOM IN MY LIFE TO DO WHATEVER YOU WISH. KING JESUS, TAKE CONTROL AND BE FREE TO DO WITH ME WHATEVER YOU DESIRE. AMEN.

FINE POTTERY

O, man, who art thou that repliest against God? Shall the thing formed say to him that formed it, Why hast thou made me thus? Hath not the potter power over the clay?

—ROMANS 9:20–21

Once we grasp the purposeful will of God for our lives, we no longer desire to kick against the pricks. Instead, we will find ourselves free from fear, in humble submission to His will. But if we are not acquainted with His character, we have trouble releasing ourselves into His purpose.

The Potter takes the clay made from the dust of the ground, puts it on His wheel, and begins to shape it. Perhaps you have so many trials and tribulations in your life until you can't focus and start to lose your grip. You may feel as if you can't hold on much longer. But the Potter never takes His loving eyes away from you. God is working His plan in your life.

You are not going to fall off the wheel; you are not going to perish in the depths of your trial. His eyes and His hands are upon you. You are that weak and perishable container being formed to radiate the glorious power and light of God.

LORD, I AM YIELDED CLAY IN YOUR HANDS. SHAPE ME INTO WHATEVER VESSEL YOU DESIRE TO BE POURED OUT FOR YOUR PURPOSES. I AM YOURS, O LORD. THOU ART THE POTTER AND I AM THE CLAY. AMEN.

HE LEADS US

For my thoughts are not your thoughts, neither are your ways my ways, saith the LORD.

—ISAIAH 55:7

G od's character is not our character; His thoughts are not our thoughts; and His ways are not our ways. But He has revealed Himself to us through His Son, Jesus Christ, who said, "He that hath seen me hath seen the Father" (John 14:9).

God not only revealed Himself to us through His Word, but through the life and ministry of Jesus, who was the Word of God incarnate (John 1:1). As we read His words and observe His life, the mind, heart, and ways of God are revealed to us.

Follow Jesus, and let Him lead you to the Father. Let His Spirit guide and direct you into all truth. Listen to the voice of the Good Shepherd. Let the life of Jesus flow through you by the Spirit. As you study and meditate on the life and ministry of Jesus in the Gospels, you will have a more intimate relationship with Him.

JESUS, I WANT TO BE LIKE YOU. I WANT TO LIVE AND MINISTER IN EVERY WAY, EVERY DAY, JUST LIKE YOU. JESUS, TEACH ME TO LIVE FOR YOU. AMEN.

CLING TO THE ROCK

From the end of the earth will I cry unto thee, when my heart is overwhelmed: lead me to the rock that is higher than I.

—PSALM 61:2

S ometimes faith is not much more than clinging to Christ with all your might. Charles Haddon Spurgeon tells of the limpet, a type of mollusk that fastens itself to the rocks of the English seashore. Those wanting to harvest these creatures can walk softly up to the rocks on which they are clinging, strike them a quick blow with a stick, and off they will come. However, you have warned the limpet clinging next to it. He heard the blow you gave his neighbor, and now clings with all his might. It is impossible to pry him loose!

The limpet doesn't know much. He isn't acquainted with the geological formation of the rock. He only knows that he has found something to cling to for his security and salvation.

It is the limpet's life to cling to the rock, and it is ours to cling to our Rock, Jesus, with all our might. He is an immovable Rock, strong and mighty. He will never let you go so never let go of Him.

JESUS, YOU ARE MY ROCK. I CLING TO YOU TODAY NO MATTER WHAT ANYONE SAYS OR DOES TO ME. YOU ARE MY ROCK AND MY SECURITY. TO YOU ALONE I CLING. AMEN.

THE ANOINTING IS ON THE SEED

Except a corn of wheat fall into the ground and die, it abideth alone: but if it die, it bringeth forth much fruit.

—JOHN 12:24

Archaeologists found seeds stored in the tomb of the Egyptian Pharaoh Tutankhamen when it was opened in 1922. Those seeds were planted and watered, and they grew and bore fruit.

Your finances are like that seed. They have miracle-working power and resurrection potential inside them. Although a seed dies when planted, it resurrects itself and bears fruit. What you hold onto will never multiply. But let go and allow that seed to die. Then it will multiply abundantly bringing a bountiful harvest for both the Lord and you.

God's anointing is on the seed. The seed has life inside itself; it is only waiting for someone to plant it.

Consider a kernel of corn. Inside that kernel is the stalk, the ears, and the grain. You cannot see them now, but they are there. You can count the number of kernels on a corn cob, but you cannot number the ears of corn in one seed. Only God knows the abundant potential of the harvest. You sow and trust the harvest to Him. The seed in your hand has the potential to produce abundantly.

LORD, GRANT ME THE TRUST IN YOU TO SOW GENEROUSLY, HAVING FAITH IN YOUR HARVEST. LET MY SEED DIE SO THAT YOUR SEED MAY LIVE. AMEN.

WHOM DO YOU SEEK?

Jesus therefore, knowing all things that should come upon him, went forth, and said unto them, Whom seek ye?

—JOHN 18:4

Jesus knew all that was to come. He asked this question not because He was wondering what was happening, but to reveal whom they sought. The soldiers came to arrest one they thought was a fleeing peasant but found themselves confronted by the Commander-in-chief of a heavenly army.

The Greek phrase "I am he" comes from two Greek words. In Exodus 3:14 this phrase is expressed as "I AM who I AM" and is taken from the word YHWH, which means "Ever Present." Jesus declared His deity in John 8:58 when He said, "Before Abraham was, I AM" and again to the soldiers in the Garden of Gethsemane. The very power of the words, "I am He" hurled them backwards (v. 6). The soldiers did not take Jesus captive any more than Jesus lost His life. He gave it willingly for all mankind.

Seek the ever-present God of the universe for who He is . . . not for what He can do for you. Desire the Giver . . . not the gifts. Seek His face and His presence, knowing that in His presence you will be changed.

JESUS, I DESIRE YOUR PRESENCE IN MY LIFE. I KNOW THAT I CANNOT BE OR DO ANYTHING WITHOUT YOU. KEEP ME CLOSE TO YOU. AMEN.

THREE CROSSES OF SIN

Where they crucified him, and two other with him, on either side one, and Jesus in the midst.

—JOHN 19:18

H istorians of Jesus' day tell us crucifixions were common. Hundreds at a time would be crucified when the Romans came into a new region.

But on this day in infamy there were only three . . . not the usual thirty or a hundred. Only two were sentenced to die with Jesus. The Roman guards would not even have time to finish the task before the Passover celebration began.

There were three crosses. The cross in the middle bore the One who died *for* sin; another bore the one who died *to* sin; and the third bore the one who died *in* sin. Although both criminals originally railed Jesus, one asked for forgiveness and Jesus promised that man a home in Paradise. The other ridiculed His choice and now is spending eternity in hell.

Jesus died for your sins, but have you died to sin for Him? If you want to live, you must die. Surrender at the Cross of Calvary today. Lay down every treasure and every burden at the foot of the Cross. Nail every sin and every expectation to the Cross.

JESUS, AT THE FOOT OF YOUR CROSS I LAY DOWN MY BURDENS, MY EXPECTATIONS, MY SUCCESSES, AND MY FAILURES. WASH ME CLEAN WITH YOUR BLOOD, AND FILL ME WITH YOUR SPIRIT. AMEN.

FINISHED FOR THE DEVIL

When Jesus therefore had received the vinegar, he said, It is finished: and he bowed his head, and gave up the ghost.

—JOHN 19:30

I do not care what your situation looks like. I do not care what the devil has been trying to do in your life. I do not care what kind of lie he has tried to sell you. Settle it in your spirit once and for all that the devil is defeated. The devil may know your past, but you know his future. He is finished. He is destroyed. He is defeated.

Jesus came to earth "to destroy the works of the devil" (1 John 2:7). The word works in this verse means the kind of energy that produces power or action. Jesus came to strip the devil of his power. The only power the enemy has over you is what you give him through believing his lies.

When Jesus hung His head on the Cross and said, "It is finished," He did not mean "almost finished." The battle was won at Calvary and declared at His resurrection. Do not let the devil browbeat you any longer. Tell him he was defeated two thousand years ago, and claim your victory today. Rejoice, because when Jesus said, "It is finished," He meant it was finished for the devil and Your salvation, healing, deliverance, and victory were also settled for eternity.

I DECLARE TO THE ENEMY THAT HE IS DEFEATED. SATAN, YOU ARE FINISHED. YOU HAVE NO AUTHORITY OVER MY LIFE. ALL POWER AND AUTHORITY BELONGS TO CHRIST. HE IS THE ONE I LISTEN TO, AND I AM DEAF TO ANY LIES YOU WOULD SAY TO ME. AMEN.

RESURRECTION SEED

For whom he did foreknow, he also did predestinate to be conformed to the image of his son, that he might be the firstborn among many brethren.

—ROMANS 8:29

Mankind was careening helplessly on its way to an eternity in hell. The world needed a miracle, and there was no way humanity could manipulate its own salvation. There was no sacrifice dear enough to pay the penalty for our sins. Then God planted a seed, and that seed was Jesus.

Jesus took the penalty for our sin on His body, suffered unspeakable agony on the Cross, and died. His lifeless body was placed in a tomb. On the third day, life infused His body and He rose again, triumphant over the power of sin and death.

That first Resurrection Seed brought God a harvest of souls, those who believe on His name and are redeemed to receive the blessings of salvation, healing and abundance. For two thousand years, that original seed has continued to multiply. Jesus was the firstborn of many children and the firstfruits of the resurrection. We are part of a harvest that has never ceased.

RISEN LORD, LIVE IN ME. MAY YOUR RESURRECTION REVIVE ME—BODY, SOUL, AND SPIRIT. PLANT IN ME YOUR RESURRECTION SEED THAT I MAY BE BOTH YOUR FIELD AND HARVEST THIS DAY. AMEN.

THE TOMB IS EMPTY

And if Christ be not risen, then is our preaching vain, and your faith is also vain . . . But now is Christ risen from the dead, and become the firstfruits of them that slept.

—I CORINTHIANS 15:14,20

All of Christianity rests on the fact that Christ is risen from the dead. Romans 1:4 says "He was declared to be the Son of God with power, according to the spirit of holiness, by the resurrection from the dead."

Our hope lies in an empty tomb. What made Jesus God was not only His ability to lay down His Life (for many can lay down their lives), but only Jesus could pick it up again.

If Christ has not arisen, then there will be no sounding of the trumpet, and neither will we arise. But because we have been made one with Christ, one day we too will experience the resurrection power of the Holy Spirit—that "great getting up morning."

He is risen. And they which are asleep in Christ along with those that remain will most surely arise to meet Him in the air (1 Thessalonians 4:13–18). This is our blessed hope.

JESUS, I REMAIN READY AND PREPARED FOR YOUR RETURN. I LIVE IN THE HOPE OF YOUR RESURRECTION POWER EACH DAY. FILL ME THIS DAY WITH RESURRECTION HOPE AND THE COURAGE TO WITNESS TO THAT HOPE. AMEN.

HOLD ON FOR THE JOY

Joy cometh in the morning.

—PSALM 30:5

You may be walking through the driest, darkest, most desperate situation of your life, but hold on—joy comes in the morning. Remember, weeping lasts only for a night. The army of God goes forth in the morning and marches under the banner of light (John 9:5).

Jesus declares, "But whosoever drinketh of the water that I shall give him shall never thirst; but the water that I shall give him shall be in him a well of water springing up into everlasting life" (John 4:14). Stop drinking from the old wells of your past traditions and worldly preoccupations. Refuse to drink the stagnant, sin-infested, putrid waters of this world, and dig new wells deep into the pure waters of God.

Sing a new song unto the Lord as Israel did: "Then Israel sang this song, Spring up, O well; sing ye unto it" (Numbers 21:17). Christ is the well of living water springing up within us.

We must allow His well to flow continually and eternally from within us through the Holy Spirit. "He that believeth on me [Jesus], as the scripture hath said, out of his belly shall flow rivers of living water. (But this spake he of the Spirit, which they that believe on him should receive)" (John 7:38–39).

JESUS, FILL ME WITH YOUR LIVING WATER. NO LONGER WILL I BE CONTENT WITH THE NIGHT OR WITH A DRY SEASON. I LONG TO LIVE IN YOUR LIGHT AND DRINK YOUR LIVING WATER. AMEN.

FOREVER FREE

He answereth him, and saith . . . bring him unto me.

—MARK 9:19

Maybe you have gone to every therapist and counselor you can find, watched talk shows and listened to experts, but you still have that bad habit. You're still plagued with that addiction; you're still in bondage to your past.

The man brought his son to Jesus' disciples, the twelve to whom Jesus imparted power and authority. They each tried, but none could cast out the evil spirit that had all but destroyed his young son. Then Jesus said, "Bring the boy to me," and the lad was immediately set free.

Don't be fooled into believing vain philosophies of men or the rigors of religion can free you from any habit or addiction. Unless Holy Spirit power and anointing are present, total deliverance is impossible.

There is no mediator between God and man except Christ Jesus. You do not have to go through anybody; you can walk right up to the throne of grace and find help in time of need. Take your problems directly to the King today and be forever set free!

You have a High Priest interceding for you at the throne of God (Hebrews 8–10). Take to Him every request, need, and concern. He listens and answers every prayer.

JESUS, MY HIGH PRIEST, THANK YOU FOR INTERCEDING FOR ME EVERY MOMENT AT THE FATHER'S THRONE. KEEP ME CLOSE TO YOU. SEARCH MY HEART AND KNOW ME. AMEN.

Fresh Fire

Take up the ashes which the fire hath consumed with the burnt offering on the altar, and . . . put them beside the altar.

—Leviticus 6:10

~~~~~~

God is saying, "Take yesterday's ashes off the altar and get them out of my presence." He is saying, "Lay yesterday's spiritual experience aside." For too many, their first experience with the baptism in the Holy Ghost is their last. If we have not had a fresh experience with God today, we are late. If we did not receive a renewed filling today, we are lagging behind.

Not only are God's mercies renewed daily, but He wants to refresh our spirits so that we remain overflowing with Holy Ghost power and anointing. God has new frontiers for us to conquer. Yesterday's flame is growing dimmer. Get ignited in the Spirit!

To dwell in the presence of God requires fresh fire every day! Humble yourself before Him and say, "I am not ready to go forth until I have first been prepared by You. Touch me today."

Let the fire of the Holy Ghost daily purify and prepare you, and give you fresh passion for Him.

Lord, I long for Your fresh fire every moment of my life. Renew, cleanse, purify, refresh, and restore Your servant. Amen.

THE NARROW WAY

Not every one that saith unto me, Lord, Lord, shall enter into the kingdom of heaven; but he that doeth the will of my Father"

—MATTHEW 7:21

An all-inclusive, non-condemning, watered-down gospel promotes a generalized version of Christianity and may avoid giving offense—but it will never save one solitary soul!

Those who rewrite the Word of God preach a humanistic gospel filled with good-sounding lies or a perverted gospel, convincing others they can have sin and salvation too. One day they will proudly spread their works before Jesus, expecting a reward. Their faces will fall as they are told to depart! They will protest, "But we prophesied in your name! We cast out devils and did wonderful works in your name!" But Jesus will answer, "I never knew you" (Matthew 7:22,23).

Let's preach the gospel according to Jesus. Let's preach and teach true salvation, being bought with a price, washed in the blood, filled with the Holy Ghost, walking the straight and narrow way. This gospel will reap an eternal harvest.

JESUS, I ENTER INTO YOUR NARROW WAY AND DESIRE TO SURRENDER COMPLETELY TO ALL THAT YOU HAVE FOR ME IN MY LIFE. AMEN.

ANOINTED FOR ACTION

The Spirit of the Lord God is upon me; because the Lord hath anointed me to preach good tidings unto the meek; he hath sent me to bind up the brokenhearted, to proclaim liberty to the captives, and . . . to proclaim the acceptable year of the Lord.

—LUKE 4:18–19

⸻

Jesus not only testified to be the Son of God, but He attested that the source of His anointing was from God. Here He gives the purpose of His earthly ministry:

- to preach the gospel to the destitute and afflicted;
- to those whose spirits have been crushed by the world;
- to heal the oppressed;
- to open the spiritual eyes of those blinded by Satan;
- and to declare that today is the day of freedom.

If you are in the kingdom and filled with His Spirit, you are also anointed for this same purpose. The anointing is given to meet the needs of others. Step out in faith to minister to the hurting in your family, your neighborhood and your city.

JESUS, OPEN MY EYES TO SEE THE DESTITUTE, AFFLICTED, BROKENHEARTED, OPPRESSED, SICK, AND BLIND PEOPLE AROUND ME. ANOINT ME TO SET THEM FREE WITH THE GOOD NEWS. AMEN.

HIS PERFECT WILL

Consider it all joy, my brethren, when you encounter various trials, knowing that the testing of your faith produces endurance. And let endurance have its perfect result, that you may be perfect and complete, lacking in nothing.

—JAMES 1:2–4 NASB

As you mature in Christ, there are some things you need to accept, even though you may not understand them.

When everything in you cries, "No, Lord, no," and you say, "How could God want me to go through this?" . . . that is the time for you to bow your knee and declare, "Yes, Lord, yes." God will allow you to walk through the fire to prove that the power to deliver you is of Him and not of yourself.

He is the God who brought you in; He is the God who will bring you out. Let no thought of defeat enter your mind, but rather, "Let this mind which was in Christ be in you also" (Philippians 2:5).

When you pass through deep waters, raging storms, and terrible trials, He will see you through. Jesus delivers you from every crisis and puts your feet on solid ground—the rock of His Word.

JESUS, SEE ME THROUGH EVERY TRIAL. HELP ME KEEP MY EYES FIXED ON YOU IN ALL MY CRISES. AMEN.

IS THERE NOT A CAUSE?

And David said, What have I now done? Is there not a cause?

—I SAMUEL 17:29

In 1990 the atrocities committed against the people of Kuwait roused our nation to righteous indignation. President George Bush announced, "This aggression . . . will not stand."

While the Iraqi army continued laying mine fields and stringing barbed wire, armaments and supplies began arriving from America, Europe, and Africa, accompanied by soldiers, ships, and aircraft. Differences in uniforms, languages, customs, and manners faded as the soldiers became Desert Shield. The world had seen the outrages, and now the world had a cause.

In these last days, multitudes of nations are again gathering behind a shield. Differences in dress, language, customs, songs, and worship fade as the remnant church of Jesus Christ unites behind the shield of faith. We are preparing to go forth into battle against the devil's forces. The church has seen the outrage, and the church has a cause.

You have a cause. It is not to make others righteous. It is not to change the world, though your cause will do all of that. Your cause is Jesus. Make Him your cause today.

JESUS, YOU ARE THE REASON FOR EVERY SEASON IN MY LIFE. YOU ARE MY LIFE AND MY LIFE'S CAUSE. AMEN.

YOUR FUTURE IS IN YOUR SEED

Jesus said unto him, If thou canst believe, all things are possible to him that believeth.

—MARK 9:23

My heart breaks when I see someone suffering in physical pain, because I know the Bible provides the answer. I am troubled when I see someone bound by addiction, because I know the Bible provides the answer. I ache when I see Christians struggling financially, living from paycheck to paycheck, barely able to get by, unable to bless the kingdom of God as God intends—because I know the Bible provides the answer!

Determine today to change your future with the seed you sow, because your future is tied to your seed. Any seed that is not planted remains the same. Take the seed God has placed in your life and sow it in faith. Your past will determine your present and your future unless you sow new seed today. What you sow today will shape your future. Allow God to use what you sow to bring you from where you are to where God wants you to be. Take God at His Word and let go of the things you are holding onto so tightly.

Determine to take a step of faith beyond anything you have ever done . . . to secure a future greater than you can imagine.

JESUS, EMPOWER ME TO SOW SEEDS OF LOVE, KINDNESS, GOOD WORKS, SERVICE, COMPASSION, MERCY, AND GIVING TODAY SO THAT MY HARVEST TOMORROW MIGHT BEAR THE GOOD FRUIT OF YOUR SPIRIT. AMEN.

THE MERCY OF GOD

And God saw their works, that they turned from their evil way; and God repented [changed His mind] of the evil, that he had said that he would do unto them; and he did it not.

—JONAH 3:10

After much resistance, Jonah yielded to God to go to Nineveh to preach repentance to that great city in Assyria. Then the pronouncement was made that after forty days God would judge the city with His wrath.

With urgency, the king declared a fast that even included the animals. The people wept and begged for mercy, and with an open heart they prayed to God. Because they humbled themselves in prayer, God lifted His declaration and spoke life, and not death, over them.

Our God does not show favoritism, for His mercy extends the globe (John 3:17). The love and mercy of God can reach anyone—from the uttermost to the guttermost. He can reach out to wherever your unsaved loved ones are and set their feet on the Rock of their salvation.

Think of loved ones who are lost, and pray for their salvation today. Think of those in your city, nation, and world who are lost. Pray for their salvation today. Ask God to be merciful to them and to seed His Spirit to convict, deliver, save, and heal them today.

JESUS, I PRAY FOR THE LOST THIS DAY. I PRAY FOR MY LOVED ONES WHO ARE LOST. I PRAY FOR ALL THE LOST IN THE WORLD. EXTEND YOUR MERCY AND SEND FORTH WORKERS INTO THE HARVEST TO PROCLAIM YOUR GOOD NEWS. AMEN.

GIVE YOUR BEST

Ye offer polluted bread upon the altar . . . The table of the LORD is contemptible. And if ye offer the blind for sacrifice . . . and if ye offer the lame and sick, is it not evil?

—MALACHI 1:6–8

B y the time Malachi wrote these words, the sacrifices the Israelites brought God were nothing more than their castoffs. God commanded the people to give their best, and the priests were instructed to examine the offerings before they were made. But the people became greedy. They didn't want to give God their best. They had forgotten the law of sowing and reaping. They offered only the leftovers, the rejects, and the castoffs of what they had. They reaped destruction and ruin as a result.

Too often, we keep the best for ourselves and offer to the Lord that which costs us little. Five percent is not 10 percent. It may soothe your conscience, but it doesn't satisfy God's commands. He says, "Go ahead and offer your desecrated offering, but I won't be listening to your songs, and I won't be hearing your prayers." Give your best to God and walk in covenant blessing.

Remember that tithing touches your time and talents as well as your treasure. Are you spending the best part of your time with the Lord? Are you giving to the Lord the best of your talents?

LORD, TODAY I GIVE YOU MY BEST, NOT MY LEFTOVERS. I GIVE YOU MY BEST TREASURE, TALENTS, AND TIME SO THAT YOU CAN BE HONORED AND GLORIFIED IN MY LIFE. AMEN.

RESURRECTION WORDS

It is the spirit that quickeneth; the flesh profiteth nothing; the words that I speak unto you, they are spirit, and they are life.

—JOHN 6:63

Jesus waited four days before he went to Bethany, the home of His dear friends Mary, Martha, and Lazarus. After greeting the two grieving sisters, Jesus went to Lazarus' tomb. He prayed the prayer of faith and called Lazarus' name—and Lazarus arose and walked out of the tomb.

John 5:25 says, "The hour is coming, and now is, when the dead shall hear the voice of the Son of God: and they that hear shall live."

"Life" in the above verse is the Greek word *zoe,* which means "the God-kind of life." Jesus said that He came not only that we would have life, but that we would have it more abundantly. Let the words of David be your daily prayer: "Quicken thou me according to thy Word." Let Jesus speak His life into your situation.

Is there death in a relationship? Ask Jesus to speak life into it. Is there death in your finances? Ask Jesus to speak life into them. Is there death in your ministry? Ask Jesus to speak life into it.

JESUS, SPEAK LIFE INTO EVERY AREA OF DEATH. BRING TO LIFE ALL THAT YOU DESIRE TO LIVE AND CRUCIFY ALL MY FLESH. SPEAK YOUR WORDS OF LIFE INTO MY LIFE TODAY. AMEN.

LABOR FOR THE LORD

Therefore, my beloved brethren, be ye steadfast, unmoveable, always abounding in the work of the Lord, forasmuch as ye know that your labour is not in vain in the Lord.

—I CORINTHIANS 15:58

I receive letters every day from pastors and church workers concerning the rough road they face in the ministry. Many times people look at our church and television ministry and wish they had what I have been privileged to be a part of for so many years.

Let me encourage you with these words: "It has not always been this good." I remember starting with just seventeen people. I sometimes preached until my throat was so dry I coughed up blood. At one time doctors told me I had to stop preaching, but I knew I was born with "a microphone in one hand and a Bible in the other."

Wherever you are, draw a line in the spiritual sand and say, "Devil, I'm pressing on, no matter what you say; nothing can stop me and my God." Be steadfast and immovable, and you will abound in the Lord's work. Look forward to that day when He says to you, "Well done, good and faithful servant." Don't quit. Don't look back. Press on toward the mark in Christ Jesus.

JESUS, KEEP ME FOCUSED ON YOU. GIVE ME THE STRENGTH AND THE COURAGE TO MINISTER REGARDLESS OF THE PERSONAL COST OR THE PERSECUTION. JESUS, I LIVE FOR YOU. AMEN.

KINGDOM PRIORITIES

And if ye go to war in your land against the enemy that oppresseth you, then ye shall blow an alarm with the trumpets; and ye shall be remembered before the LORD your God, and ye shall be saved from your enemies.

—NUMBERS 10:9

I n His last discourse on earth, Jesus instructed His disciples to go and preach the gospel to all nations (Matthew 28:19). His first priority for His followers was to bring the good news of salvation to as many people as possible.

He followed this instruction with the assurance: "And these signs shall follow them that believe; in my name shall they cast out devils" (Mark 16:17).

Jesus not only intended for the gospel to be made available to all mankind but for His manifested presence to continue to destroy the works of the enemy.

The presence of Jesus Christ is alive and active in every born-again believer . . . and we have a divine mandate to set the captives free and to tear down the devil's kingdom! Keep the kingdom priorities ever before you.

JESUS, EXAMINE MY PRIORITIES. HELP ME TO ORDER MY DAY TODAY WITH YOUR PRIORITIES. HELP ME DO EVERYTHING ACCORDING TO YOUR WILL, IN YOUR WAY, AND IN YOUR TIMING. AMEN.

FIRE SHUT UP IN MY BONES

Then I said, I will not make mention of him, nor speak any more in his name. But his word was in mine heart as a burning fire shut up in my bones, and I was weary with forbearing, and I could not stay.

—JEREMIAH 20:9

Jeremiah spoke these words when the opposition was at its height. Jeremiah lamented to the Lord for calling him into the ministry. The pressure seemed too great. But just when he thought life was over and he saw no hope, something sprung up within him.

Holy Spirit fire ignited his life when Jeremiah had burnt out and was unable to continue. When he had come to the end of himself, Jeremiah was ready to quit, but he could not. He was possessed with the Holy Spirit. The fire of God burned in him, and he had strength to go on.

Fill yourself with the Word and when you think you are ready to quit, don't throw in the towel. Rest in God and watch as the Word begins to kindle in your heart, empowering you and refueling you just as you are running out of steam. When the devil is bearing down on you, the fire from heaven will rest upon your soul.

LORD, WHEN I FEEL BURNT OUT, LIGHT MY FIRE. BURN HOT IN MY BONES WITH YOUR FIERY COMPASSION, LOVE, AND ZEAL. LET ME BE YOUR LIGHT IN A DARK AND DYING WORLD. AMEN.

GOD'S DELIVERY SERVICE

Shall I bring to the birth, and not cause to bring forth? saith the LORD: shall I cause to bring forth, and shut the womb? saith thy God.

—ISAIAH 66:9

The process of fetal development is fascinating. As the weeks turn to months the mother's stomach muscles expand to adjust to the growth pattern of the infant. When the final stage arrives, the baby shifts, moving its head downward into the birth position. The beginning of delivery is heralded by labor pains and allows time to prepare for proper birth.

Through the prophet Isaiah, God declared the mother of Zion gave birth without labor pains. What is God trying to say through this analogy?

God is the author of life and the giver to birth. What God impregnates (or begins) He will not abort. This passage is alluding to revival. God birthed it at Pentecost. What He has started He will surely finish. Nothing can stop this great move in the final hours of these last days. Get ready to be delivered into the pearly gates!

JESUS, KEEP ME FROM ABORTING YOUR NEW CREATION IN MY LIFE. BIRTH IN ME YOUR NEWNESS AND CREATE IN ME A NEW MIND AND HEART THIS DAY. AMEN.

THE TRUTH OF THE MATTER

Pilate saith unto him, What is truth? And when he had said this, he went out again unto the Jews, and saith unto them, I find in him no fault at all.

—JOHN 18:38

P ilate, troubled by his wife's dream and faced with the pressure of the angry Jewish religious leaders, asked Jesus the greatest question ever asked: "What is truth?"

This is the quest of philosophers, scientists, astronomers, and lawyers—to find truth. To many, truth is relative. Truth is whatever suits their purpose. In a growing age of technology and space discoveries we have less answers to life's greatest question: "What is truth?"

Truth is what is true for all people, at all times and in all situations. Jesus is the same yesterday, today, and tomorrow. He alone is truth.

Pilate, like people today, looked everywhere but to the source for the answer, Jesus Christ. It sounds so simple, but many make it hard. It is as easy as breathing. Just say His name, "Jesus." He is the answer to every need you will ever have and every prayer you will ever pray.

JESUS, YOU ARE MY TRUTH FOR THIS DAY. YOU ARE THE STANDARD OF MORALITY AND EXCELLENCE BY WHICH I WILL LIVE MY LIFE. BY YOUR SPIRIT, GUIDE ME IN ALL TRUTH TODAY. AMEN.

UP AND GETTING UP

He that dwelleth in the secret place of the most High shall abide under the shadow of the Almighty.

—PSALM 91:1

An elderly man stood up in a testimony service, waved his handkerchief, and said, "I've been serving the Lord for fifty years, and I want to testify that in that fifty years I have never been down . . . not one day . . . not one time."

There was also a young man in that service who had recently given his life to Jesus. He stopped the old man as he was leaving and said, "I don't understand. I gave my life to Jesus, and it seems like all hell broke loose. How can you say you have never been down?"

The old gentleman replied with words of wisdom, "Son, I've never been down, because I have always either been up or getting up."

If you are fighting a little adversity, dance longer, shout louder, and pray harder. Tell the devil you are not giving up; you are enduring to the end. Born-again, Spirit-filled believers may wobble, but they don't fall down. Claim His promise today: "The steps of a good man are ordered by the LORD: and he delighteth in his way. Though he fall, he shall not be utterly cast down: for the LORD upholdeth him with his hand" (Psalm 37:23–24).

LORD, WHENEVER I STUMBLE, LIFT ME UP BY YOUR HAND. UPHOLD ME IN YOUR ARMS. COVER ME WITH YOUR WINGS. SHELTER ME IN THE ROCK. AMEN.

A KINGDOM OF PRIESTS

*And He hast made us unto our God kings and priests; and
we shall reign on the earth.*

—REVELATION 5:10

A literal translation renders this verse not "kings
and priests" but rather "a kingdom of priests."
Fifteen hundred years before Jesus ever came to the
earth, God told His people they would be a kingdom of
priests (Exodus 19:6).

But when Moses went unto the mountain with God,
the people rebelled, making a golden calf (Exodus
32:1–4). Seeing what they had done, Moses broke the
tablets of God's law, saying, "Who is on the Lord's side
let him come unto me" (v. 26). And only the Levites
came.

God is now fulfilling His original plan through you
and me—His church! Just as the priests of the Old
Testament bore the ark on their shoulders, we are to bear
His glory wherever we go—the malls, the streets, or the
workplace. We have all been called into kingdom priesthood and anointed with the power of the Holy Spirit to
minister the saving gospel of Jesus Christ.

You are part of a holy nation, a royal priesthood
(1 Peter 2:9). Live today as a priest, a minister, an inter-
cessor, and one anointed to take the gospel into every
area of life.

**JESUS, TEACH ME TO BE A PRIEST. HELP ME
TO INTERCEDE. GIVE ME THE DESIRE TO MIN-
ISTER TO YOU IN EVERY LOCALE OF LIFE.
AMEN.**

GOD'S AMBASSADORS

Now then we are ambassadors for Christ, as though God did beseech you by us: we pray you in Christ's stead, be ye reconciled to God.

—2 CORINTHIANS 5:20

True fulfillment in life comes when you stop running to and fro, grasping for things to fulfill you, and begin to realize the marvelous plan God has for you.

Of the billions of people on this planet, you have the unique role of husband, father, wife, mother, son, or daughter. God has positioned you to serve Him in whatever environment you find yourself. It is our responsibility to let a hurting world know that God, in His love, gave His Son on the Cross.

You are special, one of a kind, and essential in the kingdom of God. Without you, many will not hear the good news of Christ. Without you, many will not be saved, healed, delivered, and served in His name.

God has ordained a special place of ministry for each of us. This isn't a choice on our part. God has commissioned every believer with the ministry of reconciliation. Reflect today on the roles you alone can fill, and then determine to fulfill those roles to the very best of your God-given abilities.

USE ME, TODAY, O LORD. LET ME BE YOUR VOICE, HANDS, FEET, AND WITNESS IN THE WORLD. WHEN OTHERS LOOK AT ME, I PRAY THAT THEY WILL SEE YOU. AMEN.

USE YOUR STICK

And concerning the tithe of the herd, or of the flock, even of whatsoever passeth under the rod, the tenth shall be holy unto the Lord.

—LEVITICUS 27:32

Exodus 14 tells the story of how Moses led the Israelites out of Egypt. They came to the Red Sea, the mountains were on either side and the Egyptians were pursuing. Moses cried out to God, "What are we going to do?"

God said, "What have I put in your hand?" When Moses replied, "Just a stick," God responded by saying, "Use it!"

It was no ordinary stick that God had put in Moses' hand. It was anointed. Anything anointed of God has miracle-working power.

Many of you are hemmed in with credit cards on one side, car payments on the other and the bank pursuing- but you have a stick. God says, "Use your stick. Sow the ten dollars of the one hundred dollars you made this week that I have sanctified for your deliverance from financial bondage."

Use what you have for the Lord. It may not be much, but it will be enough. Little is much in His hands. Whatever the Lord has put into your hand, use it for Him.

LORD, I COMMIT MYSELF TO USING WHATEVER YOU GIVE ME FOR YOUR PURPOSES AND GLORY IN JESUS' NAME. AMEN.

NURTURE YOUR GARDEN

But the fruit of the Spirit is love, joy, peace, longsuffering, gentleness, goodness, faith, meekness, temperance.

—GALATIANS 5:22–23

Apples are a natural result of an appleseed uniting with the elements necessary for growth. The fruit of the Holy Spirit is the natural result of the union of God's Spirit with your spirit. You have potential for fruitful living, because Jesus is your source! You have the ability to manifest every one of the gifts of the Spirit, because He is the vine and you are a branch! Because He is love, you can love. Because He is peace, you can have peace.

If you are lacking fruit, it is because God's Spirit cannot freely flow through you. Determine to cut away every lust of the flesh, lust of the eye, and pride of life that hinders fruit from coming forth. Nurture the fruit of a Spirit-filled life with the Word of God and prayer and watch your fruit grow!

Does anything hinder the flow of His Spirit in Your life today? Tear down the walls and barriers that hinder His Spirit. Let His Spirit flow freely through your life.

JESUS, REMOVE EVERY BARRIER IN MY LIFE TO YOUR SPIRIT. HELP ME TO BEAR YOUR FRUIT SO THAT ALL AROUND ME MAY BE BLESSED AND COME TO KNOW YOU AS LORD AND SAVIOR. AMEN.

THE CIRCLE IS UNBROKEN

Who shall tell thee words, whereby thou and all thy house shall be saved.

—ACTS 11:14

My grandmother was the greatest Christian I have ever known. Her entire life was a living witness of her faith. I was concerned about the salvation of my uncle, and I wanted to be sure I did the right thing, so I would go talk to my grandmother. Every time she would pat my hand, give me that big faith-grin of hers and tell me, "Don't you worry, Rodney. All my children will be saved. I have His Word on it."

She was right . . . a few years later my uncle was gloriously saved. Never give up on anyone in your family who is lost. Pray for them daily. Share the Word with them. Love them. Minister to their needs. Commit them to the Lord. Ask the Holy Spirit to convict them.

Every year the family circle grows smaller and smaller on this side of glory. But thanks be to God, because Jesus died on Calvary and rose again from the dead, a day is coming when the circle will be unbroken.

JESUS, I LIFT UP TO YOU THIS DAY ALL IN MY FAMILY WHO ARE NOT SAVED. SAVE AND REDEEM THEM BY YOUR BLOOD. AMEN.

A MOTHER'S TRAVAIL

I call to remembrance the unfeigned faith that is in thee, which dwelt first in thy grandmother Lois and thy mother Eunice; and I am persuaded in thee also.

—2 TIMOTHY 1:5

My mother inherited my grandmother's faith and, like Timothy, I inherited that same faith.

As a young boy, I remember coming home from school ready to find Mom and the cookies she always had waiting for me. But this day, there was no Mom and no cookies. I anxiously ran up the stairs, only to find our vacuum cleaner running in the hallway and the sound of crying coming from my sister's closet. It was there I first heard my mother consumed in the prayer of travail. I heard her crying with all her might, "God, save my babies. Let them grow strong and sure in you. Raise them up to preach the gospel."

Mothers, you may never know or see the results of your prayer. Nonetheless, keep praying. God may have charged you to raise up a John Wesley or a Martin Luther. Live out your faith before them, and they will carry the torch to the next generation.

Fathers, what does it profit you to gain the whole world and lose your children? Set a godly example for them. Do not provoke them to wrath, but motivate them to seek the face of God.

> JESUS, HELP ME PASS MY FAITH IN YOU ON TO MY CHILDREN. GIVE ME WISDOM. HELP ME TO MAKE TIME FOR THEM IN MY LIFE. THANK YOU, LORD, FOR THE GIFT OF MY CHILDREN. AMEN.

SLIPPERY FAITH

He staggered not at the promise of God through unbelief; but was strong in faith . . . and being fully persuaded that, what he had promised, he was able also to perform.

—ROMANS 4:20–21

T he word translated "stagger" from the Greek means to "doubt or hesitate." Abraham did not slide back and forth between faith and fear—two mutually exclusive expectations. You cannot have faith and fear in the same heart. One drives out the other. You do not have to rebuke fear or overcome fear. Have faith in God and fear not.

Abraham was fully persuaded. Some Christians are not fully persuaded about anything—that their spouse is the right one, that their church is the right one, or their choice for lunch is the right one.

Stop wading in the shallow flatlands of weak spiritual experience and launch out into the deep. Be fully persuaded that the God you serve is able to perform what He has promised!

LORD, I AM PERSUADED THAT YOU ARE ABLE TO SAVE MY LOST LOVED ONES. LORD, I AM PERSUADED THAT YOUR PLANS FOR ME ARE GOOD AND NOT EVIL. LORD, I AM PERSUADED THAT YOU WILL PROTECT ME FROM ALL HARM. AMEN.

SEAWORTHY VESSELS

But every man is tempted, when he is drawn away of his own lust, and enticed. Then when lust hath conceived, it bringeth forth sin; and sin when it is accomplished, bringeth forth death.

—JAMES 1:14-15

I have seen great ocean liners docked in the ports of Hong Kong, vessels weighing thousands of tons with mammoth engines that propel them across the oceans. But they will be docked in the bay and a little old tugboat can hook a chain to that boat and draw it away. It would be a different story if that ocean liner suddenly started its engines and threw its gears in reverse.

The same thing is true of believers. The devil cannot take you in tow unless your engines are shut down. Second Timothy 2:26 says, "These are they that are taken captive of the devil at his will." Don't allow the devil to dry dock your spirit.

If you shut down your mind to the things of God, you will give in to your own lusts and passions, allowing the enemy to seduce you into watching soap operas or football games.

Ride the waves of adversity fueled by the Holy Ghost. Let His wind fill your sails and empower you toward His destination.

GOD, FILL MY ENGINES WITH THE FUEL OF YOUR POWER. IGNITE ME WITH YOUR SPIRIT. WITH YOUR WIND, PROPEL ME IN THE WAYS YOU WANT ME TO GO. AMEN.

SETTLE IT

For which cause I also suffer these things: nevertheless I am not ashamed: for I know in whom I have believed, and am persuaded that he is able to keep that which I have committed unto him against that day.

—2 TIMOTHY 1:12

G od is going to be God, whether the answer to your prayer ever manifests or not. Shadrach, Meshach and Abednego looked death in the eye and said, "Our God is more than able to deliver us, but even if he doesn't we will still serve Him" (cf. Daniel 3:16–18).

Settle it in your mind and in your spirit once and for all that you are committed to God and His ordinances. Determine that, come what may, you are going to serve Him in loving obedience.

We all know what to do when God is speaking to us. It is when He is silent that those who have not settled it begin to falter in their walk. You will stumble over every rock of adversity the devil tosses in your path, unless you can shout like Timothy with the conviction of knowing in whom you believe.

Ambivalence leads to double-mindedness. God cannot use a double-minded man (James 1:7–8). Settle in your mind that you will have single-minded devotion to Christ. Settle it before the storm comes.

JESUS, I HAVE SETTLED THE LORDSHIP ISSUE IN MY LIFE. YOU ARE LORD. YOU ARE MASTER. YOU ARE MY KING. YOU ALONE WILL I OBEY. AMEN.

SECURE YOUR VICTORY

My people are destroyed for lack of knowledge.

—HOSEA 4:6

When you give in to temptation, it is because you have not secured your victory for one of two reasons:

1) You are receiving His Word but choosing not to walk in it. When you know what the Bible says about your situation and walk in the light of that knowledge, you will not fall into temptation. You will see the snares of the devil and avoid them.

2) You are yielding to temptation because you are uninformed of God's instructions.

We are required to walk in the revelation of the Word, whether we have received it or not. Just because you don't know the law doesn't mean you won't get arrested for disobeying it. People get into all kinds of sin, die of cancer, and live in poverty. Why? Because they are ignorant of the power available to them.

Secure your victory by finding out what God has to say about your situation and then determine to do what He says to do about it.

LORD, TEACH ME YOUR WORD AND YOUR WAYS. I WILL READ, STUDY, MEDITATE UPON, AND APPLY YOUR WORD THIS DAY IN ALL THAT I SAY AND DO. AMEN.

GOD'S PRUNING SHEARS

I am the true vine, and my Father is the husbandman.

—JOHN 15:1

God will put people in your life to perfect the fruit of His Spirit in you. But if you say, "We have a personality conflict, and I am just going to have to get away from that person," you take the pruning shears of the Holy Spirit out of God's hands.

When He wanted to cut that thing off that hindered your growth, you said, "No, God, I won't change there. I like that fruit. Don't change that, God. Get your pruning shears away from me."

God brought that person or situation into your life, because there is an area of your life only that person, that relationship or that situation can perfect in you. They may be God's sandpaper, smoothing out the rough edges in your life. They may be the irritation, like sand in an oyster, that produces a pearl in your life. Notice the people God brings into your life, and you will begin to see the kind of person you are with God. He says, "Show that person the same love, compassion, forgiveness, patience, and tolerance I have shown you."

LORD, HELP ME STOP COMPLAINING ABOUT IRRITATING PEOPLE IN MY LIFE. USE THEM TO HELP ME GROW IN FAITH, WISDOM, AND MATURITY. THANK YOU, LORD, FOR PRUNING THE DEAD WOOD AND ROUGH AREAS OUT OF MY LIFE. AMEN.

DIG A DITCH

And he said, thus saith the LORD, Make this valley full of ditches. For thus saith the LORD, Ye shall not see wind, neither shall ye see rain; yet that valley shall be filled with water, that ye may drink, both ye, and your cattle, and your beasts.

—2 KINGS 3:16–17

The armies were dying of thirst when they received the prophet's words. God instructed them, through His prophet, to do something first in the natural: Dig a ditch! It's too late to dig a ditch after the rains come. Get prepared. Stay ready. Be armed. When God says to act, don't delay. Do exactly what He commands.

The man with the withered arm wasn't healed until he stretched forth his arm. Farmers don't expect a harvest until they sow seed. God will not send your increase until you have prepared to receive it. What will you do today to prepare to receive what God has for you?

God has something He wants to give you—so prepare for increase. If you want to make room for Him in your life, you have to dig a ditch.

JESUS, I WANT TO RECEIVE ALL YOU HAVE FOR ME. I AM DIGGING A DITCH, PREPARING A PLACE FOR ALL YOU HAVE FOR ME. I AM READY, LORD. SEND YOUR RAIN. AMEN.

WEEK 26—FRIDAY

THE DEVIL'S HIT LIST

And the Lord said, Simon, Simon, behold, Satan hath desired to have you, that he may sift you as wheat: but I have prayed for thee, that thy faith fail not: and when thou art converted, strengthen thy brethren.

—LUKE 22:31–32

On the top of the devil's hit list are those who love the Lord and walk according to His plan for their lives.

The devil wants to sift you as wheat, but you do not have to be afraid, because he has to contend with the next verse: "But I have prayed for you." Who prayed? Not Abraham, David, Peter, nor Paul. The One who prays for you is the resurrected Son of the living God, the One who conquered death, hell, and the grave. He pulled the keys of your bondage out of the defeated hands of your adversary.

Take hold of this revelation: Jesus is interceding at the right hand of your Father, calling your name aloud and praying, specifically, that your faith won't fail. Then rejoice that you have made the devil's hit list. He cannot touch or harm you. At least, you are a problem to him. At least, he has noticed your work in the kingdom of God. Rejoice when he attacks. You are doing something right, and the enemy hates it.

GOD, EMPOWER ME TO WITHSTAND THE ATTACKS AND FIERY DARTS OF THE EVIL ONE. I KNOW THAT JESUS IS INTERCEDING FOR ME, AND I WALK IN THE POWER OF HIS INTERCESSION. AMEN.

SHIELDED WITH FAVOR

For thou, LORD, wilt bless the righteous; with favour wilt thou compass him as with a shield.

—PSALM 5:12

Our righteousness is as filthy rags. Right standing with God comes only through the blood of Christ and has nothing to do with our works; it is nothing we can earn. We are made the righteousness of God, and we will never be more righteous than we are right now.

Being in right standing with God positions us for blessing. We serve a "faith God." His promises are "yes" and "amen" to those who believe, and He wants every believer to walk in those promises (2 Corinthians 1:20).

Because God wants to bless you, He will give you supernatural favor with all men. God will cause your boss to give you a raise when he knows he can't stand you. He will cause the owner to sell you a house at a bargain price without knowing why. He will even cause your enemies to bless you. Because God rejoices as you come into His presence, you are wrapped in His blessing and favor—an impenetrable covering and shield of His loving grace and mercy.

GOD, RELEASE YOUR FAVOR UPON MY LIFE. COVER ME WITH YOUR BLESSING AS I GO OUT AND COME IN. THANK YOU, JESUS, FOR BEING MY RIGHTEOUSNESS. AMEN.

BE GOD'S STANDARD BEARER

Is this not the fast that I have chosen? . . . That thou hide not thyself from thine own flesh?

—ISAIAH 58:6,7

This text is the foundation for our becoming one of God's standard bearers. Too often the church has gone rushing into battle with dirty garments and soiled uniforms. Too often the church has tried to call the world to repent before she has left the night of sin. We need to come out of our deserts—soiled with past battles and sins—and be washed by living water.

In this text the Spirit of God admonishes us not to hide ourselves from our own flesh. We have been so busy playing the victim and blaming someone else for our failure to obey the commands of God that we have forgotten we were the ones who made the conscious decision to sin.

Before you can progress and rise to the rank of a mighty standard bearer in the kingdom of God you must first hear and respond to His primary call. God's first trumpet call to raise up standard bearers in the church is not to battle but to repentance.

Before we can become clear, transparent, shining, bright as the sun, we must repent and convert so that when the refreshing, revival, and restoration of God comes, we can receive all God has for us as His standard-bearers.

PURIFY MY HEART, O GOD. MAKE ME BEAUTIFUL, CLEAN, AND PURE AS THE MOON REFLECTING YOUR LIGHT. MAKE ME TRANSPARENT, SHINING, AND BRIGHT AS THE SUN. MAKE MY LIFE A LIGHT SHINING FOR JESUS. AMEN.

LIVING WATER

I sink in deep mire, where there is no standing: I am come into deep waters, where the floods overflow me.

—PSALM 69:2

O ver the course of time rivers often change course. Where a mighty river once coursed, only stagnating pools of water remain.

Jesus said, "He that believeth on me, as the scripture hath said, out of his belly shall flow rivers of living water" (John 7:38). He was speaking about believers who would be carried along in the power of the Holy Spirit.

David cried out to God, "Deliver me out of the mire, and let me not sink" (Psalm 69:14). Resolve to keep your spiritual river from turning into a swamp, and be ever ready to move in the power of the Holy Ghost.

As we observe in Ezekiel 47, the river of God first flows to our ankles, covering our spiritual walk. It then rises to our knees, covering our prayer lives. The river then flows to our waists, speaking of our service and finally becomes so deep that we must swim in the river, allowing it to take us with its flow. Decide today to become totally immersed in the river of God.

RIVER OF GOD, FLOW INTO, THROUGH, AND OUT OF ME. RIVER OF GOD, IMMERSE ME AND TAKE ME BY YOUR CURRENT INTO YOUR PERFECT PLAN AND FUTURE. AMEN.

DON'T TRUST YOUR FEELINGS

And when he thus had spoken, he cried with a loud voice, Lazarus, come forth.

—JOHN 11:43

ear hinders, but faith marches into enemy territory. Fear appears logical and authentic, but is only a product of our senses—what we see, hear, touch, taste, and feel. Operating in the realm of the natural only leaves us vulnerable to the devil's tactics (John 12:31).

When Jesus approached the grave of Lazarus, He saw the stone firmly in place. His sense of smell told him the man was dead. He heard with His own ears the weeping mourners. He could taste the bitterness of His own tears. But Jesus did not let His senses lead Him away from the tomb. He was not looking at the situation with the eyes of man, but with the eyes of faith. He cried out, "Lazarus, come forth!" Death fled when He looked past the natural and operated in the spiritual.

You senses may tell you to fear. Your thoughts may give you many reasons why defeat and death are your only options. But God is the God of the impossible. With God, defeating death is not impossible because He is the resurrection and the life. Trust Him to do the impossible in spite of your natural feelings and reason.

Never trust your feelings because we walk by faith, not by sight (2 Corinthians 5:7). Put your trust in God alone.

LORD, WITH YOU ALL THINGS ARE POSSIBLE. HELP ME TO TRUST YOU EVEN WHEN MY THOUGHTS AND SENSES TELL ME THAT THINGS ARE IMPOSSIBLE. AMEN.

THE FATHER'S PLAN

The steps of a good man are ordered by the LORD: and he delighteth in his way.

—PSALM 37:23

Y ou are no accident. God looked down through the corridor of time and space. He knew your mother, grandmother, and ancestors ten and twenty generations before them. "And in thy book all my members were written, which in continuance were fashioned, when as yet there was none of them" (Psalm 139:16). He knew where they would have to move and what they would have to do to bring you into existence at exactly the right time.

He told Jeremiah, "Before I formed thee in the belly I knew thee" (Jeremiah 1:5). God watched as you grew in your mother's womb. David knew this when he proclaimed, "When I was made in secret, and curiously wrought in the lowest parts of the earth. Thine eyes did see my substance, yet being unperfect" (vv. 15–16).

God knew every event that would take place in your life before you even had a life. You have not been abandoned to run amok like a mouse in a maze, trying to find its way through the labyrinth. Your Father has a plan for you.

Your every thought, feeling, attitude, and action are known to God. He is intimately acquainted with your ways. You are not alone. He is with you always even to the end of the world (Matthew 28:20).

FATHER, THANK YOU FOR ALWAYS BEING THERE FOR ME. I CHERISH EACH MOMENT WITH YOU. DRAW ME UNTO YOURSELF. AMEN.

TESTED AND TRIED

And as she was going to fetch it, he called to her, and said, Bring me, I pray thee, a morsel of bread in thine hand.

—I KINGS 17:11

rought had caused great famine in the land and had driven Elijah to ask the widow for bread and water. Her response is probably similar to ones you have made when someone has made seemingly unreasonable demands on your resources. When we focus on the possibility of failure, we see only our limitations.

But the widow trusted Elijah because she knew he heard from God. She trusted enough to give sacrificially out of what she needed to survive herself! This is a divine principle of kingdom living that God has set before us: "seek ye first the kingdom of God, and His righteousness; and all these things shall be added unto you" (Matthew 6:33).

It is not so much what is in our hand that matters as much as how we hold it. Give freely and joyfully, and the results will be as amazing as it was with this woman. Always remember, whatever you give to God never leaves your life . . . only your hand.

LORD JESUS, MAKE YOUR KINGDOM THE FIRST PRIORITY IN MY LIFE. FILL ME WITH JOY AS I SERVE AND GIVE. I TRUST YOU TO TAKE CARE OF ALL MY NEEDS. AMEN.

APPREHENDED

Not as though I had already attained, either were already perfect: but I follow after, if that I may apprehend that for which also I am apprehended of Christ Jesus.

—PHILIPPIANS 3:12

The word *apprehended* means "taken hold of." When Paul wrote to the Christians at Philippi, he told them his goal was to take hold of the purpose for which God had taken hold of him.

God has something he wants to do with your life. Before you knew Him, God set in motion the plan He wanted to accomplish. At the right time, He broke through to you and revealed Himself as your Lord and Savior, bringing you to repentance and salvation.

You may not have even been looking for Him at the time, but God knew exactly where to find you. "But God commendeth his love toward us, in that, while we were yet sinners, Christ died for us" (Romans 5:8). He sought you out to bring you in, and He did it for a specific purpose.

Take hold of God's purpose for your life; zealously pursue it. Press "toward the mark for the prize of the high calling of God in Christ Jesus" (Philippians 3:14).

JESUS, YOUR PURPOSE FOR ME HAS COMPLETE CONTROL IN MY LIFE. I SURRENDER TO YOUR PURPOSE, WILL, AND DIRECTION. LEAD ME DEEPER AND DEEPER INTO YOUR PRESENCE. AMEN.

WEEK 28—MONDAY

LET GOD BE GOD

Thus saith the LORD the King of Israel, and his redeemer the LORD of hosts; I am the first, and I am the last; and beside me there is no God.

—ISAIAH 44:6

We serve a sovereign, holy God. It is good gospel news that what God does for us is not contingent on what we are able to do. He is going to be God, regardless of what you and I do. You are not going to make God what you want Him to be. You may make a god, but it will not be *the* God.

He is more than able for every situation of our lives. The kingdom of darkness is subdued, and the blood-stained banner of His Cross is exalted. He is sitting high upon His throne, far above every principality, power, might, and name that is named (Ephesians 1:20).

It is time to destroy our idols and manmade temples and return to the pursuit of the God we are supposed to be serving—an omnipotent, all-powerful, holy God of mercy and grace.

When you truly let God be God in your life, you will be able to attain the unattainable and reach the unreachable.

JESUS, IN YOU I AM REACHING FOR THE HIGHEST HEIGHTS AND SEEKING THE DEEPEST REVELATION BY YOUR SPIRIT. TAKE ME TO YOUR PLACE WHICH IS BEYOND MY REACH AND MY IMAGINATION. AMEN.

CHANGE THE CHANNEL

But we all, with open face beholding as in a glass the glory of the Lord, are changed into the same image from glory to glory, even as by the Spirit of the Lord.

—2 CORINTHIANS 3:18

L ife is like a television with a remote control. If you do not like the channel, change it. If you do not like the way life is treating you, change the way you treat life. If you do not like the way people have been treating you, change the way you act.

I learned a long time ago that I can change myself a whole lot faster than I can ever change you. If your spouse, or child, or boss needs changing, let God change them. Pray for them, but stop trying to change them.

If I do not like the way you are treating me, I cannot do much about you, but I can change myself right away. I cannot remain depressed when I think about His goodness and what He's done for me. The devil hates a smile, and he'll train you to frown if you let him. He will pull a cloud of doom over your every thought, relationship, and situation if you do not resist him. Change the channel of your life today, and resist the devil in everything you say and do.

JESUS, GIVE ME THE PATIENCE TO TRUST YOU TO CHANGE OTHERS. CHANGE ME, LORD, SO THAT I CAN BE MORE AND MORE LIKE YOU. AMEN.

WEEK 28—WEDNESDAY
THE HELP OF THE KING

Every valley shall be exalted, and every mountain and hill shall be made low: and the crooked shall be made straight, and the rough places plain.

—ISAIAH 40:4

The Promised Land was not a level plain. It was a land of rocks, hills, and valleys. Our Promised Land will also have its ups and downs. Paul tells us to set our affections on things above, not on things on the earth (Colossians 3:2). That means not only to seek heaven but also to set your mind on the things of God and His kingdom.

This does not mean the absence of life in this world. It is rather the ability to see the things of this world in the light of eternity. Is your perspective limited by time or released by eternity? Do you see life from God's perspective or only from a human perspective?

Place your thought life, your emotions, and your will in God's hands. Let Jesus smooth out your mountains of adversity and fill in your valleys of despair. He is the One who makes our high places low and our rough places plain. Keep Him ever before you as you make His kingdom your home.

JESUS, LIFT MY EYES AND AFFECTIONS TO THE MOUNTAINTOPS OF FAITH AND HOPE. GIVE ME YOUR PERSPECTIVE IN EVERY DECISION OF MY LIFE. AMEN.

WEEK TWENTY-EIGHT**   **165**

SETTLE YOUR ACCOUNTS

Therefore is the kingdom of heaven likened unto a certain king, which would take account of his servants.

—MATTHEW 18:23

J esus used the parable of the king who wanted to settle accounts with his servants to explain one of the laws by which citizens of His kingdom are to abide.

He said, "I'm holding you to a higher standard—my standard." If Jesus could forgive you while you were still a sinner—cheating and stealing, still running around on your spouse, lying to your friends and stealing from your employer—He expects you to be able to forgive just as fully and completely.

He goes on in verse 24 to say that if we don't settle our accounts by being forgiving, God will have a rough account to settle with us! God's forgiveness, though freely given to repentant sinners, is nevertheless conditional. He forgives us as we forgive others. Keep your accounts in order. Forgive as He forgave you.

JESUS, TODAY I FORGIVE _____.
HELP ME TO FORGIVE QUICKLY SO THAT I
MIGHT RECEIVE YOUR FORGIVENESS. AMEN.

KINGDOM LIVING

Who hath delivered us from the power of darkness, and hath translated us into the kingdom of his dear Son.

—COLOSSIANS 1:13

When the children of Israel were poised to enter the Promised Land, God told them to go in, possess the land, and dwell therein.

For us as Christians, the Promised Land means crossing from the natural into the supernatural realm. God has called us to come out of the kingdom of the world and to come into the kingdom of God. He calls us to walk by faith and not by sight.

The kingdom of God has different laws from our old kingdom, and we must learn to operate in them. Jesus said in Matthew 5:19 that those who both do and teach God's laws in the Old Testament "shall be called great in the kingdom of heaven." God's commands are His blueprint for successful kingdom living.

Praise Him today for giving us the Holy Spirit, who enables us to live above condemnation and to grow in obedience to God's commands (Romans 8:1–39).

JESUS, I PRAISE YOU FOR TAKING ME FROM THE KINGDOM OF DARKNESS INTO YOUR KINGDOM OF LIGHT. TEACH ME TO OPERATE BY FAITH AND NOT BY SIGHT. AMEN.

A LIFE SURRENDERED

And so will I go in unto the king, which is not according to the law: and if I perish, I perish.

—ESTHER 4:16

Don't be afraid of making decisions, because the devil wins all standoffs. God teaches us through our mistakes. Your steps will be ordered of the Lord if you seek Him in every endeavor. Don't allow the devil to gain a toehold in your life through procrastination and indecision.

The children of Israel stood on one side of a valley week after week—until a young shepherd boy with a slingshot came along and made a decision to do something about the situation.

D. L. Moody said, "It is yet to be seen what God would do through one man's life surrendered totally to Him. I determine to be that man." Moody was never ordained, but he shook three continents with the power of God, because he realized "all things are possible to those that believe" (Luke 1:37). Be decisive for Christ. Commit to Him now. Don't worry about how the world will respond. Jesus will see you through every circumstance and valley.

JESUS, SEE ME THROUGH. HELP ME TO BE DECISIVE AND TO ACT IMMEDIATELY UPON YOUR EVERY COMMAND. GIVE ME THE COURAGE TO FOLLOW YOU WHEREVER YOU LEAD. AMEN.

DAILY SURRENDER

Then was Jesus led up of the spirit into the wilderness to be tempted of the devil.

—MATTHEW 4:1

Surrender to the Holy Spirit is not a one-time occurrence that happens when we are born again. We must surrender daily, moment by moment.

It is easy to spot those who are yielding to the Holy Spirit and those who are not. A believer who is led by the Spirit will have victory over sin (Galatians 6:15), power to witness (Acts 1:8), and will possess the fruit of the Holy Spirit: love, joy, peace, patience, kindness, goodness, faithfulness, gentleness, and self-control.

A Spirit-controlled life does not happen overnight. It takes patience and submission. It requires obedience, and it demands confession of our sins.

Today and every day give your life back to God as a living sacrifice and surrender your life to the Holy Spirit's guidance and control.

> KEEP ME YIELDED TODAY, O LORD. GIVE ME PATIENCE. EXPOSE MY SINS. I REPENT OF EVERY SIN AND DESIRE TO OBEY EVERY WORD YOU SPEAK. AMEN.

SAY "YES"

Moses was very meek, above all the men which were on the face of the earth.

—NUMBERS 12:3

Moses was a prideful and arrogant man, ready to take care of God's people (his way) when he lived in Pharaoh's palace. God took all of that away, when He sent him into the wilderness. Moses went from presiding in the palace to watching sheep in the desert.

It took God forty years to purge Moses of everything that blocked His ability to use him to deliver the children of Israel. Forty long years in the desert changed haughtiness to humility and hostility to harmony with God.

God's purpose in our lives is to bring us to a realization that everything we have of value is from Him alone. God has a plan and purpose for you, and He will remove anything that will hinder your effectiveness in fulfilling His plan—your job, your friends, your surroundings, your money—anything. God will break all threads of independence until we bow our knee and say, "Yes, Lord."

In your marriage or family, say, "Yes, Lord." In your finances, say, "Yes, Lord." In your emotions and thoughts, say, "Yes, Lord." In your work, say, "Yes, Lord." In your relationships, say, "Yes, Lord." In your service and your church, say, "Yes, Lord."

JESUS, TO EVERYTHING YOU SPEAK INTO MY LIFE, I SAY, "YES, LORD." AMEN.

PURSUIT IS PROOF

As the hart panteth after the water brooks, so panteth my soul after thee, O God.

—PSALM 42:1

I told a friend of mine one time that I would love to play the piano like he did. He replied, "No you wouldn't. If you really wanted to play the piano you would be taking lessons and practicing every chance you could. Are you doing those things?"

Well, no, I wasn't. If I really wanted to play the piano I would have been taking some action and making some plans instead of just talking about it. When you really want something, you pursue it with your whole heart.

You say that you want the things of God, you want to operate in the gifts of the Holy Spirit and you want to have an anointing on your life—but are you pursuing Him? Are you climbing the mountain of God and, like Jacob, refusing to let go until He blesses you? When was the last time you spent time in prayer and in the Word?

Pursue Him with all your might. The proof of your desire is in your pursuit. The pursuit of God will lead to holiness, purity, passion, zeal, and power in your life.

GOD, I PURSUE YOU THIS DAY WITH ALL MY BEING. I GIVE YOU MY HEART, MIND, SOUL, AND STRENGTH IN LOVE. AMEN.

HE FEARS YOU

Now about that time Herod the king stretched forth his hands to vex certain of the church. And he killed James the Brother of John with the sword. And because he saw it pleased the Jews, he proceeded further to take Peter also. (Then were the days of unleavened bread).

—ACTS 12:1–3

Notice that Herod vexed "certain of the church." He did not launch a full-scale persecution of the Church or try to arrest every person who had become a Christian. He was only after certain ones. Anxious to carry favor with the Jewish leaders, he made himself a willing tool of the devil to attack James and Peter.

The devil chose these men because they were filled with the Holy Ghost, preaching the gospel and bringing thousands into the kingdom of God. People who love and serve the Lord are a threat to the devil, and he fights back.

You too may have suffered the sting of his fiery darts. He is not after you because of who you are, but because he knows what God can do through you. He has heard your prayers and felt the deadening blows of the Word of God coming from your lips. He is afraid of you!

LORD, I THANK YOU THAT THOSE WHO LOVE YOU ARE A THREAT TO THE ENEMY. LORD, HUMBLE ME SO THAT WHEN I RESIST HIM, HE WILL FLEE. AMEN.

BELIEVING FAITH

Have faith in God. For verily I say unto you, That whosoever shall say unto this mountain, Be thou removed, and be thou cast into the sea; and shall not doubt in his heart, but shall believe that those things which he saith shall come to pass; he shall have whatsoever he saith.

—MARK 11:22–23

The greatest thing that will ever happen to your faith is when the Word of God takes that eighteen-inch drop from mental assent in your head to believing faith in your heart.

When God engraves His Word in your heart, there isn't enough doubt, discouragement, or disaster to ever remove it. The devil doesn't have an eraser big enough to remove God's Word from your spirit once He has placed it there.

In what will you place your trust today? Money, work, strength, education, status, or power? Only faith in God can move mountains and resist the devil. Only faith in God can do the impossible. Only faith in God can produce powerful prayers. In what or Whom do you trust today?

JESUS, I CANNOT LEAVE THIS ALTAR OF PRAYER WITHOUT FIRST CONFESSING THAT I PLACE ALL MY TRUST IN YOU. AMEN.

FAITH IN THE BLOOD

Whom God hath set forth to be a propitiation through faith in his blood, to declare his righteousness for the remission of sins that are past, through the forbearance of God.

—ROMANS 3:25

Have faith in God, but also have faith in what He has done. Calvary was proof of God's righteousness, not only for your yesterday, but also for your today and your tomorrow.

God never said because you believe in Jesus you are automatically declared righteous. He gave us the basis for forgiveness of sin and the basis on which He could declare sinners righteous—faith in the shed blood of Jesus.

Jesus is the foundation on which our faith stands. His sinless blood blotted out your sins forever; but for that blood to be effective in your life, you must have faith to believe.

Faith in the atoning blood of Jesus means protection and provision in our daily walk. Plead the blood of Jesus over your mind, your body, your work, and your walk with Him. Apply the blood to the doorposts of your life, your family, your church, your work, and your friends.

LORD JESUS, THANK YOU FOR SHEDDING YOUR BLOOD TO ATONE FOR MY SINS. I APPLY THE BLOOD TO EVERY RELATIONSHIP IN MY LIFE FOR YOUR PROTECTING, CLEANSING, HEALING, AND SAVING POWER. AMEN.

HIS PROMISE... YOUR PURPOSE

I am the vine, ye are the branches: He that abideth in me, and I in him, the same bringeth forth much fruit: for without me ye can do nothing.

—JOHN 15:5

I f you are abiding in Him, God gives you the desires of your heart. You can only receive what comes through the vine. If your delight is right, your desire will also be right. If your delight is wrong, your desire will be wrong.

Our purpose for being on this planet is to glorify God. The chief end of man is to glorify God. It is not miracles that glorify God. It is not talking in tongues or sitting in church on Sunday morning.

When the life of Christ flows through us to touch and change lives for all eternity, we bring glory to Him.

Your success will not come from your rules, your religion, your rituals, or your regimen. Your success will come because of your relationship to the vine. The greater your relationship, the greater your results. Never touch His glory. Always give Him glory and intimacy with Him will increase dramatically in your daily abiding in Him.

HOW I LONG TO ABIDE IN YOU, O SAVIOR. I CAN DO NOTHING WITHOUT YOU. KEEP ME CLOSE TO YOU, FOR WITHOUT YOU I AM NOTHING. AMEN.

TEMPTATION IS KNOCKING

And it came to pass in an evening tide, that David arose from off his bed, and walked upon the roof of the king's house: and from the roof he saw a woman washing herself; and the woman was very beautiful to look upon.

—2 SAMUEL 11:2

We are never out of reach of the tentacles of temptation. You can be in a crowd of thousands or alone in your thoughts, and temptation will sit down beside you.

Was the seed of temptation already in David's heart, or was he only seeking a place of solitude when temptation overtook him? Instead of fleeing the roof when he saw Bathsheba, he fed temptation by inquiring about her. The result of allowing temptation to stay in your heart will be as devastating to you as it was to him.

Guard your heart with all diligence (Proverbs 4:23). Do not feed your spirit with the chaff of this world, but keep it strong through reading and meditating on the Word of God and communing with your heavenly Father.

What are the strongest temptations in your life? How are you avoiding or resisting them? How do you need God's help in resisting temptation?

JESUS, I DESIRE TO RESIST EVERY TEMPTATION THAT COMES MY WAY. GRANT ME DISCERNMENT AND WISDOM IN RECOGNIZING AND AVOIDING TEMPTATION. AMEN.

A NEW PLACE OF WORSHIP

And he said, Take now thy son, thine only son Isaac, whom thou lovest, and get thee into the land of Moriah; and offer him there for a burnt offering upon one of the mountains which I will tell thee of.

—GENESIS 22:2

God told Abraham to go to a new place to worship Him. Frequently we too must go to a new place in our worship—a place far from the religious traditions of reciting confessions and going through prayer cards. Tradition will smother the presence of God in our times of worship.

God tested Abraham's faith and obedience, and He will test yours. We may hear Him tell us to lay something on the altar that is precious to us. God does not ask for those things because He needs them, but because we need to be set free from their power in our lives. Every sacrifice we ever make will take us into a new place of worship with Him.

Abraham dearly loved Isaac. Did He love him more than the Lord? No, his faith was tested and he obeyed God. Give your children to the Lord. Give your spouse to the Lord. Give your church to the Lord. On the altar of your surrender you will discover a deeper level of worship and intimacy with God.

LORD, I COME TO WORSHIP YOU IN A NEW PLACE. TODAY I PLACE EVERYTHING AND EVERYONE I HAVE SOUGHT TO CONTROL ON THE ALTAR. I DESIRE ON THIS ONE THING—TO WORSHIP AND GLORIFY YOU. AMEN.

GOD'S ORDER

And Laban said, It must not be so done in our country, to give the younger before the first-born.

—GENESIS 29:26

Everything in the Bible is given to show us God's order and purpose. Jacob tried to cut corners. He wanted to circumvent repentance and holiness in his quest for joy and happiness. Too often we want the reward without the labor, the honor without the fight. We desire gain without pain and victory without sacrifice.

We serve a God of plan and purpose, not one of short-cuts. Laban told Jacob he would have to marry the older sister, Leah, before he could marry Rebecca, the one he truly loved. It is easy to fall in love with happiness and joy, but there is a Leah of holiness our soul must learn to love first. We will never wear the crown if we do not first carry the cross.

Labor as Jacob did, in willing service to our Lord, as we await the wedding supper of the Lamb. When the time for the wedding feast arrives, Jesus will wash away the pain and toil of our labor.

LORD, YOU DESIRE FOR CERTAIN THINGS TO HAPPEN IN MY LIFE THAT I KNOW I AM RESISTING. TEACH ME TO ACCEPT WHATEVER YOU WANT FROM ME SO THAT I MAY KNOW YOU AND YOUR WILL COMPLETELY. AMEN.

DECISIONS

And God said, Let us make man in our image, after our likeness: and let them have dominion.

—GENESIS 1:26

❦

Your character is the sum total of every decision you have ever made. There is no such thing as an unimportant decision. God never intended for man to be a salve of circumstances. We were made to have dominion on the earth, and dominion only comes through exercising our will to make decisions. Your new character is the sum total of one decision which you have made—to follow Jesus.

If your decisions line up with the will of God for your life, though all hell breaks loose you will weather the storm. You will set your chin like flint and say, "I am going to the other side! I don't care that my boat of life is being tossed to and fro. I know Who rides in my vessel, and I will fear no harm. He will keep me safe."

Out of your new character in Christ, you will have the power and courage to make right decisions. Compare every decision to His character. If that decision measure up to Jesus, who is Truth, then you will do what is right. Anything that does not measure up to Christ, discard from your life. Making right decisions is always doing what Jesus would do.

THANK YOU, JESUS, FOR BEING TRUTH IN MY LIFE. FILL ME WITH THE KNOWLEDGE OF YOUR TRUTH AND THE COURAGE TO CHOOSE WHAT IS RIGHT. AMEN.

THE BEGINNING OF MIRACLES

*This beginning of miracles did Jesus in Cana of Galilee . . .
and his disciples believed on him.*

—JOHN 2:11

Jesus' first miracle was to turn water to wine. What Jesus began is not finished; the Miracle-worker has never changed: "Jesus Christ the same yesterday, and to day and for ever" (Hebrews 13:8).

The last miracle did not end with the last apostle named in the Bible; for this to be true there would have to be a complete absence of miracles. Even one miracle would disprove this erroneous statement.

In Mark 16:15–20, Jesus confirmed that miracles are not special gifts for a few, but are for all believers. Those claiming that the age of miracles has ended deny the power of prayer. For God to hear and answer your prayer is a miracle.

You may feel that today you do not need a miracle. All of us stand in need of miracles every day. Every breath is a miracle. Every act of kindness is a miracle. Every time you forgive and receive forgiveness, it's a miracle. Every prayer is a miracle. Miracles are signs pointing to God. Expect God to act miraculously in every moment of your life.

When you pray, expect God to hear and answer your prayer. Healing is for today. Deliverance is for today. Signs and wonders are for today!

JESUS, OPEN MY EYES TO ALL THE MIRACLES YOU ARE DOING EVERY MOMENT THAT I MAY GLORIFY YOUR NAME AND GIVE YOU ALL HONOR AND PRAISE. AMEN.

NEW WINE

And when they wanted wine, the mother of Jesus saith unto him, They have no wine.

—JOHN 2:3

S igns and wonders are given to us to reveal Jesus' glory, and for no other reason. John said that because of the miracle of turning the water into wine at the wedding at Cana, Jesus' disciples then believed that He was the Messiah (John 2:11).

When Jesus arrived, He was met with mankind's universal problem: They had no wine! Wine is always symbolic of joy in the Bible, and this is the area that always starts to deteriorate first as we face the day-to-day problems of life.

But what was Jesus' action? First, He commanded the servants to bring the water pots to Him. As living vessels, we must first present ourselves in our current state, to the Lord.

Jesus then requested, "Fill the vessels to the brim." If we will give Him what we are, He will change us into what we should be. If we will pour out all that we have—our dreams, our hopes, our plans for the future— He will fill us with joy unspeakable and full of His glory!

JESUS, I THIRST FOR YOUR NEW WINE IN MY LIFE. REFRESH ME. MAKE ME NEW SO THAT I MAY CONTAIN YOUR NEW WINE. FILL ME WITH UNSPEAKABLE JOY. AMEN.

HE SENDS THE WINE

And the floors shall be full of wheat, and the vats shall over-flow with wine.

—JOEL 2:24

G od intends for our hearts to overflow with His joy. He fills you with joy as a result of your spirit man being in tune with Him.

Nehemiah 8:10 declares, "The joy of the LORD is your strength." His joy sustains you when the doctor says you will not have long to live, when your kids are on crack, or when you don't have a dollar to change. True joy is unaffected by your circumstances.

When you become filled with the Holy Spirit, you receive His joy. In Acts 2, those present in the Upper Room became "intoxicated" with the Holy Ghost, causing the crowd to believe they were drunken with wine. In Luke 10:21, Jesus rejoiced in the Holy Spirit. Romans 14:17 reveals that the kingdom of God is not meat and drink; but righteousness, peace, and joy in the Holy Ghost.

They became drunk with joy! The early disciples of Jesus were drunk with the new wine of His Spirit and with the joy of the Spirit. Thank Him for His incomparable joy permeating your spirit.

THANK YOU, JESUS, FOR FILLING ME WITH YOUR JOY. GUARD MY HEART SO THAT NOTHING WILL ROB ME OF YOUR JOY. I WILL REJOICE IN ALL THINGS, GIVING YOU PRAISE. AMEN.

HEARTS OF KINGS

The king's heart is in the hand of the LORD, as the rivers of water: he turneth it whithersoever he will.

—PROVERBS 21:1

Satan is just another would-be king. He wanted to be king of the universe, to exalt his throne above the throne of God. But God gave the command for Satan to be cast down from heaven, and he fell to the earth like lightning. He usurped the first Adam's dominion on this planet and now rules a recaptured kingdom with an expiring lease.

The devil wants to be king of your life. He wants to be king of your mind, ruler of your home and monarch over your finances. But God said, "Satan's heart is in my hand. When I speak, he moves. I am King of kings!"

The psalmist declared, "Lift up your heads, O ye gates; even lift them up, ye everlasting doors; and the King of glory shall come in. Who is this King of glory? The Lord of hosts, he is the King of glory" (Psalm 24:9–10).

So lift up your head and open your heart. Cast out the pretender and allow the King of glory to enter in!

JESUS, RULE MY LIFE. ISSUE YOUR ORDERS AND I WILL OBEY. THE PRETENDER'S VOICE FALLS UPON MY DEAF EARS. I CHOSE TO LISTEN ONLY TO YOUR VOICE AND TO OBEY YOUR COMMANDS. AMEN.

GOD'S AGENTS

And these signs shall follow them that believe; in my name shall they cast out devils; they shall speak with new tongues; they shall take up serpents; and if they drink any deadly thing, it shall not hurt them; they shall lay hands on the sick, and they shall recover.

—MARK 16:17–18

We are God's agents in the earth, and He desires to manifest His miracle-working power through us. But in order to be used, you must not only be willing to be used, you must also be ready to be used.

Don't wait until you need a miracle to start polishing your vessel. Don't wait until the devil has ravaged your family, wrecked your health, and destroyed your finances to seek a relationship with your heavenly Father.

Ready your vessel by keeping your spirit strong in the Word, in prayer, and in fellowship with your Father. Speak forth His praises and acknowledge Him as your healer, your deliverer, and your provider. Today and every day, confess that you walk in divine health because the Spirit of life resides in you. Confess that His promises are made manifest in your life daily.

What will you do today to ready your vessel to receive all that God wants to pour into your life?

POUR INTO ME, O LORD, YOUR LIVING WATERS. I AM READY TO RECEIVE TODAY ALL THAT YOU DESIRE TO POUR INTO ME AND OUT OF ME. AMEN.

SET YOUR SIGHTS

According to my earnest expectation and my hope, that in nothing I shall be ashamed, but that with all boldness, as always, so now also Christ shall be magnified in my body, whether it be by life, or by death. For to me to live is Christ, and to die is gain.

—PHILIPPIANS 1:20–21

J esus was Lord in the apostle Paul's life, and his example to us today is unparalleled. Paul's entire purpose in life was to boldly speak forth for Christ's sake and to become more like Him with each passing day. Paul disciplined himself, setting goals and priorities to glorify God.

Each one of us has the same amount of time before us today, but how we use that time is going to determine just how far we go in the things of God. We are each responsible for the depth of our own lives.

How much time today will you spend on yourself and the pursuit of material things? How much time will you spend with God? How much time will you spend on building the relationships you have with others?

Set your sights today on living your life as Paul did, magnifying Christ in everything you lay your hands to do, your every step, and your every breath.

CHRIST, IT IS MY DESIRE TO MAGNIFY YOU IN ALL THAT I DO AND SAY TODAY. MAY YOU BE EXALTED IN ALL THAT I AM AND ALL THAT I DO. AMEN.

ANOINTED APRONS

And God wrought special miracles by the hands of Paul: so that from his body were brought unto the sick handkerchiefs or aprons, and the diseases departed from them, and the evil spirits went out of them.

—ACTS 19:11-12

God used Paul in an extraordinary demonstration of His supernatural power. The tangible anointing was carried from the apostle to the oppressed through anointed aprons and handkerchiefs.

These handkerchiefs were strips of linen, used to tie around your head while you worked. The aprons were also similar to the ordinary ones we use today. But they all were turned into miracle cloths when the anointing touched them.

Because of the widespread use of witchcraft in that day, Luke wanted the readers of his letter to know that the source of Paul's miracles was God and God alone. He distinguished what was happening through Paul by calling these special miracles.

God has already planned your miracle. Remember the source and give Him praise.

JESUS, I THANK YOU FOR EVERY MIRACLE YOU HAVE DONE, ARE DOING, AND WILL DO IN MY LIFE. YOU ARE THE SOURCE OF ALL POWER AND AUTHORITY FOR MIRACLES IN MY LIFE, AND I GIVE YOU ALL THE GLORY. AMEN.

A FACE OF FAITH

The same heard Paul speak: who stedfastly beholding him, and perceiving that he had faith to be healed, Said with a loud voice, Stand upright on thy feet. And he leaped and walked.

—ACTS 14:9–10

A man, lame from birth, sat in the crowd the day Paul preached the gospel in Lystra. The Bible doesn't tell us what Paul said, but whatever he said produced faith in this man.

Heard, as it is used in this verse, implies the abiding results of a past action—the preaching of the Word. Paul's preaching gave birth to faith, and it began to grow in the man the more he *heard* Paul expound. "Faith cometh by hearing, and hearing by the word of God" (Romans 10:17).

The seed of the Word of God was planted in this man's spirit. Paul continued to exhort the crowd when suddenly that seed of faith blossomed in his heart.

The man began acting as if he were already healed. Paul was able to see beyond his outward expression and see the condition of his heart. Paul, speaking words of faith, commanded him to stand—and he did, to the glory of God.

Are you living in defeat or confessing and acting in victory? You may not yet have seen your victory, but you know by faith that the victory has already been won at the cross. So live like a victor, not a victim!

HELP ME LIVE VICTORIOUSLY TODAY, LORD JESUS. AMEN.

TAKE YOUR MEDICINE

Now no chastening for the present seemeth to be joyous, but grevious: nevertheless afterward it yieldeth the peaceful fruit of righteousness unto them which are exercised thereby.

—HEBREWS 12:11

A ustin was sick when he was only two and had to take some terrible-tasting medicine. It is not easy getting a two-year-old to take something that tastes bad. But we were not making him take it because we did not love him. We were giving him what we knew would help him get better.

Now that he is older, he understands how much we love him, and he trusts us to always do what is best for him. He may not always like the medicine, but he knows when he takes it he will get better.

If you are wondering why things never get better in your life, perhaps you have not yet learned to take your medicine. God created you to live like Him, but if you absolutely refuse to take your medicine, He will let you live your life your way. Determine to take your medicine and live in the fullness of the life God has for you.

What medicine is God wanting you to take today? How is your attitude? Are you submitting or resisting God?

LORD, I DESIRE TO RECEIVE WHATEVER YOU HAVE FOR MY GROWTH AND BENEFIT. HELP ME TO SUBMIT TO YOUR WILL, EVEN WHEN I DO NOT UNDERSTAND. AMEN.

THE MEASURE OF FAITH

For I say, through the grace given unto me, to every man that is among you . . . to think soberly, according as God hath dealt to every man the measure of faith.

—ROMANS 12:3

You may say, "How is it possible to believe before you ever come to God?" Because God gave every man the measure of faith (Romans 12:3).

Don't ever say, "I don't have faith to be healed, or for my family's salvation, or for my finances to improve." God gave you the faith to believe!

You know this is true by the very fact that you are saved. With your heart you believed when you didn't know anything about God, because He gave you the ability to believe.

Believe what? That God *is*. Wherever you are, God was there first.

God is not a rewarder of casual acquaintances. His Word was given to us so we could know Him. But don't base your faith on the Word of God; base it, instead, on the God of the Word.

Seek Him with your whole heart and mind. Seek Him early in the morning and late at night. Seek Him while you are driving and while you work. Seek Him in worship and praise. Seek Him in the Word. Seek Him and live!

LORD, I SEEK YOU IN EVERY MOMENT OF MY LIFE. I SEEK YOU NOT FOR WHAT YOU CAN DO FOR ME BUT SIMPLY FOR YOUR PRESENCE. HOW I LONG TO BE CLOSE TO YOU. AMEN.

OUR FATHER HAS A PLAN

And Abraham called the name of that place Jehovah-Jireh: as it is said to this day, In the mount of the Lord it shall be seen.

—GENESIS 22:14

G od's plan is to establish your future and to do you no harm (Jeremiah 29:11). Just as He provided the ram to take Isaac's place in Genesis 22:8, God the Father provided God the Son to take your place.

Jehovah-Jireh, "the One who provides," sent Jesus to be our mediator (Hebrews 8:6), our guarantee (Hebrews 7:22) and our messenger (Malachi 3:1) of the covenant.

You are not bound to this world system. What your boss or the banking system has planned for you has nothing to do with your Father's plan.

Decide which kingdom you are living in, and be determined to obey the King. In God's kingdom there are no limits. He can bring the increase to break the yoke of poverty, and He can deliver you from every sickness and infirmity. Thank Him today for His plan for you and your family.

I THANK YOU, FATHER, FOR THE GOOD PLAN YOU HAVE FOR MY LIFE AND MY FAMILY. I PRAY FOR YOUR GUIDANCE AND DIRECTION IN LIVING OUT YOUR PLAN. AMEN.

Back to Bethel

And God said, unto Jacob, Arise, go up to Bethel, and dwell there: and make there an altar unto God, that appeared unto thee when thou fleddest from the face of Esau thy brother.

—Genesis 35:1

God calls us to live a lifestyle with an altar always ready for sacrifice, always ready for instantaneous repentance.

When trouble comes, wherever you are and whatever situation or condition you are in, you always have two avenues of escape available to you.

First, there is the altar of sacrifice and repentance to God. Present yourself humbly before the Lord as a living sacrifice, eager to repent.

Second, after you have truly repented and changed your ways, renew your consecration and dedication daily through prayer and study of His Word.

Both these methods are available to you twenty-four hours a day. Don't hesitate. Be willing at anytime to go back to Bethel and build an altar before the Lord. You will never climb upon an altar of God without the God of the altar showing up!

GOD, COME TO BETHEL TO MEET WITH YOU. YOU ARE MY BETHEL. TO YOU I MAKE EVERY SACRIFICE. I REPENT OF SIN AND DESIRE TO BE CLEANSED BY YOUR BLOOD THIS DAY. AMEN.

TANGIBLE AND TRANSFERABLE

And it shall come to pass in that day, that his burden shall be taken away from off thy shoulder, and his yoke from off thy neck, and the yoke shall be destroyed because of the anointing.

—ISAIAH 10:27

The anointing is a tangible force. Many people have difficulty understanding that truth, but I want you to comprehend the fullness of God's most precious anointing.

It is not something God dangles in front of you like a carrot for a horse. It is completely within your grasp, and God wants you to have it.

It is tangible, and it can be transferred. It was transferred from Elijah to Elisha through a mantle. It was transferred from Paul through handkerchiefs and aprons to those who were sick and afflicted.

The anointing of God comes from the very throne of heaven. It comes full of power, full of energy to root up, to pull down and to destroy every yoke of bondage the devil tries to put on you.

JESUS, HOW I NEED YOUR ANOINTING TO BREAK ALL THE YOKES OF BONDAGE IN MY LIFE. TOUCH ME THROUGH THE LAYING ON OF HANDS AND THROUGH THE PRAYERS OF THOSE AROUND ME. ANOINT ME TO DO YOUR MINISTRY. AMEN.

CALLING DISTANCE

But we had the sentence of death in ourselves, that we should not trust in ourselves, but in God which raiseth the dead: who delivered us from so great a death, and doth deliver: in whom we trust that he will yet deliver us.

—2 CORINTHIANS 1:9–10

Remember the times God has set you free, the times He has moved on your behalf, and the times He has come through when it seemed no answer would or even could come.

He is not going to begin failing you today. He will answer your prayers today, because He never changes. God will turn your tragedy into triumph and your trial into a testimony when you trust and depend upon Him.

Dependence on Him is not defeat; dependence is simply staying in constant contact. Trusting God means realizing He is the source of your deliverance, and then staying within calling distance of Him.

JESUS, YOU ARE THE SOURCE OF MY DELIVER-
ANCE, MY HEALING, AND MY RESTORATION. I
WILL STAY CLOSE TO YOU SO THAT I MAY
HEAR YOUR VOICE AT EVERY TURN AND
THROUGH EVERY SITUATION. AMEN.

SIGNS AND WONDERS

Behold, I and the children whom the LORD hath given me are for signs and for wonders in Israel from the LORD of hosts, which dwelleth in mount Zion.

—ISAIAH 8:18

P haraoh asked scornfully, "Who is the LORD?" (Exodus 5:2) At God's command, Aaron threw down his rod and it became a snake. Pharaoh's magicians laughed as their rods also turned into snakes, but the laughter died when Aaron's snake (rod) devoured theirs.

God proclaimed, "I will multiply my signs and my wonders in the land of Egypt" (Exodus 7:3). As ten plagues ravaged the land, Pharaoh, his magicians and all of Egypt came to know beyond a doubt who the Lord is.

God is multiplying His signs and wonders in our generation. Just as in the days of Moses, God is revealing himself to the scoffers, the doubters, the cynics and the sinners who scornfully ask, "Who is the Lord?"

You do not need to prove or defend God to skeptics. Simply lift up the name of Jesus and speak about your faith with simplicity and clarity. Love your enemies, thereby demonstrating who God is to them.

LORD, I TRUST YOU TO REVEAL YOURSELF THROUGH SIGNS AND WONDERS. LET YOUR ENEMIES SEE WHO YOU ARE. AMEN.

THE PRICE OF GLORY

And it came to pass, when Moses came down from mount Sinai with the two tables of testimony in Moses' hand . . . that Moses wist not that the skin of his face shone while he talked with him.

—EXODUS 34:29

Moses spent forty days in the mountain with God. When he finally returned to camp with the Ten Commandments inscribed on stones, he had to cover his face because it shone with the glory of God (Exodus 34:33). Moses shone with the tangible presence of God—everyone who looked at Him knew He had been with God.

If you will leave everything else behind . . . if you will be bold and persevere in your times of prayer, God will meet with you and talk to you just as He did with Moses. Second Corinthians 3:14–18 tells us that the veil covering our hearts is removed when we turn to the Lord and reflect His glory.

Stay in the mountain with God until you shine with His glory. Don't leave your house without His presence. Get in the mountain with God and receive His glory. Remember that you reflect His glory; you do not shine with your own glory.

JESUS, I DECLARE YOUR GLORY. I DESIRE TO STAY IN YOUR PRESENCE SO THAT I MAY REFLECT YOUR GLORY. CHANGE ME FROM GLORY TO GLORY. AMEN.

HOLD FAST

Seeing then that we have a great high priest, that is passed into the heavens, Jesus the Son of God, let us hold fast our profession.

—HEBREWS 4:14

Whatever you talk about is your confession. If you are continually confessing how much trouble the devil is causing, how bad your finances are or how rotten your spouse is, rest assured that your words will ring true.

When the Bible directs us to "hold fast" to our profession, we are being told to hold onto what the Bible says about our situation with bulldog faith—the kind that does not let go.

You are going to have trouble in this life, but if you will hold fast to your confession of faith you can be assured of victory, because you have been blessed with every spiritual blessing (Ephesians 1:3). You have been redeemed, forgiven, and are a recipient of His lavish grace (Ephesians 1:7–8). You have been delivered (rescued) from the domain of darkness (Satan's rule) and transferred to the kingdom of Christ (Colossians 1:13). You have been given a spirit of power, love, and sound mind (2 Timothy 1:7).

JESUS, I AM HOLDING FAST TO YOU. I HOLD FAST TO THE TRUTH OF MY CONFESSION IN YOU AS LORD AND SAVIOR. I HAVE THE ASSURANCE THAT YOU WILL SEE ME THROUGH EVERY VALLEY AND LEAD ME THROUGH EVERY STORM. AMEN.

WHAT IS SIN?

For if, when we were enemies, we were reconciled to God by the death of his Son, much more, being reconciled, we shall be saved by his life.

—ROMANS 5:10

I remember the story about the time John Wesley asked his mother the riveting question, "What then is sin?" She replied that sin is anything that impedes the tenderness of your conscience; anything that obscures your sense of God; anything that weakens your reason or dulls your desire for spiritual things or exalts the lordship of your soul and body over that of your spirit. That thing to you is sin.

You may believe that you are God's friend, but the Bible calls you His enemy. What makes you an enemy of God? Sin! And what is sin? It is missing the mark, God's glory.

Sin is what caused our Kinsman-Redeemer, our High Priest, to leave His eternal throne and invade earth through a lowly manger. Sin brought Jesus from heaven's majesty to a disgraceful, shameful death on a cross so that He could reconcile, revive, refresh, and restore the standard bearer to the Father's side.

But the first message you must hear and the initial call you must obey was first uttered by the Savior and has been echoed by His standard-bearers throughout history. "Repent!" Are you willing to repent?

LORD JESUS, I COME BEFORE YOU, REPENTING OF MY SIN AND RECEIVING YOUR FORGIVENESS AND GRACE. WHEN I RESIST THE CONVICTION OF YOUR SPIRIT, DRAW ME BY YOUR LOVE TO REPENT. AMEN.

THE SPIRIT OF LIFE

For the law of the Spirit of life in Christ Jesus hath made me free from the law of sin and death.

—ROMANS 8:2

John Lake was a missionary in Central Africa when an epidemic broke out. Thousands of people were dying. One of the doctors sent by the local government asked him what he used to inoculate himself with against the virus.

Lake directed the doctor to put a sample of the living virus under a microscope, and view the masses of living germs. He then took the sample in his hand for a moment and then returned it to the microscope. To the doctor's amazement the germs were dead.

"That is the law of the Spirit of life in Christ Jesus," he declared. "As long as I keep my soul in contact with the living God . . . no germ can attach itself to me. My spirit and body are so filled with the blessed presence of God, it even oozes from my pores."

The "law of the Spirit of life" is the regulating, activating power, and life of the Holy Spirit that has set us free from the power of sin, hell, and the grave.

FILL ME LORD WITH YOUR SPIRIT OF LIFE. EMPOWER ME TO OVERCOME THE POWER OF SIN, HELL, AND THE GRAVE IN YOUR MIGHTY NAME. AMEN.

ACTIVE FAITH

And all things, whatsoever ye shall ask in prayer, believing, ye shall receive.

—MATTHEW 21:22

The devil cannot hinder those who believe they receive when they pray.

A woman in our church was abandoned by her husband. She prayed for his return, and she believed she received when she prayed. There was no evidence to support her belief as one year turned into two and then three.

One day she said to me, "Pastor, my family thinks I am crazy, because I am still waiting. But I believed I received when I prayed, and there is nothing I can do now except thank God that I shall have it."

That faithful woman believed for twelve long years. One day she called and said, "My husband came to my house and said he had an experience with God. He asked if I could forgive him and let him back into the family."

How long are you willing to wait on God—a day, a week, a month, a year, a lifetime? Are you willing to wait for as long as it takes?

I had the joy of renewing their marriage vows, and they are still happily married today. Why? She believed she received when she prayed.

LORD, I WILL WAIT ON YOUR WILL, IN YOUR WAY, AND IN YOUR TIMING. I KNOW THAT BY TRUSTING IN YOU, I WILL RECEIVE YOUR BEST. AMEN.

FAITH COMES BY HEARING

So then faith cometh by hearing, and hearing by the word of God.

—ROMANS 10:17

Y ou have faith in what you can see, touch and understand. You did not stand in front of your chair and debate whether or not it would hold you before you sat down. Why? You trusted the chair. You had prior experience with the chair and knew the chair had always held you. Your knowledge surpassed your fear that the chair would fail. You had faith.

Faith in God comes through the study of His Word, learning who He is, how He behaves and that He is a rewarder of those who diligently seek Him. As the Holy Spirit leads you into truth, you learn that God loves you and is ready to do anything for you. That knowledge produces understanding, understanding produces trust, and trust produces the faith to believe for your miracle.

Seek Him in His Word. Learn about Him. Let the Holy Spirit show you the Father's heart. Faith is simply knowing God. Faith says, "I can trust Him to be who He says He is. I can trust Him to do what He says He will do."

Hearing goes beyond listening and understanding. The faith that comes by hearing is a hearing that obeys God. Do you have ears to hear and a heart to obey?

LORD, TUNE MY EARS TO HEAR ALL THAT YOU SAY. GIVE ME A NEW HEART TO OBEY ALL THAT I HEAR FROM YOU. AMEN.

YOUR SOURCE

And thou say in thine heart, My power and the might of mine hand hath gotten me this wealth.

— DEUTERONOMY 8:17

W hen things are going well, it could be easy to take credit for your prosperity. You may think it is your job or your college education that has given you the ability to get wealth. Your intelligence and cunning are not the source of your supply: God is.

During times of great need, you can't depend on anything of this world, including your job or your education. People who hold several degrees and have worked for corporations for decades have been fired from their jobs, thrown into the workforce, and are finding that their age and experience are not a help, but a hindrance.

The woman sick with an issue of blood spent her living—everything she had—on physicians, relying on their intelligence and education, but only grew worse (Matthew 9:20). We are warned not to forget God in our abundance, or we will eventually lose everything (v. 19).

Realize exactly how dependent you really are on God, for He alone is your true source.

JESUS, YOU ARE MY SOURCE AND MY SUPPLY. YOU ARE MY RESOURCE AND MY RESUPPLY. I NEED YOU OVER AND OVER AGAIN TO RENEW AND REVIVE MY LIFE. WITHOUT YOU MY LIFE LOSES ITS CHARGE AND VITALITY. AMEN.

TRUTH AND EVIL DON'T MIX

And this did she many days. But Paul, being grieved, turned and said to the spirit, I command thee in the name of Jesus Christ to come out of her. And he came out the same hour.

—ACTS 16:18

This slave girl performed sorcery and divination for the profit of her owners. When Paul and Silas arrived in Philippi she followed them around shouting, "These men are the servants of the most high God, which shew unto us the way of salvation" (Acts 16:17).

Second Corinthians 2:11 warns us not to be ignorant of Satan's methods. What she said was true, but her source was demonic. Although this seemed like good advertising, she was only trying to expose them so they would be arrested, beaten, or run out of town.

The devil is not to expose us; we are to expose him (Ephesians 5:11). If Paul had let her go on, people would link the gospel with the things of the devil. Expose Satan at every turn. Expose him in the horoscopes and in the psychics. Expose him in the ritual and the religious. Expose him in the lies and in the deceptions. Give no place to his work in your life.

Don't allow Satan any opportunity to wreak havoc in your life, but resist the devil and he will flee (James 4:7).

JESUS, EMPOWER ME TO TEST THE SPIRITS AND EXPOSE THE DEVIL WHEREVER HE REARS HIS UGLY HEAD. DEVIL, YOU ARE UNDER MY HEEL AND I BRUISE YOUR HEAD IN JESUS' NAME. AMEN.

WHERE IS YOUR FAITH?

Who his own self bare our sins in his own body on the tree, that we, being dead to sins, should live unto righteousness: by whose stripes ye were healed.

—I PETER 2:24

Everyone has faith. We all believe in something or someone. In order to believe there is no God, atheists must have faith far greater than that of Christians. Why? To believe that the complexities of life and the universe are all accidental takes blind faith. And that's what they are—blind to the realities of a wonderful, creator God.

Hebrews 11:6 tells us that without faith it is impossible to please God. Because of a lack of faith, Jesus left the town of Nazareth, unable to perform many miracles (Matthew 13:58). Their problem wasn't really a lack of faith, however—their faith was misplaced in things instead of placed in Him.

The world may promise great things, but Jesus provides the truth. Promises rest on the future; facts stand in the present. Healing is a past fact, not a future promise. It is not something to look forward to, but a truth in which we can walk.

LORD, I BELIEVE YOUR WORD. CREATE NEW LIFE IN ME TODAY. RESTORE AND HEAL ME THROUGH YOUR SHED BLOOD. AMEN.

HOT OR COLD?

I know thy works, that thou art neither cold nor hot: I would thou wert cold or hot. So then because thou art lukewarm, and neither cold nor hot, I will spue thee out of my mouth.

—REVELATION 3:15–16

My mother used to can food. She would put vegetables and fruits into jars and then place them in a pressure cooker. The extreme heat and pressure not only sealed the contents in the jars, but most importantly, destroyed all the disease-producing bacteria.

Do you know why God said He would rather you be hot or cold? Lukewarm is the only temperature in which germs can grow. Extreme heat or cold will kill them, but germs thrive in a lukewarm environment.

A lukewarm heart toward God will allow germs of sin (doubt and unbelief, pride and criticism, grumbling and complaining) to invade your mind, your ministry and destroy your destiny!

How passionate are you for Jesus? Does love for Him burn hot in your heart? Are you willing to following Him anywhere?

Set your sights on God and not the world. The world will cool your heart. Keep your eyes on God, and keep Holy Ghost fire in your heart!

JESUS, I PASSIONATELY LOVE YOU AS THE LOVER OF MY SOUL. I WILL NOT SETTLE FOR BEING LUKEWARM FOR YOU. I LOVE YOU WITH ALL MY HEART, MIND, SOUL, AND STRENGTH. AMEN.

LIVE IN THE SPIRIT

Now we have received, not the spirit of the world, but the spirit which is of God; that we might know the things that are freely given to us of God.

—I CORINTHIANS 2:12

Most Christians do not know much about the realm of the Spirit. It is as if they are separated from the Promised Land by the Jordan River. Once in a while, when no giants are around, they may rush across the water and take some fruit from the trees and then run back. This is a long way from dwelling in the land!

Perhaps they hear a rousing sermon by a strong evangelist. For a brief time their spirits are stirred up, and they reach out and take hold of their healing, their strength, their joy, their peace, or their deliverance. But when the stirring fades, they go back to walking in the natural.

We were not meant to rush in and out of the spiritual realm; we are meant to live there. Why wonder where our spiritual blessings are? They are dangling over our heads in the spiritual realm. We must enter in and take hold of what is ours.

We live and move and have our being in Christ Jesus. We never have to depart from His presence because His Spirit both indwells us and surrounds us when two or more gather in His Name (Matthew 18:20).

JESUS, INDWELL AND SURROUND ME. KEEP ME EVER CLOSE TO THEE. SHOW ME ALL OF THY WILL AND THY WAY—THIS DAY AND EVERY DAY. AMEN.

NO MAN

For an angel went down at a certain season into the pool, and troubled the water: whosoever then first after the troubling of the water stepped in was made whole of whatsoever disease he had. And a certain man was there, which had an infirmity thirty and eight years.

—JOHN 5:4–5

esus asked the man if he wanted to be made whole, and he answered, "Sir, I have no man." He was so caught up with thinking he needed someone to help him, he could not see that his miracle was standing right in front of him!

When you have no man to help you—nowhere to turn but God—you are a prime target for a miracle! No man can do for you what Jesus can do for you.

When you quit depending on your job, the preacher, your family, or the next healing line, you are positioned for your breakthrough. Family may let you down, the preacher may disappoint you, and your friends may forsake you, but Jesus is the friend who sticks closer than a brother. Rely on Him alone, and He will meet you at the very point of your deepest need.

Even your closest friends or family can let you down. But don't be discouraged. You can always trust in your best friend—Jesus.

JESUS, NO MAN CAN DO FOR ME WHAT YOU CAN DO. I KNOW THAT YOU ARE MY BEST FRIEND. I WILL TRUST YOU IN EVERYTHING BECAUSE YOU ARE MY BEST FRIEND. AMEN.

PUT YOUR PAST BEHIND YOU

Brethren, I count not myself to have apprehended: but this one thing I do, forgetting those things which are behind, and reaching forth unto those things which are before, I press toward the mark for the prize of the high calling of God in Christ Jesus.

—PHILIPPIANS 3:13–14

Many people need to be delivered from the skeletons of their past. "Those things which are behind" may include failed marriages, broken promises, failures, disappointments, setbacks, and betrayals.

You can be standing waist high in ocean water and watch as water begins to ebb quietly away from you . . . then the force of the wave begins to increase, propelling you forward.

Just as the tide pulls the water back, forming a wave of power, God draws you to Himself.

Don't fight against God's pulling and tugging at your spirit. Allow yourself to be drawn to Him and enveloped in His presence. Trust Him with your very life, and He will propel you forward into your destiny.

Put all of your past behind you. Bury it under His mercy and grace. Refuse to dig it up again or to listen to the old, tired accusations of the devil.

JESUS, GIVE ME THE STRENGTH TO LOOK FORWARD AND NOT LOOK BACK. KEEP ME FROM DREDGING UP MY PAST SIN WHICH YOU HAVE ALREADY FORGIVEN AND FORGOTTEN. KEEP MY HEART FIXED ON YOU. AMEN.

WEEK 35—THURSDAY
LORD, OPEN OUR EYES

And they talked together of all these things which had happened. And it came to pass. . . . Jesus himself drew near, and went with them. But their eyes were holden that they should not know him.

—LUKE 24:14–16

Two weary men headed for home, their hopes for liberation dashed on a bloody Cross. The man they believed was their Messiah had been murdered.

Although Jesus Himself joined them in the way, they did not recognize Him. They had heard Peter and the others testify that the tomb was empty, yet grief, fear, hopelessness, and tragedy blinded their eyes. They were focused on their circumstances rather than on their promise.

They had had expectations that were unfulfilled. But Jesus did not come to meet our expectations. He came to fulfill the will of the Father.

But as Jesus journeyed alongside these disheartened men, He revealed the triumph they could not see. Their eyes were opened, and they knew him (v. 31).

Don't let your expectations blind you to what the Father is doing. Are you confused over your circumstances and disappointed that God has not moved as you expected? Let the One who walks beside you open your eyes to His plan and His purpose.

JESUS, OPEN MY EYES TO SEE YOU AND MY EARS TO HEAR YOU. AS YOU WALK BESIDE ME IN THE WAY, REVEAL YOURSELF AND THE FATHER TO ME, I PRAY. AMEN.

GIANT KILLERS

David therefore departed thence, and escaped to the cave Adullam . . . And every one that was in distress, and every one that was in debt, and every one that was discontented, gathered themselves unto him;

—I SAMUEL 22:1-2

When David and his men went into the cave, they were discouraged, in debt, and defeated. In the natural they had plenty to be discouraged about, but they were in the cave with God's anointed King. They became intimately acquainted with David, and the anointing on David's life rubbed off on them. When David's men came out of the cave, they were mighty, valiant men of war! Spend intimate time with God and receive His anointing on your life.

In the presence of the anointing, you will grow stronger and more assured than ever before. Stay in the presence of the Anointed One—Jesus the Christ. Refuse to leave His presence. There you will come to know intimately the One who died for you.

You will come out stronger and surer than when you went into the cave with God. Your steps are ordered of the Lord, so expect signs and wonders to follow you. Proclaim boldly, "I have been with the Lord God Jehovah, and I am ready to reap the harvest He has prepared!"

LORD, BEFORE I KILL ANY GIANTS, LET ME SPEND TIME WITH YOU, THE KILLER OF GIANTS. I KNOW THAT YOU HAVE DEFEATED ALL THE GIANTS IN MY LIFE. DRAW ME CLOSE TO YOU SO THAT I MIGHT BE IMMERSED IN YOUR ANOINTING. AMEN.

A SOUND FROM HEAVEN

And suddenly there came a sound from heaven as of a rushing mighty wind, and it filled all the house where they were sitting.

—ACTS 2:2

Sound is the vibration of air molecules; the Greek word translated "sound" here is *echoes,* which means "to reverberate." Acts 2:6 says, when this was noised abroad, the multitude came together. The word noised" is *phoneo,* meaning "to publish" or "to proclaim."

Luke is telling us in these two verses that the multitude heard a voice echoing like a mighty rushing wind and the phenomenon was made public. On Pentecost, God spoke life to the church in much the same way He created heaven and earth. Ezekiel prophesied to the wind, and the army came alive (Ezekiel 37).

When God speaks to us, His Spirit reverberates in our human spirit. We can then speak the oracles of God and allow His message to reverberate in the hearts and spirits of others (1 Thessalonians 1:8).

What has the Spirit deposited in your heart that you are burning to speak? What message from the Lord are you passionate to share with others?

LORD, OPEN MY MOUTH AND BAPTIZE ME IN FIRE SO THAT I MAY SHARE YOUR WORD WITH ANYONE WHO WILL LISTEN. EMPOWER ME TO SPEAK YOUR MESSAGE. AMEN.

WILT THOU BE MADE WHOLE?

When Jesus saw him lie, and knew that he had been now a long time in that case, he saith unto him, Wilt thou be made whole?

—JOHN 5:6

Jesus asked the man beside the Pool of Bethesda if he wanted to be made whole. This may seem to be an odd question, but it really is not. Many appear to be seeking a miracle, but do not really want a miracle. They have grown comfortable with their condition, enjoying their self-pity and the attention they receive. Or they may be wishing for a miracle, but don't really expect one to come.

How long will you wait on the banks, while rivers of living water course past you? Say good-bye to sympathy and complacency. Cast aside the maybe, the perhaps, and the someday. Do not allow yourself to become an impotent Christian, lying by the water, too blind to see God, and with no power to overcome. What keeps you from reaching out to Jesus? Is it fear, shame, or laziness? Whatever it is, get over it! Go beyond yourself to the One who will make you whole—Jesus.

Take the initiative. Get to know Jesus. Get to know His Word. Stop waiting for a man to help you. Stretch out your hand, and allow Jesus to lift you up.

JESUS, I AM GETTING UP FROM WHERE I AM AND OVERCOMING EVERY OBSTACLE FOR THE SOLE PURPOSE OF BEING MADE WHOLE BY YOU. THANK YOU FOR OFFERING TO MAKE ME WHOLE. AMEN.

RAISE THE STANDARD

Thou has given a banner to them that fear thee, that it may be displayed because of truth.

—PSALM 60:4

I wo Jima was the site of one of the bloodiest battles of World War II. Many marines lost their lives while pulling the enemy forces out from the caves and tunnels where they were hiding.

A war is also raging on the fertile soil of our hearts, and too many lives have already been lost. We will never win our families—let alone a world—to Christ, until we raise the standard in our own lives.

God is calling God's people to the front lines to raise the standards of service, holiness, prayer, thanksgiving, praise, and worship far above the status quo of church as usual.

Determine to go into their dens of adversity, defeat, and strife and drag the enemy out of your life. Our children cannot live and your marriage cannot survive unless the devil is banished from your lives.

It is time for us to storm the beach, take the mountain and plant the banner of Jehovah-Nissi, our banner of completed victory!

JEHOVAH-NISSI, I RAISE YOUR BANNER AND STANDARD HIGH. I DECLARE YOUR VICTORY IN THE FACE OF EVERY SITUATION I FACE. EQUIP ME TO BE YOUR STANDARD-BEARER. AMEN.

NO QUESTION

But if thou canst do any thing, have compassion on us, and help us.

—MARK 9:22

I n this Scripture Jesus explained to the desperate father of a demon-possessed boy, "It's not a question of what I can do." God flung the stars into the heavens, put the oceans in their boundaries, sprinkled sand around the shores, and then sent the world spinning and commanded the oceans not to spill a drop. It was this blind man healer, this leper-cleansing man, this water-walking Jesus who said, "Light be" . . . and light was and has never ceased to be, because He never commanded it to stop. He is a supernatural, miracle-working God. He can do anything.

There is no mountain high enough to keep Him from getting to the other side. The devil can't come up with a problem in your life that God can't solve. It is never a question of what God can do, but only of what you believe He can do. Believe He can work miracles, He can make your feet like hind's feet, and that you too will leap and bound over every obstacle the enemy puts in your path! No question.

Are you facing an insurmountable mountain today? Have it move aside by faith in Jesus. Only you can limit what He does through you.

JESUS, MOVE MY MOUNTAINS, SHATTER MY BONDAGES, AND SET ME FREE FROM EVERY-THING THAT HINDERS MY WALK WITH YOU. AMEN.

TRUTHFUL HEARTS

Behold, thou desirest truth in the inward parts: and in the hidden part thou shalt make me to know wisdom.

—PSALM 51:6

God wants nothing less than complete honesty from us. The word in Hebrew for "truth" is *amet*. It means to be totally honest and transparent. Who we are on the outside is to be absolutely consistent with who we are inside. He who comes to God with the acknowledgment of his sin comes in truth—a sinner saved by grace. His grace requires nothing more than truth from the truly repentant.

A sincere heart is not a perfect heart, a holy heart, or even one dedicated to service—it is a heart willing to reveal itself just as it is and nothing more.

You need not be afraid of shocking God. There is nothing about you He does not already know. Even the hairs of your head are numbered.

Be honest with God. He who searches the hearts of men will never withhold His grace and mercy from you.

JESUS, I EMBRACE YOUR TRUTH AND YOUR WAYS. MAKE ME TOTALLY TRANSPARENT TO YOU. I DESIRE TO SERVE YOU ALONE. GUIDE AND DIRECT ME IN ALL TRUTH, I PRAY IN JESUS' NAME. AMEN.

TEACHER

Take my yoke upon you, and learn of me; for I am meek and lowly in heart: and ye shall find rest unto your souls.

—MATTHEW 11:29

Jesus' earthly ministry included preaching, healing, miracles, and teaching. You may have bowed your knee to call Him Savior, but do you know Him as "Teacher"?

The disciples sat under His instruction for three years before their spirits were truly teachable and ready to receive the baptism of the Holy Spirit.

A teachable spirit seeks the Spirit of the Lamb of God, meek and lowly in heart. Jesus' entire work in us is a divine teaching. The Holy Spirit who dwells in us—the very Spirit of Christ—shall teach us all things (John 16:13) if we submit our spirits to become meek and teachable.

Take up His yoke today and learn His meekness and lowliness of heart, because with that learning comes the teachable, pliable spirit that does nothing of its own will but says, "not my will, but thine be done."

HOLY SPIRIT, TEACH ME. GUIDE ME IN ALL TRUTH. REVEAL TO ME THE TRUTH—JESUS CHRIST. AMEN.

THE POWER OF PRAYER

Pray without ceasing.

—1 THESSALONIANS 5:17

Prayer is our communication link with God. Open, constant communication with Him keeps us within calling distance. When we neglect our prayer life, we experience a major breakdown in communication from headquarters. Then we can't receive orders from our Commander-in-Chief.

When that line of communication is down, our spirit man cannot receive direction from God. We become vulnerable to the enemy and are subsequently motivated by our flesh instead of our spirit. Our ears become deafened to the still, small voice of the Holy Spirit, and the whispered lies from the enemy begin to sound believable.

When you pray, you have access into the spirit realm where God is; and He will reveal to you the root cause of any battle you are facing.

Prayer in private equals power in public. Battles are won in your prayer closet on your face before God interceding in prayer, seeking His wisdom and receiving His direction.

TEACH ME, LORD, HOW TO PRAY WITHOUT CEASING IN BOTH MY PRIVATE AND PUBLIC MOMENTS. HELP ME TO KEEP MY MIND AND HEART CONTINUALLY COMMUNICATING WITH YOU. AMEN.

UNCONDITIONAL SURRENDER

But when he saw Jesus afar off, he ran and worshipped him.
—MARK 5:6

Jesus said, "All power is given unto me in heaven and in earth" (Matthew 28:18). When Jesus arrived in the country of the Gadarenes, immediately he was confronted by a man who was possessed by so many demons that he gave his name as Legion.

These demons were not only many, but powerful. No man could bind him with chains. "Because that he had been often bound with fetters and chains, and the chains had been plucked asunder by him, and the fetters broken in pieces: neither could any man tame him" (Mark 5:4).

Yet when the demoniac saw Jesus coming from a distance, he flung himself at Jesus' feet. Absolute, unconditional surrender!

Any time you think about the devil, immediately add the word "defeated." Is the devil attacking you? No, the defeated devil is attacking you. Call on the One who holds all power in heaven and in earth, and drive the defeated devil out of your life.

Jesus demands no less from you than absolute surrender. Are you ready to surrender all to Jesus?

LORD, I SURRENDER ALL TO YOU. I KNOW THAT NOTHING CAN SAVE, DELIVER, OR BREAK MY BONDAGE EXCEPT YOU. I YIELD TOTALLY TO YOUR WILL. AMEN.

HE PRAYS FOR YOU

Who is he that condemneth? It is Christ that died, yea rather, that is risen again, who is even at the right hand of God, who also maketh intercession for us.

—ROMANS 8:34

Jesus announced to Peter: "Satan hath desired to have you, that he may sift you as wheat" (Luke 22:31), and then added these words of comfort: "but I have prayed for thee, that thy faith fail not" (v. 32).

Not after Satan had done his worst but before Satan ever laid a hand on Peter, Jesus said, "I have prayed for you." He did not tell Peter he should start praying for himself. When you are a blood-bought child of God and you're headed for the last inning with all the bases loaded, before Satan can hurl the ball to take you out, Jesus calls the play and declares you are, "Safe!"

What prayer of the Son has the Father not heard? There is no such prayer. Wherever you are and whatever situation you are in, Jesus Christ is praying for you. And if Jesus is praying for you, you cannot fail.

INTERCEDE FOR ME, LORD JESUS. TAKE MY EVERY NEED TO THE FATHER. SEARCH AND KNOW ME. EXPOSE MY SIN AND BRING ME TO REPENTANCE. USE MY WEAKNESSES FOR YOUR GLORY. AMEN.

HE HAS GONE BEFORE YOU

Yea, though I walk through the valley of the shadow of death, I will fear no evil: for thou art with me; thy rod and thy staff they comfort me.

—PSALM 23:4

Are you walking through a valley? As you walk, Jesus is walking alongside you, ready to pick you up if you should stumble. He is holding your hand and talking with the Father about your situation.

He is constantly presenting you to the Father. This is His only purpose in heaven. He calls your name before the throne, and He points to the mercy seat covered by His precious blood.

Today is no surprise to God. Tomorrow's headlines will not surprise Him either! He knows tomorrow better than you know yesterday. He has gone before you and prepared the way. You never walk alone. He is Jehovah-Jireh, the God who provides your need before you have a need.

If He is leading and you are following, you have nothing to fear. In fact, tomorrow in Christ is filled with possibilities, hope, and new beginnings.

THANK YOU, JESUS, FOR GOING AHEAD OF ME AND SECURING MY TOMORROWS. SO TODAY, I WILL REST IN YOU—SETTING ASIDE EVERY FEAR, ANXIETY, AND WORRY. AMEN.

VICTORY WALK

I sought the Lord, and he heard me, and delivered me from all my fears.

—PSALM 34:4

Maybe fear is telling you that you cannot handle another thing. Maybe you feel as if you have gone down for the last time.

The fact that you have a problem is proof God has provided the answer. He will slip His everlasting arms underneath you! You need not fear; you are going to make it.

The key to receiving God's answer is found in Psalm 34:4—seek the Lord! You do not need a healing—you need Him. You do not need deliverance—you need Him. You do not need joy or victory—you need Him.

Since He has provided the answer to every prayer you will ever pray, you can walk in total victory! As God becomes your passion, everything else will fall into place.

Everything is in the Lord. Every victory, need, longing, desire, plan, possibility, and dream is in Him. Don't despair. He is your all in all.

CHRIST, IN YOU ALL THINGS HOLD TOGETHER. I DON'T NEED ANYTHING BUT YOU. IN YOU I FIND MY RESTING PLACE AND MY CONTENTMENT. AMEN.

GROW IN GOD

My little children, of whom I travail in birth again until Christ be formed in you.

—GALATIANS 4:19

Most Christians do not progress beyond their first experience with God: salvation. They are justified but not sanctified. They are baptized by water but not by His Spirit.

If God intended our relationship with Him to stop at salvation, then we'd get saved and He would immediately take us to heaven. God's intent was for us to get saved, to be conformed to the image of His Beloved Son, and to become mature Christians walking in the Spirit.

Paul said that he travailed in the Spirit until Christ be truly formed in the believers he led to the Lord. Have you had your desire for the things of God renewed lately?

Search yourself and ask some hard questions: Is my relationship with God the same as it was when I first got saved? Do I know Him better? Am I walking closer to Him? Have I received fresh revelation from His Word?

Set your sights higher in God. Don't allow yourself to become satisfied with where you are. Launch out into the deep. Be sanctified, set apart, and made holy by the Spirit of God. Go deeper than you ever imagined yourself going with God.

JESUS, I WANT TO GROW DEEPER IN MY RELA-TIONSHIP WITH YOU. SHOW ME WHAT I NEED TO RELEASE IN ORDER TO GROW CLOSER TO YOU. BAPTIZE ME WITH YOUR SPIRIT AND FIRE. AMEN.

OUR CONFIDENCE

And this is the confidence that we have in him, that, if we ask any thing according to his will, he heareth us.

—1 JOHN 5:14

I do not know who this God is who does not answer prayer. I cannot find Him in my Bible! The Bible describes a God who says, "Ask and it shall be given you; seek and ye shall find; knock, and it shall be opened unto you" (Luke 11:9).

You have an adversary, and the answer to your prayers may have to withstand a battle before it breaks through. Daniel prayed for twenty-one days before an angel appeared to deliver his answer. When the angel arrived, he informed Daniel of the battle he encountered with the adversary along the way—but he prevailed because of Daniel's constant, confident prayer (Daniel 10:12–13).

Too often we stop praying just as our answer is ready to be delivered. Remember, your darkest hour and greatest opposition will come at the point of your breakthrough. Persevere in prayer. Be confident that God hears, and He will answer.

Remember that prayer is a dialogue, not a monologue of you talking at God. Spend as much time listening as talking. Take time to hear His answer. Be still and know what God is speaking into Your life by His Spirit.

JESUS, HELP ME TO LISTEN TO YOUR VOICE. PREPARE MY HEART TO RECEIVE AND ACT UPON YOUR ANSWERS TO MY PRAYERS. AMEN.

THE KINGDOM OF HEAVEN

Thy kingdom come. Thy will be done in earth, as it is in heaven.

—MATTHEW 6:10

J esus came to bring the kingdom of heaven to earth; to establish godly, heavenly authority in the hearts and lives of all mankind.

God said, "I will put my laws into their mind, and write them in their hearts: and I will be to them a God, and they shall be to me a people: And they shall not teach every man his neighbour, and every man his brother, saying, Know the Lord: for all shall know me, from the least to the greatest" (Hebrews 8:10–11).

We do not live in a kingdom cut off from the King, nor do we live bound by impersonal laws that control every aspect of our lives. In the kingdom of heaven, Jesus Christ dwells inside every Spirit-filled believer, teaching us and guiding us every step of the way. As our indwelling constant companion and counselor, the Holy Spirit reveals to us the heart of the Savior.

Jesus came to bring heaven to earth, to bestow the gift of sonship and bring you into relationship with your heavenly Father. The kingdom dwells within you. Celebrate the reign of the King of kings in your life.

> JESUS, I REJOICE OVER YOUR REIGN IN MY LIFE. MAKE EVERY DECISION. GUIDE ME EVERY STEP OF THE WAY. KEEP ME IN YOUR PATH. AMEN.

CHANGE YOUR MIND

And be not conformed to this world: but be ye transformed by the renewing of your mind, that ye may prove what is that good, and acceptable, and perfect will of God.

—ROMANS 12:2

What must happen for the kingdom of heaven to come? Renew your mind according to the Word of God.

Christians sometimes sing, "When we all get to heaven, what a day of rejoicing that will be!" Why wait? You are in the kingdom of heaven right now! Rejoice! When you change your mind, you also change your attitudes and your actions. Your responses change. When life gets tough, start rejoicing instead of rebelling. When difficulties arise, start praising instead of protesting.

You are a child of the King. Begin to think like a King's kid. Instead of praying for the rapture when trouble comes, transform woeful thoughts into words of faith: "Things may look bad, but I am in the center of God's perfect will for my life. I am a citizen of heaven, seated in heavenly places together with Christ Jesus. The kingdom has come because the King has come!

> JESUS, RENEW MY MIND. CHANGE MY ATTITUDES AND MY ACTIONS. RENEW AND CONFORM ME TO YOUR IMAGE THAT MY EVERY WORD AND ACTIONS WILL PROCEED FROM YOU. AMEN.

WE SERVE A HEALING GOD

If thou wilt diligently hearken to the voice of the LORD thy God . . . I will put none of these diseases upon thee . . . for I am the LORD that healeth thee.

—EXODUS 15:26

God promised divine health to those who not only hear His commands but are faithful to obey them. Our heavenly Father's redeeming provision for us is as vast as the consequences of the fall: He provides forgiveness for sin, eternal life for death, and healing for sickness. What an awesome God we serve!

Jesus revealed God's will in action as He went to the cities and villages around Galilee "healing every sickness and every disease" (Matthew 9:35), and His atoning death on the Cross sealed the matter: we have been redeemed, spirit, soul, and body.

Once you have a revelation of Jehovah-Rophe—the Lord who heals all our diseases—no infirmity, sickness nor disease will ever have power over you again. God's will for you is health. God's provision for your healing is the blood of Jesus Christ—by His stripes you are healed.

HEAL ME, JESUS. HEAL MY HURTS AND BROKEN-NESS. HEAL MY DISEASES. HEAL MY EMOTIONS. HEAL MY BODY. O GREAT PHYSICIAN, YOU ARE THE HEALING BALM OF MY LIFE. AMEN.

WHOM WILL YOU BELIEVE?

And what shall I more say? for the time would fail me to tell of Gideon, and of Barak, and of Samson, and of Jephthae, of David also . . . Who through faith subdued kingdoms, wrought righteousness, obtained promises, stopped the mouths of lions. . . .

—HEBREWS 11:32–33

S ometimes when we are confronted by the cares of the world, we find ourselves believing in a God who is different from the God of the Bible. Not believing God is who He says He is probably accounts for most of the uncertainty and defeat in our lives.

Believe in Him! The God of the Bible always hears and answers your prayers. The God of the Bible does not cower in the presence of the devil and will never leave you nor forsake you. The God of the Bible cannot fail.

He is the God of battles, the Lord of Hosts, and the God of victory. He will never surrender in the face of adversity because the war is over and He has emerged victorious! Just believe in Him and the battle is already won!

Never consider defeat when He is in the plan and the battle. Never allow doubt to distort His Word or truth. Above the roar of the battle, only one voice rings out the truth—the voice of God. Listen to His still, small voice whispering His truth in your heart.

GOD, HOW I LISTEN INTENTLY FOR YOUR VOICE IN YOUR WORD, IN WORSHIP, IN THE STILLNESS, IN THE SPIRIT, AND IN THE PROPHETIC MOMENTS. SPEAK TO ME AND I WILL BOTH LISTEN AND BELIEVE. AMEN.

SEALED

In whom ye also trusted, after that ye heard the word of truth, the gospel of your salvation: in whom also after that ye believed, ye were sealed with that holy Spirit of promise, which is the earnest of our inheritance until the redemption of the purchased possession, unto the praise of his glory.

—EPHESIANS 1:13-14

When Mom took the canning jars from the pressure cooker, she lined them up on the kitchen table. My job was to watch and listen for them to pop as they cooled. If the jars didn't pop they were not sealed, and this meant germs on the outside could get inside and spoil the contents. Mom would have to pour the contents out and repeat the process.

The devil cannot contaminate our lives when we stay sealed by the Holy Spirit. Seek God daily to reveal areas in your life that are exposed to the influences of the world. Bring those areas under the Lordship of Jesus Christ.

Let the Holy Spirit seal you against evil and teach you to "walk worthy of the vocation wherewith ye are called" (Ephesians 4:1). Be careful to guard your heart so that nothing is permitted to break the seal on your life. Keep yourself free from garbage and contaminates that will pollute the holiness of your life.

HOLY SPIRIT, KEEP ME PURE AND HOLY. HELP ME TO ABSTAIN FROM ALL IMMORALITY. SEAL ME WITH YOUR PURITY. AMEN.

NOT FOR SALE

And Jacob said, Swear to me this day; and he sware unto him: and he sold his birthright unto Jacob. Then Jacob gave Esau bread and pottage of lentils; and he did eat and drink, and rose up, and went his way: thus Esau despised his birthright.

—GENESIS 25:33–34

As Isaac's firstborn son, Esau was entitled to the birthright and inheritance—but we do not speak of "Abraham, Isaac, and Esau." Esau sold his birthright for one meal. When Jacob offered food and asked for his birthright, Esau could have said, "No! It is not for sale," but he did not. He sold out the eternal for a moment's temporal satisfaction.

You were bought with a price—the precious blood of Christ. Nothing in you or that you have is for sale. You and everything about you belongs to Jesus.

The devil will offer you momentary satisfaction as he reaches for your birthright. He will tell you it is all right to keep your tithe, all right to keep your offering and satisfy the lusts of the flesh and of this world. He will tempt you to sell your time for momentary pleasure. He'll encourage you to barter away your godly inheritance.

Resist the devil's counsel. He promises the rainbow—but only delivers the rain.

> **JESUS, I BELONG TOTALLY TO YOU. I THANK YOU FOR THE AWESOME PRICE IN YOUR SHED BLOOD THAT YOU PAID FOR ME ON CALVARY. AMEN.**

NO VACANCY

Finally, brethren, whatsoever things are true, whatsoever things are honest, whatsoever things are just, whatsoever things are pure, whatsoever things are lovely, whatsoever things are of good report; if there be any virtue, and if there be any praise, think on these things.

—PHILIPPIANS 4:8

You can probably look back right now and see a time where you opened the door in your mind and let the devil in—where you did not submit to God, where you did not resist the devil; therefore, he did not flee.

When you are rejoicing, the devil cannot get in your mind. When you are shouting, he cannot get in your body. When you are praising God and thanking Him for His goodness and mercy, the devil has no access to your life.

Build up your spirit by praying in the Holy Ghost. Renew your mind with the Word of God, and fill your mouth with His praises. Hang out a "NO VACANCY" sign for the devil, and when he tries to enter in, slam the door by lifting up your voice in praise and thanksgiving.

Strive after Jesus Christ's excellence and perfection. If you are tempted to think thoughts beneath what is true, just, pure, lovely, and virtuous, then stop thinking and start meditating on His Word. Replace every worldly thought with His Word.

JESUS, FILL MY MIND WITH THOUGHTS THAT ARE TRUE, HONEST, JUST, PURE, LOVELY, EXCELLENT, AND VIRTUOUS. AMEN.

THE WAGONS ARE COMING

And they told him all the words of Joseph, which he had said unto them: and when he saw the wagons which Joseph had sent to carry him, the spirit of Jacob their father revived.

—GENESIS 45:27

Jacob's love for Joseph aroused his ten older sons to jealousy, prompting them to sell Joseph into slavery and then to cover their deed with a lie. In the years that followed, Joseph rose from slavery to power in Egypt, while famine fell upon his family (Genesis 41:56–57).

As his sons journeyed to buy food in Egypt, Jacob looked around and saw his expectations for his sons and his land reduced to dry dust. But Jacob had God's Word. Day after day he reminded himself, "In blessing, I will bless thee and in multiplying, I will multiply thee" (Genesis 22:17).

One day he heard a sound—the wagons were coming! But they weren't creaking and rattling like when they left. No! They were heavy and full of provision and promise! Hold on, don't despair! The wagons are coming, overflowing with the goodness of God.

God's provision is worth waiting for. Don't settle for good. Wait for His best. His provisions last while worldly stuff rusts and corrodes. Don't settle for rusty iron when He has silver and gold for you.

LORD, I DESIRE YOUR BEST. NOTHING ELSE WILL DO. SO I WILL WAIT FOR YOUR TREASURES AND WILL STOP TRYING TO MAKE THINGS HAPPEN MY WAY. AMEN.

NEVER REGAINED

For ye know how that afterward, when he [Esau] would have inherited the blessing, he was rejected: for he found no place of repentance, though he sought it carefully with tears.

—HEBREWS 12:17

Y ou may lose some things through disobedience that you can never regain. The loss of the birthright did not mean that Isaac rejected his son, nor did God reject him. The loss of the birthright meant that Esau's golden opportunity for God's provision was lost forever. He could not regain what he lost in that moment (Genesis 25:33–34).

Determine today that your inheritance is not for sale. No price is dear enough to pay for your salvation by the blood. Decide today that divine healing and the baptism in the Holy Ghost cannot be bought from you. Stand fast in your faith and refuse to listen to the subtle sales pitch of your adversary.

Refuse to believe the lies of the world. Nothing it offers you can begin to compare with the treasure laid up for you in eternity. Reject compromising the truth and selling part of your integrity for temporal gain. Stockpile your treasures in heaven, not on earth.

JESUS, YOU ARE MY TREASURE. I REFUSE TO COMPROMISE. I REJECT THE TEMPTATION OF A MOMENT OF WORLDLY PLEASURE. KEEP ME PURE THROUGH THE POWER OF YOUR HOLY SPIRIT. AMEN.

BLOOD COVENANT

But he is a Jew, which is one inwardly; and circumcision is that of the heart, in the spirit, and not in the letter, whose praise is not of men, but of God.

—ROMANS 2:29

Y ou are in covenant with God not because of a blood line, but because your heart has been circumcised by the Holy Spirit who pours the love of God into your heart (Romans 5:5). You were born in sin but there is life after birth. You can be born again in Christ (John 3:3).

The message woven throughout the Bible is that God made a covenant of love with mankind; everyone who chooses can become part of this covenant through Jesus Christ.

The desire of God's heart is to be God to us and for us to love Him with all our hearts. Everything God has ever said to His people, and every covenant He has ever made, builds on the fulfillment of that one desire.

If you are not seeking Him today with a pure heart, cleanse your heart of all deceit, all bitterness, and all envy. Allow the Holy Spirit to fill you with the love of God. The purpose of all your worship and devotion is to love Him with all your heart (Matthew 22:37). This is the covenant of love—the strongest of all covenants.

LOVER OF MY SOUL, HOW I LOVE YOU, JESUS.
BE THOU MY BRIDEGROOM. MY PASSIONATE
LOVE IS GIVEN TO YOU ALONE. AMEN.

PET SKUNKS

No man can serve two masters: for either he will hate the one, and love the other; or else he will hold to the one, and despise the other. Ye cannot serve God and mammon.

—MATTHEW 6:24

What sin are you tolerating in yourself that you would never tolerate in someone else? What is that pet sin you hold so close? Your "pet" is nothing more than a skunk . . . and a stench in the nostrils of God.

That pet sin of yours tells God that you have only given Jesus a vote of approval in your mind, that you have never chosen to make Him Lord of your life. The only thing God looks for in us is our desire to conform our will to His.

When we lose a pet that has been with us for years, there is a void in our lives. We grew accustomed to having it with us wherever we went.

Do not become comfortable with sin. Refuse to give place to what is unholy and despicable to God in your life. Search your heart today. Make a decision to let go of that pet resentment or habit, and let God replace the void with the presence of His Holy Spirit.

ALMIGHTY GOD, REMOVE EVERY STENCH IN MY LIFE. I REPENT OF ALL MY PET SINS AND ASK FOR YOUR FORGIVENESS AND CLEANSING IN JESUS' NAME, AMEN.

GO TO THE KING

And he hath on his vesture and on his thigh a name written, KING OF KINGS, AND LORD OF LORDS.

—REVELATION 19:16

Have you ever heard the nursery rhyme about Humpty Dumpty? "Humpty Dumpty sat on a wall. Humpty Dumpty had a great fall. All the king's horses and all the king's men couldn't put Humpty together again."

I always want to stop in the middle of that rhyme and shout, "Wait! Why are you wasting time with the king's horses and the king's men? Why don't you just go to the King?" Many Christians waste time today taking their problems to everybody except the One who has the power to fix them.

Is something broken in your life? Have all your friends and therapists, doctors and counselors, failed at putting you back together again. Don't give up. Don't end up like poor Humpty Dumpty. Bypass the middlemen and head straight for the King! Don't go to your co-workers about your boss—go to Jesus. He is King of kings, and Lord of lords! Why don't you just have a little talk with Jesus today? Turn every situation over to Him, and allow Him to begin to move in your life and put things together again.

> HOLY SPIRIT, YOU ARE MY COUNSELOR AND GUIDE, MY TEACHER AND COMFORTER. GUIDE ME IN ALL TRUTH. DISCERN AND HEAL MY BROKENNESS IN JESUS' NAME. AMEN.

A COMPASSIONATE HEART

And Jesus went forth, and saw a great multitude, and was moved with compassion toward them, and he healed their sick.

—MATTHEW 14:14

Here, as throughout the Gospels, Jesus unveiled the compassionate heart of God to the people. In both the Old and New Testaments, the words "mercy" and "compassion" are derived from the same word and carry the same meaning: bestowing sympathy and selfless tenderness.

Psalm 145:8 says, "The Lord is gracious, and full of compassion; slow to anger, and of great mercy." Our Father is a God of boundless love.

It is not our faith in God's power that brings about His wonder-working presence, but faith in His love and in His will for us: to pour out His blessing upon us. Micah 7:18 says that He is constantly searching for those He can bless. He is not only willing but eager to pour out His blessings on those who call Him Lord.

The Lord is eagerly seeking you out today. Are you eagerly seeking Him out? Are you passionately in love with the Savior today? Seek Him out today as eagerly as He is seeking you.

JESUS, I EAGERLY SEEK YOU TODAY. THIS DAY WILL NOT BE FULL WITHOUT YOUR SPIRIT FILLING EVERY MOMENT WITH YOUR GRACE AND POWER. HOW I LOVE YOU, LORD. AMEN.

SPIRITUALLY ALIVE

For as in Adam all die, even so in Christ shall be made alive.

—1 CORINTHIANS 15:22

The spirit realm is a world greater and more awesome than this world could ever be. We who are spiritually alive can cross into that realm and hear the voice of God. We can live without fear, for we have eternal life by the blood of the Lamb.

The spiritually dead cannot see what we see or hear what we hear. I have seen them wandering the earth by the thousands: milling in and out of theaters and shopping malls, driving on the freeways, mowing their lawns, and dragging themselves through life. Like weary prisoners who march until they drop, the spiritually dead walk without hope, defeated prisoners of a lie. They believe the lie that they will live and die, and nothing lies beyond.

One day the trumpet will sound, but they will go on with their weary lives . . . typing, welding, baking, and driving as though nothing had happened. Those who are spiritually alive will hear the sound no one else hears and skyrocket into the presence of God (1 Thessalonians 4:16–17).

JESUS, I LONG TO LIVE DAILY IN YOUR SPIRITUAL REALM. HELP ME TO LIVE WITHOUT FEAR AND TO OBEY YOUR VOICE EACH AND EVERY DAY. AMEN.

CALL ON HIM

Call unto me and I will answer thee, and shew thee great and mighty things, which thou knowest not.

—JEREMIAH 33:3

A prominent theologian stated, "Prayer is doomed," and "I don't see that the church of the twentieth century will have any more need of prayer than it does any other form of magic."

Well, I disagree. The Bible says God hears our prayers, and He will answer them.

I used to just pray for a wife, until I saw some of the candidates that were showing up. When I learned to pray specifically, God brought Joni into my life. Follow these keys to prayer:

- Decide what you want.
- Know the will of God.
- Verbalize your request.
- Bind doubt and unbelief.

After you have prayed, here is the major key: Give thanks. Rejoice that God has heard and answered your prayer. Because we know He hears us, we have confidence that He has granted our requests.

I THANK YOU, FATHER, FOR REVEALING YOUR WILL TO ME. I DESIRE TO KNOW AND TRUST YOU WITH ALL MY HEART. I GIVE YOU PRAISE FOR ANSWERING MY PRAYER EVEN BEFORE I ASK. AMEN.

GIVE THANKS ALWAYS

Speaking to yourselves in psalms and hymns and spiritual songs, singing and making melody in your heart to the Lord; Giving thanks always for all things unto God and the Father in the name of our Lord Jesus Christ.

—EPHESIANS 5:19–20

Prepare your heart to praise the Lord. Prepare to give thanks for all the blessings He has bestowed upon you. Praise Him when you rise in the morning. Praise Him as you go to work and as you return home. Praise Him in the evening for another day finished. Praise Him before you go to sleep for a restful night and a new sunrise when you awaken.

The more you praise Him and give thanks, the more the devil flees from your presence. Praise and prayers of thanks to the Lord are your greatest defenses against the wiles of the devil.

"What shall I render unto the LORD, for all his benefits toward me?" (Psalm 116:12). Give God thanks today for His boundless grace and mercy in your life. Praise Him today with your whole being. Praise Him!

JESUS, I GIVE YOU ALL MY PRAISE TODAY. I PRAISE YOU FOR ALL THAT YOU HAVE DONE IN MY LIFE. I PRAISE YOU FOR ALL THAT YOU ARE DOING IN MY LIFE. I PRAISE YOU FOR ALL THAT YOU WILL DO IN MY LIFE. AMEN.

THE LORD OF GLORY

So shall they fear the name of the LORD from the west, and his glory from the rising of the sun. When the enemy shall come in like a flood, the Spirit of the LORD shall lift up a standard against him.

—ISAIAH 59:19

To fear the Lord is to reverence Him, to recognize Him for who He is. Even devils know there is a God—and they shudder (James 2:19). When the presence of God overshadows you, there is nothing the enemy can do to harm you. God rises up and causes the enemy to scatter.

God's presence covers and protects us on every side. He goes before us into every battle and He is our rear guard. He is ever-watchful.

Behold the battle-scarred Lord of glory. He stands before you, a shepherd's rod in His right hand—stained with the blood of your defeated enemy. Now look down and see the roaring adversary, laying mortally wounded at His feet.

This is the victorious Lord who says, "Fear thou not; for I am with thee" (Isaiah 41:10). His strength is in you; His anointing is upon you. Nothing is impossible when you believe in Him.

JESUS, YOU ARE THE LORD OF GLORY. YOU ARE THE GOOD SHEPHERD. I PRAISE YOU FOR DEFEATING THE ENEMY. AMEN.

MY HELPER

*So that we may boldly say, The Lord is my helper, and I will
not fear what man shall do unto me.*

—HEBREWS 13:6

A s Paul wrote to the Hebrews, "Let brotherly love
continue. Be not forgetful to entertain strangers:
for thereby some have entertained angels unawares"
(Hebrews 13:1–2).

We should always be ready to do the Lord's work
without fear of what man will say or do. The prophets of
old suffered more persecution and torture than we can
ever imagine today; yet the spirit of fear still holds us
back from speaking out for the Lord.

The anointing of God is sent to meet needs. If you
never step out in love, you will never experience the help
of His anointing. But for His grace, we could be the ones
in need. Since God has blessed us with His help, we
should be bold in service for Him. We should help those
we can help and pray for those we can't.

Step out boldly for Christ, so that in the day of judgment He may step out boldly for you.

JESUS, EMPOWER ME TO STEP OUT IN FAITH
TODAY. I AM WILLING TO TAKE RISKS IN ORDER
TO SERVE YOU. THANK YOU LORD FOR REMOV-
ING FEAR AND UNBELIEF FROM MY LIFE.
AMEN.

DO NOT EXCUSE YOUR SIN

But every man is tempted, when he is drawn away of his own lust, and enticed. Then when lust hath conceived, it bringeth forth sin: and sin, when it is finished, bringeth forth death.

—JAMES 1:14–15

Jesus says, "I am the way" (John 14:6). We cannot bypass sin and expect to get through to God. Jesus is the only throughway to repentance, the only access road. In our ignorance and wickedness we try to bypass the reality of our sin.

Don't try to excuse your sin. Sin is always a deliberate act of your will. You decide to sin. Notice the path that leads you into sin and the end result.

The tool of sin is lust. Your own lusts, desires, wants, and cravings grasp for what you should not have or do not need.

The device of sin is enticement. Sin uses your lust to draw you away from God and toward the world. Like a fish lured by bait or an animal enticed by a trap, you find yourself drawn away from the safety of a loving Father and into the arms of the devourer.

The effect of sin is death. Lust conceived, bears sin. Sin gradually and seductively steals from you until you are robbed of life itself.

The only way out of sin is Jesus. Are you turning away from sin and toward the way, truth, and life—Jesus?

JESUS, BREAK THE POWER OF SIN IN MY LIFE THROUGH YOUR PRECIOUS BLOOD. GIVE ME DISCERNMENT THAT I MAY AVOID EVERY TRAP OF SIN TODAY. AMEN.

HE IS GREATER

And one of the multitude answered and said, Master, I have brought unto thee my son, which hath a dumb spirit . . . And ofttimes it hath cast him into the fire, and into the waters, to destroy him: but if thou canst do any thing, have compassion on us, and help us.

—MARK 9:17,22

You may be facing failure, or perhaps you just received a bad report from the doctor. You may desperately need Jesus, but a faithless disciple may have destroyed your faith. One of the greatest obstacles to seeing lost souls won to the kingdom is the failure in the lives of professing Christians to live for Christ. They say one thing on Sunday—but on Monday, it's business as usual.

Jesus responded by telling the one who came to him the problem was not with what He could do, but in what the man could believe. Jesus said, "Don't let the failures of my disciples destroy your faith in me. Look beyond their failures, Satan's antics and your own disappointment."

With God . . . all things are possible. God is greater than demons, death, and disappointments. God can do anything!

JESUS, I WILL STOP TRUSTING IN MY OWN STRENGTH AND I WILL TRUST IN YOURS. I CONFESS THAT YOU ARE GREATER THAN ANY OBSTACLE I FACE. AMEN.

EVER-ABIDING PRESENCE

And I will pray the Father, and he shall give you another Comforter, that he may abide with you for ever; Even the Spirit of truth; whom the world cannot receive, because it seeth him not, neither knoweth him: but ye know him; for he dwelleth with you, and shall be in you.

—JOHN 14:16–17

During Jesus' ministry on the earth, He was constantly teaching and training His disciples. He even imparted His power and anointing to them. But very little change took place in their lives, because His influence and His power were still external.

But when Jesus returned to heaven, there was a tag team handoff! The Father sent the third person of the Trinity—the Holy Spirit—to fill them with His ever-abiding presence.

The Holy Spirit came down as a "mighty rushing wind" to invade the innermost recesses of the disciples' lives and to fulfill Jesus' promise to them (Acts 2:4).

Acknowledge God's ever-abiding presence. Allow His internal presence to transform you and empower you to be a bold witness for Christ!

JESUS, TRANSFORM AND EMPOWER ME TO BE A BOLD WITNESS FOR YOU. HELP ME OVERCOME ANY RELUCTANCE OR FEAR I HAVE OF WHAT MEN MAY THINK OF ME. AMEN.

PENTECOSTAL POWER

And they were all filled with the Holy Ghost, and began to speak with other tongues as the spirit gave them utterance.

—ACTS 2:4

The rushing wind that blew into the room that day was the unexpected fulfillment of expected promise and prophecy. Isaiah and Joel had both foretold the coming of this day (Isaiah 28:11; Joel 2:28–29). Jesus had told them to watch for it.

Though he had denied Christ only days before, a downcast Peter waited with the others. When the wind came, Peter changed. He became steadfast and bold in Christ. He spoke with tongues of fire in languages he didn't even know! He became a man whose shadow would heal the sick. In spite of his shortcomings, Peter had been filled with the Holy Ghost!

It is the commandment of God-and the privilege of God's people—to be filled with His Spirit in spite of our shortcomings. When we are immersed in Him, we are given supernatural power, grace, and ability. The church needs Pentecostal power for these last days. Invite Him to fill you and transform you today.

> JESUS, BAPTIZE ME WITH YOUR SPIRIT. EMPOWER ME TO LIVE IN YOUR SUPERNATURAL POWER AND GRACE. AMEN.

OUR SHEPHERD

Thou preparest a table before me in the presence of mine enemies: thou anointest my head with oil; my cup runneth over.

—PSALM 23:5

Psalm 23 is often called "The Shepherd's Psalm," because it describes the loving care the Lord provides for His flock. David said in the first verse, "The Lord is my Shepherd, I shall not want," because you will never experience a need our heavenly Father will not supply.

David went on to say, "Thou anointest my head with oil" (v. 5). He was alluding to the way shepherds poured oil on the heads of their sheep before they were sent out to graze. The oil soaked into their wool; and if they happened to cut their heads on stones while grazing, the healing oil was already there to soothe and cleanse the wound.

God is not only the loving Jehovah-Rohi, (the Lord our Shepherd), He is also Jehovah-Jireh, the God of more than enough who provides for your every need before your need arises.

Imagine all of your enemies watching as God blesses and provides for you. They will witness the goodness and faithfulness of God poured out upon your life. Don't worry about getting back or getting even with your enemies. It is enough that the Shepherd prepares a table for you in the presence of His enemies.

THANK YOU, FATHER, FOR THE TABLE THAT YOU ARE PREPARING BEFORE MY ENEMIES. I EXALT YOUR NAME FOR ALL TO HEAR. AMEN.

HIS STRENGTH

And the Lord looked upon him [Gideon], and said, Go in this thy might, and thou shalt save Israel from the hand of the Midianites: have not I sent thee?

—JUDGES 6:14

The angel of the Lord told Gideon, "The Lord is with thee." God told Gideon he didn't have to rely on his own might, but God's. He said, "You do not have to be strong in yourself, because you have my strength."

Satan will never attack our strengths, because he knows he's defeated in those areas of our lives. But he is also defeated in our weaknesses, because God is made strong in the midst of our weakness.

Gideon was terrified because he couldn't see past his own weaknesses and limitations. He started making excuses as to why he couldn't do what God wanted Him to do. God doesn't make mistakes. Don't waste your time questioning God when He prompts you to move. Lay your fears onto Him in prayer. Rely on His strength to carry you through to victory, and go forth in the strength of His might.

Do you need strength? God will strengthen you— not for yourself but to be and do what He requires of you.

LORD, YOU ARE MY STRENGTH. IN YOU IS THE POWER TO LIVE A FULL AND ABUNDANT LIFE. BE THOU MY STRENGTH! AMEN.

THE GIFT OF REPENTANCE

Or despisest thou the riches of his goodness and forbearance and longsuffering; not knowing that the goodness of God leadeth thee to repentance.

—ROMANS 2:4

R epentance does not mean making a slight change in course. It is a 180-degree turn. You cannot turn away from something without turning *toward* something. God never delivers you "from" without also delivering you "to" something.

He delivered the children of Israel *from* Egyptian bondage *to* the Promised Land. When we repent, we turn away from our former ways, as we turn to live for God.

He delivers you from deception to truth . . . from despair to hope . . . from disease to health . . . from brokenness to wholeness . . . from hell to heaven.

Imagine that God set before you a dish of dog food and a T-bone steak, pointed to the dog food and said, "That is what you have been eating." Then he points to the steak and says, "This is what you can have. The choice is yours." God will never deliver you from something good to something bad. He is a God of increase, not decrease. When He delivers you, you will always take a turn for the better! It is His goodness that leads us to repentance.

JESUS, HOW I CHERISH YOUR DELIVERANCE. I REPENT AND TURN AWAY FROM ALL THAT IS BAD AND EMBRACE ALL THE GOOD THAT YOU ARE. AMEN.

HOUSEHOLD SALVATION

They shall take to them every man a lamb, according to the house of their fathers, a lamb for an house.

—EXODUS 12:3

The night before the great Exodus, God instructed each Hebrew household to slay a lamb and apply its blood on their doorposts. When the death angel saw the blood of the spotless lamb, he knew to pass over that home . . . and the entire household was spared God's wrath.

Parents, the Bible says if you believe Jesus is who He said He is—the Lamb that died for the sins of the world—you are to apply His sinless blood to your life and that of your family, and believe God for your entire household to be saved! (Acts 16:31).

Stop walking the floor and complaining to God, "My children are on drugs," or "Mine is a homosexual," or "Mine has been married fourteen times." Walk around your home and announce, "I plead the blood of the Passover Lamb over my home. I don't care what my family's situation looks like, or what it sounds like. I don't care what anyone says about it. The blood is applied!"

LORD JESUS, I APPLY THE BLOOD TO MY FAMILY. COVER AND PROTECT MY SPOUSE AND MY CHILDREN, MY PARENTS, AND MY GRANDCHILDREN. BY YOUR BLOOD, REDEEM, DELIVER, SAVE, HEAL, AND RESTORE EVERY MEMBER OF FAMILY. AMEN.

WAITING

And he [Jesus] must needs go through Samaria . . . being wearied with his journey, sat thus on the well.

—JOHN 4:4,6

These verses don't say Jesus just happened to go through Samaria, or that Samaria was on His way. In fact, it was out of the way for Him to go through Samaria. Jesus went there and waited, knowing the Samaritan woman would soon arrive.

Sometimes it may seem as if your family is going through the greatest trial of your lives, but you are right on time. God is just getting your family to Samaria. You may not know where your fourteen-year-old is, or your sixteen-year-old may be on crack, but don't fear. Jesus is waiting at the well.

I wanted to be a trial attorney and was on my way with a basketball scholarship when I blew my left knee out of joint . . . and my scholarship out the window. In the ashes of that brokenness, God said, "You are right on time. I just have to get you to a cornfield in Columbus, Ohio. I want you to plant a church there."

So don't worry over your children. They don't have to find God. He knows where they are, and He is waiting for them to arrive.

LORD, I WILL GO WHEREVER YOU LEAD. THROUGH WHATEVER TERRAIN OR WILDERNESS, I WILL FOLLOW YOU. AMEN.

A GOOD GOD

Every good gift and every perfect gift is from above, and cometh down from the Father of lights, with whom is no variableness, neither shadow of turning.

—JAMES 1:17

Y ou can always be sure that the good things in your life have come from God. You can always rely on His loving character to remain the same. God will not change. You will not come to Him one day and find Him in a good mood, and approach Him the next day and find Him angry and hostile. He is not a God of mercy on Monday and a God of unforgiveness on Tuesday. "I am the Lord, I change not" (Malachi 3:6).

What a comforting thought! Not only is God reliable and consistent, but James 1:17 couples that assurance with the fact that He is the giver of all good gifts. God's generosity does not waver. He does not provide good things one day and withhold them the next day.

You do not have to hesitate to approach God for your needs. You can always count on Him to be the changeless, loving provider of every good and perfect gift.

JESUS, I THANK YOU FOR FORGIVING MY SINS. KEEP ME PURE AND HUMBLE IN YOUR SIGHT. I PRAISE YOU FOR EVERY GOOD AND PERFECT GIFT. AMEN.

ALL THINGS

And we know that all things work together for good to them that love God, to them who are the called according to his purpose.

—ROMANS 8:28

No matter what obstacle has upset your plans, we have a promise from our Father in heaven: *everything* works together for good to them that love God.

In everything circumstance, God works for good bringing light out of darkness for us. God can bring good out of the direst circumstances and the most difficult situations. Are you willing to let God work in everything?

While God has given us a free will, He still is sovereign. He knows everything that happens in our lives. Just as an earthly father may allow his child to make decisions while living under his roof, so our Father allows us free choice. You may think you are putting something over on God, but He will take your sinful acts and use them to accomplish His purpose on the earth.

He will even use the deeds of sinners to bring His plan for mankind to pass. He turned the evil of Joseph's brothers into the salvation of the entire Hebrew nation!

Are you striving to work according to His purpose or yours? Don't let yourself become upset over any interruptions to your plans, but rather, rejoice that God is in control of the situation.

LORD GOD, YOU ARE IN CONTROL. YOU HAVE BOTH THE PLAN AND THE ABILITY TO ACCOMPLISH YOUR PLANS. I SUMMIT EVERYTHING TO YOU IN ORDER TO KNOW YOU AND LIVE OBEDIENTLY. AMEN.

HIS TEMPLE

And what agreement hath the temple of God with idols? for ye are the temple of the living god; as God hath said, I will dwell in them, and walk in them; and I will be their God, and they shall be my people.

—2 CORINTHIANS 6:16

Your church is not the temple! Your body is a temple, and inside it resides the Holy Spirit. In the Old Testament the tabernacle of God was comprised of the outer court, the inner court, and the Holy of Holies.

The outer court is your body. The inner court is your soul: "The Holy of Holies is the temple not made by man" (Hebrews 9:1–11). Within our spirit is an altar to Jehovah God! And God said, "It is in that place that I will come in and I will sup with my people" (Revelation 3:20).

Prepare and maintain your temple for His Presence. Let the Shekinah glory of God fill you and radiate from you. Seek Him who dwells in your heart today and hear the still, small voice of the Lord.

Remember that you are a refection of His glory (2 Corinthians 3:18). You are not the source of His glory. Never take glory. Always give Him honor and glory.

ALMIGHTY GOD, LET YOUR SHEKINAH GLORY REFLECT IN MY LIFE. FILL ME TO OVERFLOWING WITH YOUR GLORY AND POWER. AMEN.

FOLLOW THE LEADER

Then said Jesus unto his disciples, If any man will come after me, let him deny himself, and take up his cross, and follow me. For whosoever will save his life shall lose it: and whosoever will lose his life for my sake shall find it.

—MATTHEW 16:24-25

Two thousand years ago, Jesus Christ came to earth in the flesh and commanded us to follow Him—and to this day no one has ever followed Christ down a road to prostitution, crime, addiction, or suicide.

Fathers, as the most influential leader your son or daughter will ever have, determine to lead them in the path they should go (Proverbs 22:6). Teach your children to live as Jesus lived, in loving service to others, and they will grow to be mature, responsible members of society.

Children will instinctively follow the leader, so if you are following Christ yourself, your children will follow your lead. Your personal example is the greatest teaching tool you possess. Teach them to follow the Leader of the heavenly hosts—the one who holds the keys to death, hell, and the grave.

LORD JESUS, MAKE MY LIFE AN EXAMPLE TO MY FAMILY AND CHILDREN OF YOUR LOVE AND SERVICE. MAY ALL THOSE IN MY FAMILY SEE YOU SHINING THROUGH ME. AMEN.

Righteous Seed

But whoso shall offend one of these little ones which believe in me, it were better for him that a millstone were hanged around his neck, and that he were drowned in the depth of the sea.

—Matthew 18:6

G od made a covenant with Abraham and pronounced a multitude of blessings upon him. Why? Because God knew Abraham would raise his children in the fear and admonition of the Lord.

Abraham became the father of many nations, and the entire earth has been blessed through his seed. You are engrafted into the family of Abraham and are blessed because of his righteous seed.

Our children are our righteous seed, and Satan is after them. He has turned our public schools into cesspools of godless propaganda where God is publicly mocked and reviled.

It is time to take a stand against the devil. The blood-bought saints of God must rescue this generation with the blood of Jesus, with the Word of God, and with prayer. Pray a hedge of protection around the children in your life.

What stand is Christ calling you to make in Your family, at work, in church, and in your community? Are you will to stand up for Jesus no matter what the cost?

Jesus, give me the courage to stand firm on Your truth. Guide me in raising my children in the fear of God. Protect my children and family from every attack. Amen.

OBEDIENCE

And ye shall take a bunch of hyssop, and dip it in the blood that is in the basin, and strike the lintel and the two side posts with the blood that is in the basin; and none of you shall go out at the door of his house until the morning.

—EXODUS 12:22

W e can plead the blood of Jesus continuously, but if we are not obedient to the Word of God, we will be wasting our breath.

God told the Israelites to stay inside their homes that Passover night. If they had disobeyed His instructions and crossed their thresholds, the blood would not have covered them.

Even though the Israelites believed what God said, if they didn't follow His instructions to them, the blood could not keep them from harm.

Be obedient to God's commands, and abide under the protective covering our loving Father has provided for you and your family. Are you obedient to the Word of God? Are you obedient to the leading and voice of the Holy Spirit? Will you repent of those areas of disobedience in your life?

JESUS, I REPENT OF ANY DISOBEDIENCE IN MY LIFE. CONVICT ME OF ANY UNKNOWN AREA OF DISOBEDIENCE. IN JESUS' NAME, AMEN.

KEYS TO THE KINGDOM

And I will give unto thee the keys of the kingdom of heaven: and whatsoever thou shalt bind on earth shall be bound in heaven: and whatsoever thou shalt loose on earth shall be loosed in heaven.

—MATTHEW 16:19

If you have keys to your home, you have authority in your home. If you give the keys to someone else, you also give them authority. Would you give the keys to your home to someone you didn't trust? Jesus gives the keys to His kingdom to those who acknowledge Him as Lord of the kingdom and submit to His Lordship within the kingdom.

You can't just casually wander into Jesus' kingdom, either. You may enlist in an army. You might join an organization. You are hired as an employee. But as a child of God—a citizen of His Kingdom, you must be born (John 3). As a matter of fact, He compared it to the process of birth! It is not something to be taken lightly, and it requires earnest commitment (Philippians 3:14).

But praise to God, once we are born again as citizens of His kingdom, we have power over all oppression operating outside His kingdom. We have protection from everything the powers of darkness would try to array against us!

BY YOUR SPIRIT, LORD, BIRTH ME INTO YOUR KINGDOM. I LONG TO BE YOUR CHILD AND A LOYAL, ETERNAL CITIZEN OF THE KINGDOM OF HEAVEN. AMEN.

IGNITION

But ye shall receive power, after that the Holy Ghost is come upon you; and ye shall be witnesses unto me both in Jerusalem, and in all Judaea, and in Samaria, and unto the uttermost part of the earth.

—ACTS 1:8

Have you ever watched a space shuttle lifting off? While the shuttle is still on the launch pad, all kinds of supports hold it in place. When blast-off comes, if the rockets don't fire, the shuttle falls back to the ground.

When God launched the church, there were no Christian broadcasting networks—Christian television or radio. The wind of Pentecost blew away the disciples' props of religious tradition. There was nothing to hold them, and nothing for them to depend on but God and His promise. They preached the Gospel throughout the known world with a passport straight from heaven.

It is time to set aside your church committees and programs, your prayer cards and your "steps to successful prayer." Allow the Holy Ghost to ignite a fire and a passion within you that cannot be quenched and to endue you with power to tread on serpents and to overcome the enemy.

JESUS, TAKE FROM ME ALL THE GIMMICKS, RITUALS, AND QUICK SPIRITUAL FIXES. INSTEAD, GIVE ME YOUR CROSS AND BAPTIZE ME IN THE FIRE OF YOUR HOLY SPIRIT. AMEN.

SPOILS OF VICTORY

To whom also Abraham gave a tenth part of all; first being by interpretation King of righteousness, and after that also King of Salem, which is, King of peace.

—HEBREWS 7:2

braham had just come from defeating four kings when he brought Melchizedek, king of Salem, the spoils of his victory. Offerings given from the spoils of victory say, "Our enemies came, we conquered them; and here is our proof of victory."

Fear and greed are two of the greatest obstacles to claiming our spiritual possessions. God can't bless us when greed and fear have overtaken us. But if we drive fear and greed from our hearts, we can enjoy the bounty of the kingdom! God is not going to put blessings into our possession for them to be turned over to the devil.

He who brings the spoil of the battle to the Father will be given even more. But to he who has no spoil, even what he has will be taken away. (Matthew 12:12).

Consider this: "Nay, in all these things we are more than conquerors through him that loved us" (Romans 8:37). Already you are a victor over sin and death in Christ Jesus. The spoils of battle—eternal life—is yours. So, bring your tithes and offerings to God with an open hand, rejoicing in your victory!

LORD, I REJOICE THAT YOU HAVE WON THE VICTORY OVER SIN AND DEATH AND DEFEATED SATAN. I GIVE YOU MY ALL. I REJOICE IN YOUR VICTORY, AND I WILL LIVE WITHOUT FEAR OR GREED. AMEN.

WHY THE WITHERED?

If a man abide not in me, he is cast forth as a branch, and is withered; and men gather them, and cast them into the fire, and they are burned.

—JOHN 15:6

I n Ohio we have a lot of clay reserves. In some areas the topsoil is very thin, while underneath there is a hard layer of clay called a "hardpan." We can have an all-out downpour, and within hours the topsoil will be as dry as powder.

Some Christians shout victory on Sunday, but by Monday they have no joy, no victory, and no peace. They are as hardhearted as our Ohio clay, and their fruit withers on the vine. They are without patience, mercy, gentleness, meekness, temperance, or compassion. They are just going through the motions.

Others wither as soon as the hot winds of temptation, trouble, and tribulation blow their way.

Keep your faith fresh and alive by constantly tilling the soil of your heart. Pray for the Holy Ghost to send the rain. Stay in union with the source of all life, and your faith will blossom and bear fruit in season.

HOLY SPIRIT, SEND YOUR RAIN. KEEP ME UNITED WITH YOUR VISION. BEAR YOUR FRUIT IN MY LIFE. AMEN.

SPIRIT-LED

If we live in the Spirit, let us also walk in the Spirit.

—GALATIANS 5:25

The greatest asset of Christian families today is the leading of the Holy Spirit. We must all learn to discern the prophetic voice of God and learn to obey Him. A gentle nudging of the Holy Spirit to pray may make the difference between life and death in your family. You may only hear a gentle, "Do not go to the store right now; stay and worship me." While you are worshiping Him, the devil's plan to meet you head-on with a swerving truck is thwarted because you heard-and obeyed.

Satan hates a godly family because he knows its spiritual strength. The devil would like nothing better than to sow strife and discord into your family life, opening the door for him to attack.

Determine to join hands with your family members every morning and to pray a hedge of protection around each other before anyone leaves the house!

SPIRIT OF GOD, LEAD ME. TEACH ME HOW TO BE A SPIRITUAL LEADER IN MY FAMILY, CHURCH, AND WORK. BY YOUR POWER, HELP ME CLOSE AND LOCK EVERY DOOR OF ATTACK FROM THE ENEMY. AMEN.

Week 44—Wednesday
CRUMBLING FOUNDATIONS

If the foundations be destroyed, what shall the righteous do?
—PSALM 11:3

E very day the world is witnessing murders of every kind in every country, as innocent people die needlessly from senseless crimes and terrorism. America is witnessing the assassination of the spiritual power and prowess of the body of Christ. We have sown to the wind, and we are now reaping the whirlwind. We have spent a generation raising irreverent children, training them to question authority at every level instead of teaching them that "to obey is better than to sacrifice" (1 Samuel 15:22).

Where are your children today? What is the condition of their spiritual lives? Where will they be five years from now if they continue on the path they are on now?

Hitler said what we teach our children will mold the nation. You cannot mold your children into what you want them to be, but you can help them become what God wants them to be.

Keep the foundations of our Christian heritage strong by giving your children the Rock of Jesus upon which to build their lives.

JESUS, GIVE ME WISDOM IN RAISING MY CHILDREN. PUT YOUR WORDS ON MY LIPS AND YOUR KNOWLEDGE IN MY HEART THAT MY CHILDREN MIGHT SEE YOU IN ME. AMEN.

TRAIN UP

Train up a child in the way he should go: and when he is old, he will not depart from it.

—PROVERBS 22:6

S atan's strategy since the Garden of Eden has been to tear down the spiritual foundation in the family. He will move against our children any way he can. He will try to attack them with sickness, accidents, violence, spirits of rebellion, and spirits of the occult. He will try to invade their minds with ungodly philosophies and doctrines of demons that undermine the teachings of their parents and their church.

In too many homes, family worship and Bible study have been cast aside for the television set. It is time for Christian families to take the power and authority God has given to us and use it against the enemy!

It is time to re-establish the home as the spiritual foundation God intended it to be. Parents and grandparents, consecrate and dedicate your home and your family to God. Declare today that, "As for me and my house, we will serve the Lord" (Joshua 24:15).

JESUS, AS FOR ME AND MY HOUSE, WE WILL SERVE, HONOR, AND OBEY YOU. WE RESPECT YOUR AUTHORITY AND HUMBLE OURSELVES BEFORE YOU IN ALL THINGS. AMEN.

GOD'S KIDS

For we are God's workmanship, created in Christ Jesus to do good works, which God prepared in advance for us to do.

—EPHESIANS 2:10

O ur children are special creations of God's loving workmanship. In fact, the word "workmanship" is the Greek word for "poetry." Our children are the poetry of a loving Creator.

Let your children know they are uniquely wonderful, with gifts and talents like no one else. Tell them that they were created to mirror Him.

We live in a society that puts conditions on everything. Kids join gangs because they want to belong. Tell your kids they don't need acceptance from their peers, because God has not only accepted them, but He has forgiven them of everything they have ever done wrong. "God commendeth his love toward us, in that, while we were yet sinners, Christ died for us" (Romans 5:8).

Help your children understand that God loves them unconditionally—not for what they do but for who they are—God's kids. Refuse to love your children conditionally. Love them as the Father does—unconditionally. Say to your children, "There is nothing you can do that will make me stop loving you!"

FATHER, FILL ME WITH YOUR UNCONDITIONAL LOVE FOR MY CHILDREN. MAY THEY SEE YOUR LOVE IN MY LIFE. AMEN.

THE SANCTITY OF MARRIAGE

For this cause shall a man leave his father and mother, and shall be joined unto his wife, and they two shall be one flesh. This is a great mystery: but I speak concerning Christ and the church.

—EPHESIANS 5:31–32

God sanctioned and blessed only two institutions: the family and the church. He even used the marriage relationship to illustrate the relationship between Christ and the church, showing us the high value He places on marriage.

Ephesians 5 discusses in detail the way God intends marriage to be. A sanctified marriage is a harmonious union between a man and a woman who cherish each other and willingly give up their own self-interests on behalf of the other.

The church is the model for wives, submitting to their husbands just as the church follows the leadership of Christ. Jesus is the model for husbands, who are told to "love your wives, even as Christ also loved the church, and gave himself for it" (v. 25). Couples who commit to living out Ephesians 5 in their marriage are a living witness to all those around them. Make your commitment today!

JESUS, MAKE OUR MARRIAGE HOLY. SANCTIFY US AS ONE IN YOU. GIVE US THE SAME LOVE FOR EACH OTHER THAT YOU HAVE FOR THE CHURCH. AMEN.

STAY HOME

But know this, that if the goodman of the house had known in what watch the thief would come, he would have watched, and would not have suffered his house to be broken up.

—MATTHEW 24:43

The devil wants to grieve you by taking your loved ones and your most treasured possessions. He wants to torment you by taking your peace and security. He wants to rob you of your health, your finances and your cherished dreams. Most of all, he wants to shake your faith in the Word of God, so you will be powerless to stand against him. He will strike at your life, taunting, "Why didn't God prevent this?" He will laugh at your sorrow and sneer, "Curse God and die!"

A thief does not have to be strong to steal. All he has to do is wait until there is no one home! This is what the devil does. He preys on people who are not "at home" spiritually. He stalks those who do not believe he is real, because he knows they will not be on guard against him. He lurks behind Christians who believe he is real—but leave themselves open to his oppression.

Be watchful, stay alert, and stand guard! Guard the home of your heart. Stand spiritual watch over your family through intercession and teaching the Word.

JESUS, DON'T LET ME LOWER MY GUARD AGAINST THE ENEMY. KEEP ME ALERT AND IN THE WORD ALL THE TIME. AMEN.

AGREE WITH GOD

If ye abide in me, and my words abide in you, ye shall ask what ye will, and it shall be done unto you.

—JOHN 15:7

T he Bible is God's Word to us. It is the operator's manual, given to mortal men by an eternal God. God and His Word are alive and inseparable. His Word does not change, nor can it fail, nor will it return unto Him without accomplishing what it was sent to do (Isaiah 55:11).

When you confess what God's Word says about you, you are agreeing that what He has said concerning you is true. There is infinite power in that agreement.

Decree that you have what God says you have. Proclaim that you are who God says you are. God said He would hasten after His Word to perform it, to bring it to pass in your life.

When you speak the Word, angels hearken to that command (Psalm 103:20), and all of heaven will back you up. You have God's written guarantee.

GOD, I BELIEVE WHAT YOU SAID IN THE WORD. I KNOW THAT YOUR WORD IS LIFE AND TRUTH. I WILL COMMAND ALL THAT YOU HAVE SPOKEN BY THE POWER OF YOUR SPIRIT. AMEN.

THE MIRACLE REBIRTH

For I will take you from among the heathen, and gather you out of all countries, and will bring you into your own land.

—EZEKIEL 36:24

F or centuries, theologians puzzled over the references to Israel in the Book of Revelation. Israel had ceased to exist as a nation, and it seemed impossible for the prophecies in the Bible to be literally true. Many books were written by scholars who tried to interpret Revelation while omitting Israel.

After World War II, American bulldozers unearthed the grim evidence of the Holocaust. The concept of a nation of Israel had never seemed so remote. But God meant what He said in His Word. On May 14, 1948, Israel became a nation—overnight! This event marked one of the greatest miracles in history and the fulfillment of an end time prophecy!

God kept His Word and is gathering His covenant people from all over the world. He is establishing them once again in their land, where He promised they would be at the close of the age.

In Matthew 24:32, Jesus warns us, "Now learn a parable of the fig tree: When its branch is yet tender, and putteth forth leaves, ye know that the summer is nigh; So likewise, ye, when ye shall see all these things, know that it is near, even at the door." In history, Israel is God's fig tree serving as a harbinger of Christ' return. Are you ready for Jesus to return today?

COME QUICKLY, LORD JESUS. THANK YOU FOR THE SIGN OF THE FIG TREE IN THIS GENERATION HERALDING YOUR RETURN. AMEN.

PROPHETIC TECHNOLOGY

But thou, O Daniel, shut up the words, and seal the book, even to the time of the end: many shall run to and fro, and knowledge shall be increased.

—DANIEL 12:4

I n the past sixty years more inventions, discoveries, scientific, and medical breakthroughs have occurred than in the entire history of the world. Every three years our knowledge doubles! The astounding magnitude of new knowledge is just one of many signs that identifies our generation as the end time generation.

At the beginning of this century, no one imagined man would ever fly. In 1950, space travel only occurred in science fiction movies. In 1960, tape recorders were still bulky machines with seven-inch reels, and no one had ever heard the phrase "compact disc." In 1970, computers took up entire rooms. The information super-highway was only an idea in 1980. But today the world is linked via satellite, computer modem, and cellular telephone.

The gospel is being proclaimed through technology our ancestors never envisioned. The whole planet is rapidly being reached with the gospel. Jesus promised, "And this gospel of the kingdom shall be preached in all the world for a witness unto all nations; and then shall the end come" (Matthew 24:14). We are living in the final hour!

> JESUS, USE ME AS AN INSTRUMENT IN PRO-CLAIMING THE GOSPEL TO THE ENDS OF THE EARTH. USE MY GIVING, MY SERVICE, AND MY LIFE TO WITNESS TO EVERYONE I MEET ABOUT YOUR WONDERFUL SALVATION. AMEN.

SIGNS FROM HEAVEN

And great earthquakes shall be in divers places, and famines, and pestilences; and fearful sights and great signs shall there be from heaven.

—LUKE 21:11

Worldwide famine in these days when there should be none tells us that Jesus is coming. The major wheat producers grow enough food to feed every starving person in the world, yet famine abounds.

There have been more earthquakes worldwide in the last fifteen years than in the other eight decades of this century. New and powerful strains of bacteria emerge to mock the efforts of doctors to fight them.

Jesus warned us that in these times men's hearts would fail them for fear (Luke 21:26), but He was not talking about you. The people who fear the turbulent events of these times are those who do not understand what is happening—but you do! Every newscast that tells us of these events is a reminder to us of our blessed hope—Jesus will come soon to take His church to heaven.

Are you ready for His return? Is your family ready? Do you have a neighbor, friend, or work associate that you need to tell today about Jesus? How tragic it would be if you looked over the abyss of hell at the final judgment and recognized a face of someone you knew on the other side—spending hell in eternity. Don't let that happen. Tell someone you know today about Jesus!

LORD JESUS, GIVE ME THE COURAGE AND THE WORDS TO WITNESS TO YOUR SAVING POWER THIS DAY. AMEN.

STAND IN THE GAP

And I sought for a man among them, that should make up the hedge, and stand in the gap before me for the land, that I should not destroy it: but I found none.

—EZEKIEL 22:30

A father does not need to be a Bible scholar to function as the priest in his home. The most powerful experiences in my childhood were the times my father gathered us to pray. He was not an eloquent man, but when he prayed I knew no devil was big enough to come against him.

Children today, more than ever, need the covering of their father's prayers. They need their fathers to speak strength and blessing into their lives and to plead the blood of Jesus over them.

You may think this message does not apply to you because you are not a father or your own children are grown. Yet you know someone who is a father; you may know of children who are hurting because their fathers are not nurturing them in the Lord. Pray for them. Plead the blood over those unprotected children. Invite the Holy Spirit to turn their fathers' hearts back home. Stand in the gap and intercede for the preservation of our righteous seed.

God needs You to stand in the gap for your family, church, and nation. He is looking for intercessors who will seek His face on behalf of others. Are you willing to stand in the gap?

FATHER, PRAY THROUGH ME WITH YOUR SPIRIT SO THAT I WILL BE ABLE TO STAND IN THE GAP FOR OTHERS. AMEN.

DISTRESS OF NATIONS

And there shall be signs in the sun, and in the moon, and in the stars; and upon the earth distress of nations, with perplexity; the sea and the waves roaring.

—LUKE 21:25

War has always been a part of man's history, but never before have there been so many continuing conflicts in the world. No clear solutions can be found, and the wars rage on with no sign of resolution. Decades after the Korean War, North and South Korea are still simmering. Rumors concerning nuclear bomb development abound in the north. Iraq and Libya continue to provoke hostility among nations. Wars seethe across the continent of Africa. Meanwhile, no earthly solution can be applied to solve the Palestinian-Israeli conflict that constantly undermines the security of Israel.

The distress of nations is being played out daily in the world. It would be easy to read the newspaper and become fearful, but do not fall into that trap. Jesus said, "When these things begin to come to pass, then look up, and lift up your heads; for your redemption draweth nigh" (Luke 21:28). Do not despair! Look toward heaven! Jesus is coming soon!

LORD, HELP ME UNDERSTAND THE SIGNS OF THE TIMES. PREPARE ME FOR YOUR RETURN. HELP ME TO LIVE FOR YOU WILL ALL MY BEING THIS DAY. AMEN.

THE DAYS OF NOAH

But as the days of [Noah] were, so shall also the coming of the Son of man be.

—MATTHEW 24:37

I n the days of Noah, people were eating and drinking, violating their marriages, and participating in revelry, lawlessness, and lasciviousness.

When the rains began to fall and the ark shifted off its housing, Noah and his family were safe inside. As the floodwaters rose, the people outside the ark screamed for deliverance, but the door was closed.

Just as God provided one solitary way of escape for Noah and his family, He has provided one solitary way for those who turn to Him in these end times. "Neither is there salvation in any other: for there is none other name under heaven given among men, whereby we must be saved" (Acts 4:12).

Those who were saved in Noah's time were sealed in the ark by God Himself before the destruction came (Genesis 7:16). When the headlines proclaim an increase in violence and corruption you can know your redemption is close at hand.

The only true safety and security in these days are resting securing in the hands of the Savior. Are you resting in Him today?

LORD JESUS, I KNOW THAT YOUR BURDEN IS EASY AND YOUR YOKE IS LIGHT. TODAY I REST FULLY IN YOU. AMEN.

Week 46—Wednesday
ESCALATING POPULATION

And he said unto me, Thou must prophesy again before many peoples, and nations, and tongues, and kings.

—REVELATION 10:11

By the most conservative calculations, in the year 2050 there will be ten billion people on the earth. With each tick of the end time clock, millions of new souls are born into the world.

More people than have ever lived in the entire history of the world are alive today. We are seeing end time prophecy come alive in the form of "many peoples and nations" living on the earth.

God has a plan for those "many peoples and nations." When the newscasts tell us of the exploding masses of people in the earth, remember that John saw them first in heaven: "And, lo, a great multitude, which no man could number, of all nations, and kindreds, and people, and tongues, stood before the throne, and before the Lamb, clothed with white robes, and palms in their hands; and cried with a loud voice, saying, Salvation to our God which sitteth upon the throne, and unto the Lamb" (Revelation 7:9–10).

Some day every knee shall bow and every tongue confess that Jesus is Lord (Philippians 2:10). Is there someone today that you know who needs Jesus? What will you do to bring them before the throne of Jesus in repentance and faith?

FATHER, MAKE ME SENSITIVE TO EVERYONE AROUND ME AND THE CONDITION OF THEIR SOULS. HELP ME TO WITNESS TO THE UNSAVED I KNOW ABOUT JESUS. AMEN.

STAY ON THE ROCK

*Be thou my strong rock, for an house of defence to save me.
For thou art my rock and my fortress.*

—PSALM 31:2–3

My wife and I made a covenant with God when we married that d-i-v-o-r-c-e would never be mentioned in our home. For us, it is simply not an option. When you marry you not only forsake all others, but you forsake your right to be right. Divorce is a product of a home ruled by selfish wants and desires and is a satanic tactic to overthrow the throne of God.

Turn off television programs depicting adultery and marital strife. If you don't, these spirits will invade your mind and, subsequently, your home. "For as he thinketh in his heart, so is he" (Proverbs 23:7).

Fill your home with the presence of God. Speak words of unity and love to one another. Paul said that we should in honor prefer one another above ourselves. (Romans 12:10). Prefer your mate's needs and desires above your own. Center your relationship around Christ. Build it on a sure foundation. Marriages built on the Rock never go "on the rocks."

Show your spouse today your love. Express your love and appreciation. Find little ways to show Your love. And most of all, pray today with your spouse.

FATHER, TOGETHER WE COME TO YOU AS ONE IN CHRIST, PRAYING TOGETHER AND SHARING TOGETHER AS ONE. KEEP US AS ONE IN YOU. AMEN.

EVERYBODY GOES TO HEAVEN

And whosoever was not found written in the book of life was cast into the lake of fire.

—REVELATION 20:15

Not long ago I burned my hand grilling hamburgers in our backyard. God did not design my skin to withstand raging flames, and it hurt when I put my hand where it was never intended to be.

Now I didn't start cursing that fire for burning me, yet every day thousands go into eternity cursing God for condemning them to a hell that was never intended for them. One of the easiest ways to identify a cult is their denial of the existence of hell. They say, "My God is a loving God and He would never send me there; everybody goes to heaven!"

Everybody does go to heaven. We just do not all get to stay. Everyone will stand before the judgment seat of God someday, but there are those whose names will not be found in the Lamb's Book of Life.

Do not allow Satan to lull you into a sense of false security. If there is sin in your life, turn from it today. Tomorrow is promised to no man.

JESUS, I CONFESS YOU AS MY LORD AND SAVIOR. I REPENT OF MY SINS AND ASK YOU FOR FORGIVENESS. I RECEIVE YOUR FORGIVENESS THROUGH YOUR SHED BLOOD AND I JOYFULLY DECLARE THAT I HAVE ETERNAL LIFE. GIVE ME THE GIFT OF YOUR HOLY SPIRIT. AMEN.

YOU HAVE THE ANSWER

For God sent not his Son into the world to condemn the world; but that the world through him might be saved.

—JOHN 3:17

Go back to the purity of the first hour you knew Jesus . . . when you wanted everyone in the world to have a chance to feel what you felt and know what you knew.

Keep that hunger and that purity that reaches out a hand and says, "I'll pray for you. I'll believe God for your miracle." We are the only hope to evangelize this world. We are the generation destined to reach out in this last hour to the depraved and the destitute with the life-changing gospel of Jesus Christ. From the uttermost to the guttermost, take a stand and declare, "This is the Bible, and it is the answer for everything!"

We are all called to be witnesses, and God has given us an anointing and a calling to reach the lost. People are hungry to know God, and you have the answer (1 Peter 3:15).

If someone asked you about Jesus, could you lead them to salvation in Christ Jesus? If you answered "yes," then pray for wisdom in saying the right thing. If you said "no," then go to a pastor, evangelist, teacher, or another Christian brother and sister and learn how to share the gospel with the unsaved. Get equipped to take the Good News to everyone you know.

EQUIP ME TO WITNESS, LORD JESUS. TEACH ME THROUGH YOUR SPIRIT AND THE LIVES OF OTHER BELIEVERS HOW TO LEAD OTHERS TO JESUS EFFECTIVELY. AMEN.

WEEKEND WARRIORS

For the weapons of our warfare are not carnal, but mighty through God to the pulling down of strongholds.

—2 CORINTHIANS 10:4

Y ou may be ready to wield your weapons on Sunday morning, when the worship has lifted you and the preaching of the Word has stirred your spirit; but how do you feel on Monday afternoon? It does no good to have your weapons ready on Sunday morning if you can't find them when you need them at 7:00 on Thursday evening.

Our adversary is an invader who will not respect your schedule or give any thought to your feelings. He will seek any entry point, and while his first attacks may seem insignificant, his purpose is to kill, steal, and destroy (John 10:10).

Today's resentment is tomorrow's hatred. Your prayers will be hindered and your interest in the Word will wane. Then the onslaught will come, like divorce, a runaway child or the loss of your job.

Don't be a weekend warrior. Stand guard over your heart and give the devil no place of entry.

JESUS, HELP ME TO GUARD MY HEART AND TO FILL MY SPIRIT WITH YOUR WORD. EMPOWER ME TO RESIST THE ENEMY. AMEN.

HEIRS OF PROMISE

And if ye be Christ's, then are ye Abraham's seed, and heirs according to the promise.

—GALATIANS 3:29

Paul said the Spirit of God revealed to him that the blessings of Abraham should come upon the Gentiles. Along with the Jews, the Gentile would also be joint-heirs and partakers of the promise (Ephesians 3:6). Christians today act as if we have to wait to get to heaven to receive the revelation of the promise! The Bible says heaven is where Jesus is, and Jesus is in us as well as among us.

Heaven is available to us today, if we will simply partake of what is rightfully ours as heirs of the promise. Do not allow the death of Jesus on Calvary to be a vain act in your life, but receive all that He purchased for you. When He gave His life willingly on the Cross, it was to give great things to all who would receive them.

Through faith in Christ, we are accounted sons (no longer servants), having all the privileges of God's children, including a heavenly Father who is intimately concerned with everything that concerns us. Seek Him for His provision, His protection, and His patient love.

You not only have His promise; You are His promise. Your life is a fulfillment of His promise as He protects, provides for, and loves others through your gifts and ministry.

JESUS, THANK YOU FOR GIVING YOUR PROMISES AND MAKING MY LIFE A PROMISE TO OTHERS. TEACH ME HOW TO TRUST ALL OF YOUR PROMISES TODAY. AMEN.

BROKEN CHAINS

The Spirit of the Lord is upon me . . . to preach the acceptable year of the Lord.

—LUKE 4:18–19

⬱

The "acceptable year of the Lord"—the Year of Jubilee—was the last in a fifty-year period. During the first forty nine years, the Israelites could own slaves, sow their fields, prune their vineyards, and gather the harvest; but each seventh year was set apart as a Sabbath for the land. At the beginning of the fiftieth year, the trumpet sounded, proclaiming the Year of Jubilee. This was a year when the ground wasn't worked, slaves were set free, and debts were erased. It was a year of rest for the entire land.

When Jesus stood in the synagogue and spoke these words, the trumpet sounded for all time and eternity declaring our freedom! "If the Son therefore shall make you free, ye shall be free indeed" (John 8:36).

The blood from Calvary's Cross declares your freedom—freedom from poverty, broken-heartedness, and death. The chains have been broken forever.

LORD JESUS, MAKE THIS SEASON IN MY LIFE YOUR YEAR OF JUBILEE FOR ME BY SETTING ME FREE FROM PAST DEBT AND GIVING ME THE HEART OF A CHEERFUL GIVER. AMEN.

THE POWER OF FASTING

Defraud ye not one the other, except it be with consent for a time, that ye may give; yourselves to fasting and prayer; and come together again, that Satan tempt you not for your incontinency.

—I CORINTHIANS 7:5

Fasting brings you through the outer court of your body, through the inner court of your soul and into the Holy of Holies of your spirit, where God resides.

When Jesus cast out the demon, He said, "This kind cometh out not but by prayer and fasting," but He didn't first go pray and fast. He immediately cast the demon out, because He was living a fasted lifestyle.

You cannot wait until the devil comes knocking on your door to pull out your Bible verses and your ten keys to deliverance.

Let us be lean, mean fighting machines in the Holy Ghost, ever ready to face the devil's onslaughts. That is what putting on the whole armor of God is about (Ephesians 6:11). Live a fasted life and be ready for the devil whenever and wherever he knocks!

In fasting, we surrender the desires of our flesh and our spirit man takes charge of our lives. Fasting creates within us an attitude for focusing entirely on Jesus and putting aside self-interests and attention.

JESUS, I SEEK YOUR WORK IN MY LIFE THROUGH PRAYER AND FASTING. TEACH ME WHEN I NEED TO PRAY AND FAST FOR A MIGHTY WORK OF YOUR SPIRIT. AMEN.

WORDS OF LIFE

My son, attend to my words; incline thine ear unto my sayings. Let them not depart from thine eyes; keep them in the midst of thine heart. For they are life unto those that find them, and health to all their flesh.

—PROVERBS 4:20–22

When we became born again, we received the eternal life of God. Eternity has no beginning and no ending, and even death has no hold on us. There is no death to a born-again believer (Galatians 2:20). We have already died the only death required of us.

The only difference physical death makes to the born-again believer is the transfer of the life of God from earth to heaven. We do not have to wait until we get to heaven to become healthy, wealthy, and wise. A victorious life is available to us on earth now.

Solomon told his son in Proverbs to pay attention to his words, because they are life—not that they are going to be or hope to be or may be in heaven—but they are life and health for you today.

JESUS, OPEN MY EARS TO HEAR YOUR WORDS CLEARLY. I HUNGER TO FEED ON HEAVENLY MANNA, WHICH IS TRUTH AND LIFE FOR ME. AMEN.

SERVANTHOOD

If any man serve me, let him follow me; and where I am, there shall also my servant be: if any man serve me, him will my Father honour.

—JOHN 12:26

The kingdom of God is built on servanthood. Isaiah gave his voice to prophesy the Savior's coming. One angel descended from the heavens to tell a young virgin she would bear the Savior of the world and another offered his voice to proclaim the Savior's birth. Mary offered her womb, while Joseph gave his fiancée. The donkey lent his back and the cattle gave their warmth. The earth volunteered the straw on which our Savior lay, while the moon gave its light. A star pointed the direction for the wise men bringing gifts. All these things were done in labor inspired by love because God gave His Son.

But it was the Son who gave all. He gave His life. He said, "No man takes it from me. I can lay it down, and I can take it up again." He could have called ten thousand angels to His aid, but He willingly died for you and me. Servanthood is giving of your time, energy, and talent, expecting nothing in return. This is the kingdom of God.

Read Philippians 2. How does your life reflect the servant attitude of Jesus Christ? In what ways does pride hinder ministry and servanthood in your life?

LORD JESUS, SHAPE MY PERSPECTIVE ON ALL OF LIFE SO THAT I MAY SEE OTHERS AS THOSE WHOM I SERVE INSTEAD OF EXPECTING THEM TO SERVE ME. AMEN.

THE MESSAGE OF HOPE

The next day John seeth Jesus coming unto him, and saith, Behold the Lamb of God, which taketh away the sin of the world.

—JOHN 1:29

The time has come for the people of God to wake up and recognize what is going on in the church. The enemy keeps gnawing away, deceiving us into accepting one lie after another, luring us into believing a compromised gospel, until the diluted body we call the church is pleasing to everyone except God.

It is time once again for the church to show the people their transgressions and point out their sins. Sin is the one thing we all have in common, but nobody likes to talk about. Sin stops us from receiving all God has for us.

The message of sin is a message of hope, for Jesus Christ is the Lamb of God who came to take away the sins of the world. We need not shrink from calling sin what it is, even at the risk of being rejected and ridiculed. Some will always turn away when confronted with their sin, but many more will be saved.

JESUS, CONVICT ME OF MY SIN BY YOUR SPIRIT. GIVE ME THE BOLDNESS AND COURAGE TO CONFRONT SIN IN MY LIFE AND MY WORLD. AMEN.

WHY DO YOU DOUBT?

And immediately Jesus stretched forth his hand, and caught him, and said unto him, O thou of little faith, wherefore didst thou doubt.

—MATTHEW 14:31

Doubt says, "I wonder if it could be." Unbelief says, "I know that it is not." Doubt is not nearly the obstacle that unbelief is. On the day of Pentecost, many in the crowd doubted the testimony of Peter and the disciples, but three thousand souls were added to the Church that very day. Doubt does not stop the mighty wind from heaven.

Doubt offers God the opportunity to prove Himself to you, and He will. He sent Elijah into an idolatrous land to challenge the priests of Baal to a contest. God was more than willing to prove himself to the doubters, and when the fire fell from heaven, no doubt remained (1 Kings 18).

Peter doubted when He took his eyes off Jesus. He saw the waves of misfortune and felt the wind of disaster beating against him. As he began to sink, he cried out to Jesus . . . and immediately Jesus reached out His hand and caught him. Jesus was there to lift him up—and He'll be there for you too.

LORD, I BELIEVE. HELP MY UNBELIEF. FILL ME WITH TRUST AND FAITH IN YOU. ANCHOR ME ON THE ROCK OF YOUR WORD. AMEN.

THE REMNANT CHURCH

I will pour out my spirit upon all flesh; and your sons and your daughters shall prophesy, your old men shall dream dreams, your young men shall see visions.

—JOEL 2:28

T he church of Jesus Christ has withstood the deadening blows of the God-haters throughout the ages. In every generation scoffers have denied the existence of God or invented their own religions to accommodate their sin. In our own generation we are seeing the fulfillment of 2 Timothy 3.

But God promised He would preserve a remnant church of the faithful, and in the last days this remnant church would rise up in Holy Ghost power. His Bride, the church, is taking possession of the land and is becoming glorious without spot or blemish. It's time for the church to take her position as the bride of Christ.

The church is beginning to come out from the world and be separate. A Bible-believing remnant is leaving behind the compromising, sin-infested church of man to take up the standard of Jesus Christ. Together we will call out to God and march forward to bring His glorious gospel to the ends of the earth.

THANK YOU, JESUS, THAT I CAN BE PART OF YOUR GLORIOUS BRIDE. PURIFY AND CLEANSE US. KEEP ME PURE AND HOLY THROUGH THE CLEANSING OF YOUR BLOOD AND THE WASHING OF YOUR SPIRIT. AMEN.

BELIEVE GOD

For the time will come when they will not endure sound doctrine; but after their own lusts shall they reap to themselves teachers, having itching ears.

—2 TIMOTHY 4:3

Turn your back on deception and stop taking the word of the world over the Word of God. Even more, stop taking anyone's word over the Word of God! Whether they are preachers, teachers, gurus, politicians, or entertainers, their words can never stand up to the inspired Word of God!

Stop listening to the intellectuals, the compromisers, the world-appeasers. You have the holy Word of God Himself! Let us reject those who twist the truth and alter the Bible to justify their self-serving agendas.

God, forgive us for the idolatrous sin of presumption—for trying to mold you into a god who fits our conceptions, rather than the God who created the universe. Put our hearts back into a reverence for your Word and a deep appreciation that we must seek out our salvation before You.

LORD, LET YOUR WORD DWELL IN MY HEART RICHLY, ILLUMINATED BY THE POWER OF YOUR HOLY SPIRIT. AMEN.

THE DAYS OF LOT

In the same day that Lot went out of Sodom it rained fire and brimstone from heaven, and destroyed them all. Even thus shall it be in the day when the Son of man is revealed.

—LUKE 17:28–30

eter tells us that God turned the cities of Sodom and Gomorrah into ashes, making them an example of the fate of those who choose to live immorally (2 Peter 2:6). He also describes how God delivered Lot, the only righteous man among them (2 Peter 2:7–8; Genesis 19:22). The destruction of the city waited until the righteous man had been removed.

The unlawful deeds of the wicked are thrust at us over the media our exploding technology has made possible. This is the most exciting time for the gospel in the history of the world. The greatest revival of all time has begun! Hundreds of thousands of souls will hear the Gospel and receive Jesus as their Savior. And when the entire end time harvest is gathered in, the righteous (those who have been saved by the blood of Jesus) will be removed before destruction falls.

In what ways do you see revival already breaking out in our day? Could Jesus bring revival to your town through you? Are you ready and prepared for all that he has for you?

JESUS, LET REVIVAL BEGIN TODAY WITH ME. IGNITE ME AND LET ME BURN FOR YOU. AMEN.

BOOT CAMP

The law of his God is in his heart; none of his steps shall slide.

—PSALM 37:31

During boot camp the new soldier is issued a weapon. The drill instructor orders him to take it apart, then put it back together. It never leaves his side. It lies beside him at night, his arm wrapped around it in his sleep. In the morning, he starts all over again, taking it apart, putting it together, and carrying it until it becomes a part of him.

When the enemy comes, it is too late to go looking for your weapon. When the enemy runs toward your foxhole with a hand grenade, it is too late to consult the training manual. You must be ready to react immediately and automatically.

When the devil comes, it is too late to start looking for your Bible. You should have been eating and sleeping with the Word—taking it apart, examining it, studying it, carrying it with you, and practicing its precepts. When the devil comes, your training will take over. When you have no strength or presence of mind to fight, the Word you have hidden in your heart will rise up and drive the enemy back.

JESUS, CONTINUALLY FILL ME WITH A HUNGER AND THIRST FOR YOUR WORD. HELP ME KNOW HOW TO FIGHT THE ENEMY AT EVERY POINT OF ATTACK. AMEN.

REPENT AND CHANGE

Jesus began to preach, and to say, Repent: for the kingdom of heaven is at hand.

—MATTHEW 4:17

G od's demand on us to become standard bearers requires us to leave the night and look forth to the morning. "Who is she who looketh forth as the morning?" She is a church filled with standard bearers who refuse to return to the night as soon as they leave the church parking lot or the mission trip. "Fair as the moon and clear as the sun" is not just for the altar or the service or the times with other Christians. Repentance, conversion, and becoming fair and clear are not for a moment but for a lifetime.

Leave sin behind at the altar once and for all! Get real about repentance. Sorrow may accompany repentance but sorrow is not repentance.

Repentance is change! Repentance involves a total change of life.

Jesus came preaching repentance. To the religious He says repent. In other words change your minds, get a new concept of God's kingdom in your hearts. To those with wealth and power He says repent. Change where you deposit your treasures. Instead of putting treasures where moth and rust corrupt, lay up treasures in heaven (Matthew 6:19–20). Instead of seeking things, seek first God's kingdom and His righteousness (Matthew 6:33).

JESUS, CHANGE ME. MAKE ME TODAY MORE LIKE YOU. TRANSFORM ME INTO YOUR GLORY. USE MY REPENTANCE AS THE TOOL TO BREAK AND REMAKE ME. AMEN.

IF THE THIEF BE FOUND

Men do not despise a thief, if he steal to satisfy his soul when he is hungry; but if he be found, he shall restore sevenfold; he shall give all the substance of his house.

—PROVERBS 6:30–31

The Bible says the thief must restore what he has taken sevenfold—if the thief be found! Sadly, many Christians cannot tell the difference between the God we serve and the adversary of our souls. Jesus said, "When he putteth forth his own sheep, he goeth before them, and the sheep follow him: for they know his voice. And a stranger will they not follow, but will flee from him: for they know not the voice of strangers" (John 10:4–5). What tragedy we will suffer if we cannot recognize the voice of our Shepherd and distinguish it from the voice of the thief!

Only when you hear the Shepherd's voice regularly will you be able to recognize it. Reading the Word and spending time in prayer and communion with Him will teach you to discern His voice. When you learn the difference between the voice of the Lord and the voice of the adversary, you will be able to stand up to the thief and demand he restore what he stole, sevenfold.

Don't allow the enemy to get away with anything. Speak the truth of God's Word aloud right now.

JESUS, I OVERCOME THE ENEMY BY THE WORD OF MY TESTIMONY THAT YOU ARE LORD AND SAVIOR AND BY THE BLOOD OF THE LAMB. I AM SAVED BY YOUR SHED BLOOD. AMEN.

WHAT IS IN YOU?

O generation of vipers, how can ye, being evil, speak good things? for out of the abundance of the heart the mouth speaketh.

—MATTHEW 12:34

A rotten egg sailed past Buddy Robinson, an old Pentecostal preacher, and struck the deacon standing next to him. As the stench of the egg covered the deacon, he started cussing up a storm.

A second egg caught Brother Robinson right in the middle of his forehead, and as it trickled down his face, he began shouting and dancing all over the platform.

The deacon said, "I don't understand it. When I was hit with the egg, I went to cussing; but when that rotten egg hit you, you went to praising."

Brother Robinson, who stuttered like Moses, gave his reply: "You already had the c-c-c-cuss in you. When that egg hit you, it just knocked the c-c-c-cuss out of you. But when I got hit with a rotten egg, I had p-p-p-praise in me, and it just knocked the p-p-p-praise right out of me."

Whatever is in you will come out of you in a time of stress, trial, or crisis. Deposit the Word in your heart that you will not sin against God (Psalm 119:11).

> **JESUS, PURIFY AND CLEANSE ME. WITH YOUR BAPTISM OF FIRE, BURN AWAY ALL THE CHAFF IN MY LIFE. AMEN.**

PRAY ALWAYS

Watch ye therefore, and pray always, that ye may be accounted worthy to escape all these things that shall come to pass, and to stand before the Son of man.

—LUKE 21:36

e are living in perilous times, surrounded by filth and violence, when men search for answers and can find none. Through this whirlwind of depravity comes the still, small voice of God saying, "Pray always," because prayer is effective! (James 5:16).

Prayer opens the door for God to do His work in a world desperately in need of His intervention. The righteous have a job to do, and it begins with prayer. The world around us is crying out for our intercession. The unsaved need our prayers to bind the hindering spirits that keep them from receiving salvation. The sick need our prayers for healing. The oppressed need our prayers for deliverance. Our families, neighborhoods, and workplaces need our prayers to rebuke the forces of darkness that threaten to sweep over them.

Too often we hear, "There's nothing left to do but pray"—but there has never been anything else to do but pray!

HOLY SPIRIT, WHEN I HAVE NOTHING TO PRAY OR DON'T KNOW HOW TO PRAY, THEN PRAY THROUGH ME TEACHING ME HOW TO INTERCEDE FOR OTHERS. LORD, ALWAYS KEEP ME PRAYING IN THE SPIRIT. AMEN.

PRESSING NEEDS

Let us therefore come boldly unto the throne of grace, that we may obtain mercy, and find grace to help in time of need.

—HEBREWS 4:16

The prayer of intercession is urgent prayer on behalf of a pressing need. We live in a world filled with pressing needs!

God said, "I sought a man among them, that should make up the hedge, and stand in the gap before me for the land, that I should not destroy it: but I found none" (Ezekiel 22:30). What a tragedy that for a lack of even one person who would pray, destruction fell on many!

The Day of the Lord is drawing near. Judgment such as the world has never known is coming upon this earth.

God is looking for spiritual warriors who will stand in the gap for the hurting, the helpless and the hopeless. Will you join the ranks?

Your commitment is to pray without ceasing, in all situations, with all kinds of prayers, and at all times.

TEACH ME LORD, HOW TO STAND IN THE GAP AND PRAY. I TRUST YOU TO SHOW ME THE NEEDS TO PRAY FOR AND THAT YOUR SPIRIT WILL PRAY THROUGH ME. AMEN.

DEAD MEN

Work out your own salvation with fear and trembling; for it is God which worketh in you both to will and to do of his good pleasure.

—PHILIPPIANS 2:12–13

W e are all commissioned to grow up in Him to the point where we accept and walk in His will in every area of our lives. It is the difference between infancy and maturity.

True maturity comes when God's will can be worked through your will. This can only happen when your flesh is dead enough, and your will becomes submitted enough and you have been truly resurrected with Christ. Then what you will is not your will, but God's.

Dead men do not have a will! When you are dead to your own will, you can get up at 4:00 in the morning to pray; you can forgive the hurt; and you can have peace in the midst of the storm.

When you have grown into the fullness of the image of Jesus your prayer will be, "Not my will, but thine be done." God will then answer your prayer and impregnate you with His will for your life.

LORD JESUS, I SUBMIT MY WILL TO YOURS. I PRAY THAT YOU DO WHATEVER YOU DESIRE IN MY LIFE. I AM YOURS, O LORD. AMEN.

TAKE NO THOUGHT

Behold the fowls of the air: for they sow not, neither do they reap . . . yet your heavenly Father feedeth them. Are ye not much better than they?

—MATTHEW 6:26

Y ou rarely see a hungry bird, or a bird with no feathers, or a bird with no tree to sleep in. Birds never sow, reap, or gather into barns. All they have is what they need at the moment. Our heavenly Father takes care of them on a daily basis.

He has an even greater plan than that for us. He doesn't just take care of us on a day-to-day basis. He is Jehovah-Jireh, the God of more than enough. He gives us the ability to plant, to harvest, and to gather the abundance into the storehouse (Malachi 3:10).

Your abundance belongs in the storehouse that God has provided—the Church. Bring your abundance into the place where God has put His name. Stop acting like a bird. Start sowing, reaping, and gathering into the storehouse so the gospel of Jesus Christ may be preached in all the earth.

JESUS, USE ME TO TEACH AND PREACH THE GOSPEL THROUGHOUT THE WORLD THROUGH MY GIVING TO THE WORK OF YOUR KINGDOM. AMEN.

CONCEIVE A MIRACLE

And, behold, thou shalt conceive in thy womb, and bring forth a son, and shalt call his name JESUS.

—LUKE 1:28,31

T he story of Mary and the conception of Jesus reveals powerful keys to receiving God's miracle-working power.

Before you can receive a miracle, you must receive a Word from God. Whether it comes from the Bible, through anointed preaching, or from the Lord speaking in your spirit, you must receive the Word that speaks to your situation.

When God told the prophet Elijah to seek out the widow of Zarephath, He had a plan for her. He intended to provide for her needs and prosper her in a time of drought and famine. When Elijah came to her, she had not yet received that Word from God. The prophet had to put a demand on her faith to bring her into God's provision. She received God's Word through the prophet, and in so doing received her miracle (1 Kings 17).

Receive God's Word for your situation, and allow Him to conceive a miracle in your spiritual womb. Give God permission to birth new creation in your life. You are born of the Spirit, not of flesh. Be born anew in Christ Jesus.

BIRTH IN ME, LORD JESUS, YOUR NEW CREATION. I DESIRE TO BE BORN OF THE SPIRIT THROUGH FAITH AND TRUTH IN YOU. AMEN.

PROTECT YOUR SEED

Guard, through the Holy Spirit who dwells in us, the treasure which has been entrusted to you.

— 2 TIMOTHY 1:14 NASB

Everything a pregnant woman takes into her body goes directly into her baby. If she smokes, drinks or takes drugs, she may harm or even abort her unborn child. Everything that comes in through your eyes, your ears, and your mind goes into your spiritual womb. If you take in doubt and unbelief, you will contaminate the miracle growing in your spirit.

Some people abort the miracle God has for them because they are full of doubt. They let go of God's promise and lose sight of their miracle.

Before raising Jairus' daughter from the dead, Jesus ordered all unbelievers to leave (Luke 8:54). If you are incubating a miracle, shun doubt and unbelief; feed your spirit with the things of God, allowing the Holy Spirit to conduct regular check-ups of your spiritual condition. Guard your miracle . . . it is His gift to you.

LORD JESUS, REVEAL TO ME THE UNHEALTHY THINGS I HAVE BEEN PUTTING INTO MY SPIRITUAL WOMB. INSTEAD OF PARTAKING OF SOMETHING HARMFUL TO MY MIRACLE, I WILL FEAST TODAY ON YOUR WORD. AMEN.

BOW YOUR KNEE

And Mary said, Behold the handmaid of the Lord; be it unto me according to thy word. And the angel departed from her.

—LUKE 1:38

⁓

The message delivered to Mary by the angel was not a command, but merely an announcement of what God intended to do. She did not ask for a sign to prove the word was true. She could have respectfully declined, but she did not. Even though she did not understand how she, a virgin, could bear a child, she believed the word from God and submitted her will to the Father's will.

God will often give us a word that requires us to receive it by faith. But remember, when God speaks, things happen. He spoke the earth into being, an impossible task according to scientists. Finite minds cannot grasp how this could be and yet standing on the earth, we are literally standing on the Word of God.

Blind submission requires blind faith. God made a demand on Mary's faith, and she accepted the challenge. Allow Him to bring you into His plan for your miracle by bowing your knee in humble submission and saying, "Be it unto me according to Thy Word."

If you had been Mary, would you have been so totally submitted to the will of God?

I SUBMIT TOTALLY TO YOU, LORD JESUS. YOU ARE MY SOLE REASON FOR LIVING. HOW I LOVE YOU! AMEN.

REST ASSURED

And the Lord shall deliver me from every evil work, and will preserve me unto his heavenly kingdom: to whom be glory for ever and ever. Amen.

—2 TIMOTHY 4:18

The Israelites suffered under the hand of the Egyptians for years. They feared they would never be delivered from the hand of their oppressor.

When they left Egypt, God was with them. He not only delivered them but also restored them. Psalm 105:37 confirms God's Word to them saying, "There was not one feeble person among their tribes" when they left. Do not fear the world or the things of this world. Don't look at God as if He trembles when the enemy approaches.

Rest assured that He is able to turn your promise into a fact (Romans 4:21). If God's Word says you are going to be right in the center of a miracle, count on it.

The God who delivers you and keeps you from the enemy is present with you now. Reassure yourself by confessing His indwelling presence (John 14:16–17). Reassure yourself by speaking His Word from 2 Timothy 4:18.

LORD JESUS, YOU WILL DELIVER ME FROM EVERY EVIL WORK, AND WILL PRESERVE ME UNTIL I REACH HEAVEN. TO YOU BE THE GLORY FOREVER AND EVER. AMEN.

NO IMPOSSIBILITIES

For with God nothing shall be impossible.

—LUKE 1:37

T he angel Gabriel brought Mary a testimony of the divine greatness of the child she was to bear—set apart from any human being who would ever walk the earth. In Luke 1:35 Gabriel tells her He will be of unique origin. Born of a virgin through the overshadowing power of the Most High, He will be—and eternally is—the Son of the Highest (v. 32). His God-given name will be Jesus, which means "God saves." Because He will be mankind's Savior, He is the One who will come as the promised Redeemer.

Unlike all other human beings, He will be wholly without sin, and therefore, the absolute Holy One (v. 35). Because He is without sin, He will be the divine King who will reign over His spiritual kingdom throughout eternity (v. 33).

Finally, Gabriel assures Mary with a truth that has stood the test of time. Everything that he announced to her was possible—even the amazing miracle of the incarnation of His Son—for with God all things are possible.

Nothing with God is impossible. Give Him every impossible area of your love, and yield to the way He will solve each problem.

GOD, I GIVE YOU ALL THAT IS IMPOSSIBLE, KNOWING THAT YOU ALONE ARE THE GOD OF THE POSSIBLE. AMEN.

WHO IS THE BABY?

And he said, Who art thou, Lord?

—ACTS 9:5

The air was filled with the sights and sounds of Christmas as I was walking through a busy shopping mall during the Christmas season.

People were bustling around carrying packages when I noticed a little boy and his mother, standing in front of a large nativity scene. The little boy asked, "Mommy, what is that right there?" and his mother answered, "That's a donkey." Then he asked, "What's that right there?" and she answered, "That's a camel." Then he asked, "Who's that man right there?," and she answered, "That's a wise man."

When they had almost gone through the entire nativity scene, the mother began to walk away. The little boy grabbed hold of her dress and said, "But wait just a minute, Mommy. Who's the baby?"

Who is he? Who is the baby? He is Jesus Christ, Savior of the world, Son of the Living God!

Do you know Him as Lord and Savior?

JESUS, TO ME YOU ARE MORE THAN A BABY IN A MANGER. YOU ARE THE LIVING CHRIST, IN WHOM THE UNIVERSE HANGS TOGETHER. YOU ARE THE MIGHTY GOD, THE EVERLASTING FATHER, AND THE PRINCE OF PEACE. AMEN.

FAVOR WITH GOD

And the angel said unto her, Fear not, Mary: for thou hast found favour with God.

—LUKE 1:30

The greatest message of the advent of Christ into this planet are the words "fear not." Why? Because you have found favor with God.

The God of all creation came to earth with the specific purpose of revealing Himself to you. If you are born again of God, you are on your way to heaven; you have been made righteous in God's eyes; and favor is part of your covenant right.

The literal translation of the word "favor" is from a Hebrew word meaning "cause for rejoicing, exultation, exuberant joy, and gladness of heart."

The precious blood of Jesus paid the price for your sin and made God's heart glad. He sits on His throne and rejoices, because He knows you will be in eternity with Him. Fear not; you have found favor with God.

JESUS, ALLOW ME TO WALK IN YOUR FAVOR, BEING FEARLESS AND BOLD FOR YOU. I LONG ONLY FOR YOUR FAVOR AND GRACE. AMEN.

THE BREAD OF LIFE

For the bread of God is he which cometh down from heaven, and giveth life unto the world.

—JOHN 6:33

Names carried great significance to the ancient Hebrews. To know the name of something was to rule it; they believed the essence of the person or thing was in its name.

Jesus was born in Bethlehem, as foretold by Micah over 450 years earlier (Micah 5:2). Bethlehem means literally, "House of Bread"—an appropriate place for God to ordain to cradle the Bread of Life that came down from heaven.

The manna which fell in the wilderness only briefly satisfied; it couldn't be stored or kept to meet tomorrow's need. But when we partake of Jesus, we can be continually filled, saved, and satisfied for all eternity.

Our clothes may wear out, our money may run out and our hair may fall out—but Christ, the "True Bethlehem," the "True Manna," gives us everlasting life. "O, taste and see that the Lord is good!" (Psalm 34:8).

LORD, I HAVE TASTED AND KNOWN THAT YOU ARE GOOD. YOU ARE THE TRUE BREAD THAT CAME DOWN FROM HEAVEN. I WILL FEED ON YOUR WORD ALL THE DAYS OF MY LIFE. AMEN.

ENDLESS PEACE

And he shall reign over the house of Jacob forever; and of his kingdom there shall be no end.

—LUKE 1:33

There is no end to the peace of God. True peace is not the absence of conflict, but His blessed assurance in the midst of all conflict. When we pray to the Father for His kingdom to come into our lives, we ask Him to become our Father and to be responsible for our supply.

Self seeks to benefit itself at the expense of others. Love seeks to benefit others at the expense of self.

You deserved to spend eternity in hell, but He forgave you. When Jesus died on the Cross and journeyed into hell, He took your place and mediated an eternal peace with your heavenly Father. He endured torture, death, and a devil's hell to benefit all mankind. This is true forgiveness, true love, and true peace.

Love as Jesus loves you, forgive as Jesus forgives you—and there will be no limit to His kingdom and His peace in your life. Find Jesus, the King, and you will find the kingdom . . . and in the kingdom you will find endless peace. Peace with God. Peace with yourself and others.

ALMIGHTY GOD, I GIVE YOU PRAISE FOR JESUS CHRIST, WHO MAKES PEACE BETWEEN ME AND YOU. I MAGNIFY YOUR NAME FOR BRINGING TOGETHER PEOPLE FROM ALL DIFFERENT RACES AND BACKGROUNDS TO BE ONE IN CHRIST'S BODY, DWELLING TOGETHER IN HARMONY AND PEACE. AMEN.

WAIT EXPECTANTLY

Wait on the LORD; be of good courage, and he shall strengthen thine heart: wait, I say, on the LORD.

—PSALM 27:14

J ust as in the natural birth process, there is a gestation period for a miracle. The Bible is filled with examples of people waiting for God's promises. Abraham and Sarah waited for God to give them their promised son. The children of Israel waited in captivity for their deliverer to appear.

David waited on God while he was being pursued by Saul's men. Israel waited for her Messiah, and the disciples waited for the coming of the Holy Spirit. We are waiting now for our blessed hope, the coming of our Lord Jesus Christ for His Church.

God always comes through for those who wait on Him. The promised Son was born; the deliverer appeared; and the enemies were defeated. The Messiah was sent; and the Holy Spirit came. One day we who are waiting expectantly will be caught up in the clouds to be with our Lord forever! God is never late, and He never forgets His promise (1 Thessalonians 4:17).

I AM WAITING ON YOU, O LORD. I KNOW THAT YOU ALWAYS ACT AT THE RIGHT TIME. SO I PRAISE YOU FOR ALL YOU DO. AMEN.

THE TROUBLED KING

When Herod the king had heard these things, he was troubled, and all Jerusalem with him.

—MATTHEW 2:3

E very year the advent of the Christmas season heralds the reminders of what Jesus came to free us from. Greedy merchants vie for our time and our money. Church pews empty as shopping malls fill. Picketers are set in place before nativity scenes in public squares, demanding their rights and denying ours.

Herod greedily welcomed the wise men, expecting a new avenue of commerce to advance his realm; but he grew troubled when he learned of their true mission.

The spirit of the world is troubled at Christmas time, as believers gather to honor and worship the King. Do not allow the traditions of Christmas to turn into empty rituals. Let your birthday celebration be more than just a reminder of your faith. Let it testify to a dying world of the awesome sacrifice Jesus made. All the glory of heaven was His, yet He gave it up to come to earth for you and for me.

Herod could not surrender the throne of life to Jesus. He sought to destroy the true King of life. Will you surrender the throne of Your life to Christ?

JESUS, RULE AND REIGN VICTORIOUSLY IN MY LIFE. MAKE OF MY LIFE A WINSOME WITNESS TO THE WORLD OF YOUR LOVE AND GRACE. AMEN.

MARY'S SONG

And Mary said, My soul doth magnify the Lord, And my spirit hath rejoiced in God my Saviour.

—LUKE 1:46–47

n her hymn of praise (Luke 1:46–55), Mary extolled the perfection of God. Through Gabriel's promise of God's fulfillment of His promises regarding the Messiah, she saw all His divine perfection: His power, His holiness, His mercy, and His faithfulness.

It is only through the incarnation of Jesus that we learn to know God in His omnipotence, holiness, mercy, and faithfulness. If He had never come to earth as a man, we would have lived forever in spiritual ignorance.

Everything Mary sang has come to pass, as the life of her Son played a revolutionary role in the life and history of mankind. Without Him all life is based on principles totally opposed to the right foundations for true life.

From the earliest times, "Mary's Hymn," commonly known as "The Magnificat," has been used in the praises of the Christian church. Make it your song of praise this Christmas season. Lift up your voice and proclaim the magnificence of the God we serve.

JESUS, I SING YOUR PRAISE. I DECLARE YOUR GLORY. I GIVE HONOR TO YOUR NAME. YOU ARE THE MAGNIFICAT OF MY LIFE. AMEN.

PRAISE OF ANGELS

For unto you is born this day in the city of David a Savior, which is Christ the Lord . . . And suddenly there was with the angel a multitude of the heavenly host praising God, and saying, Glory to God in the highest, and on earth peace, good will toward men.

—LUKE 2:11,13–14

T he angel that appeared to the shepherds that glorious night made an astounding statement. The shepherds knew Isaiah 43:11: "I, even I, am the LORD; and beside me there is no saviour." But now, an angel declares that a baby in a manger in Bethlehem is to be called "Savior." He is not "Christ your Lord" but "Christ the Lord," sovereign Lord of all creation.

The angel was suddenly accompanied by "a great heavenly host." Together they began to praise the One they served perpetually in heaven, the One who had now entered time wrapped in human flesh. The Messiah had come, and the heavens resounded with the praise of angels.

Should we not do the same? Do your lips constantly praise Him? Do you always bless and never curse His name. How will you give Jesus praise today? We have been brought from death to life, from darkness into light. Let the heavens resound with our praise!

JESUS, MY LIPS RESOUND WITH THE UNENDING PRAISE OF YOUR SALVATION. YOU ARE THE ONLY ONE WHO COULD BRING PEACE ON EARTH AND GOOD WILL TOWARD MEN. AMEN.

THE LIGHT OF THE WORLD

Then took he him up in his arms, and blessed God, and said, Lord, now lettest thou thy servant depart in peace, according to thy word: For mine eyes have seen thy salvation, which thou hast prepared before the face of all people; a light to lighten the Gentiles, and the glory of thy people Israel.

—LUKE 2:28–31

⸺

Simeon, a minister in the temple, was promised he would see the Messiah before he died. As was the custom, after eight days Mary and Joseph took the baby Jesus to the temple to consecrate Him to the Lord. (Luke 2:21–23).

Scripture tells us three times in these verses the Holy Spirit revealed the Christ to Simeon (vv. 25–27). When he saw the child, he declared the eternal significance of Christ's birth: His salvation is for "all peoples," both Jews and Gentiles. Christ fulfilled Simeon's prophecy when He later ordered His apostles to preach the gospel to all nations—making Himself a light of revelation to the Gentiles. When He added, "beginning at Jerusalem," He made Himself the "glory of his people Israel."

Are you ready for the Messiah? Have you lived your life in expectancy for His appearing? How is Jesus using your life to burn brightly in the world with His good works?

JESUS, MAKE ME A LIGHT TO OTHERS. LIGHT OF THE WORD, KINDLE IN ME A FLAME OF ZEAL AND FAITH THAT WILL LEAD OTHERS TO YOU. AMEN.

KING OF KINGS

*He shall be great, and shall be called the Son of the Highest:
and the Lord God shall give unto him the throne of his
father David.*

—LUKE 1:32

The book of Revelation shows us the Jesus who will
fulfill Gabriel's prophecy given to Mary in Luke
1:32. We are not serving a baby in a manger or a dead
man on a Cross. We serve a Jesus who is greater than any
expression we can devise for Him. He is coming back in
glory very soon with the armies of heaven, to claim His
throne.

The Gospels describe only the brief time Jesus lived
on the earth as the Son of Man, but Revelation describes
Jesus as He is now. The Book of Revelation is not the
revelation of religion; it is the revelation of Jesus Christ.
The same Jesus, whose birth we celebrate during the
Christmas season, is the victorious warrior who in righteousness "doth judge and make war" (Revelation 19:11).

Rejoice this Christmas season in the revelation of
Jesus Christ—our soon coming King.

COME QUICKLY, LORD JESUS, NOT AS A BABY
BUT AS THE KING OF KINGS AND LORD OF
LORDS. COME BACK FOR YOUR CHURCH. COME
BACK FOR YOUR SAINTS. COME BACK FOR ME.
AMEN.

THE LIGHT OF LIFE

Then spake Jesus again unto them, saying, I am the light of the world: he that followeth me shall not walk in darkness, but shall have the light of life.

—JOHN 8:12

W here the light of truth shines, darkness must flee.

When the Pharisees brought the woman caught in adultery to Christ, He said, "He that is without sin among you, let him first cast a stone at her." Those gathered to stone the woman were convicted by their own consciences, and slithered away until only Christ and the woman remained. The light of truth emanating from Jesus exposed and revealed the darkness of sin in the hearts and lives of the accusers that day. His light overcame their darkness.

It is not enough to look at the light: we must follow it, believe in it and walk in it. It is not only a light for our eyes but for our feet. We have the "light of life"— spiritual life in this world and eternal life in the next. Rejoice that as a born-again believer you never need walk in darkness again! Isaiah 60:1 tells us, "Arise, shine; for thy light is come."

LIGHT OF THE WORLD, I WILL FOLLOW YOU WHEREVER YOU LEAD. I AM LOST WITHOUT YOUR LIGHT. I AM DEAD WITHOUT YOUR LIFE. ARISE AND SHINE, LORD, IN MY LIFE. AMEN.

GOOD WILL

Glory to God in the highest, and on earth peace, good will toward men.

—LUKE 2:14

⁂

The angels celebrated the birth of the Prince of Peace by proclaiming peace on earth. They were not announcing conflict would cease and war would never again break out on the earth. They heralded the peace to be enjoyed by those who chose to live in harmony with God. The New American Standard Bible provides a more accurate translation of Luke 2:14: "Glory to God in the highest, and on earth peace among men with whom He is pleased."

The earth is plagued by conflict and strife as mankind lives apart from the peace that God alone can give. Peace on earth is a reality only among those who receive Him as Savior and Lord.

Peace is sent toward you. Joy is sent toward you. Blessing, health, happiness, and security are sent toward you. Do not let another year pass without positioning yourself to receive all He continually sends toward you. Order your steps of the Lord and walk in His perfect peace this coming year.

JESUS, I WILL LIVE THIS NEW YEAR IN YOUR BLESSING, HEALTH, HAPPINESS, AND SECURITY. I WILL SEEK TO BE AN INSTRUMENT OF YOUR PEACE IN EVERY RELATIONSHIP I HAVE. AMEN.